The Recovery of Belief

THE RECOVERY
OF BELIEF

A Restatement of Christian Philosophy

by

C. E. M. JOAD

GREENWOOD PRESS, PUBLISHERS
WESTPORT, CONNECTICUT

Library of Congress Cataloging in Publication Data

Joad, Cyril Edwin Mitchinson, 1891-1953.
    The recovery of belief.

    Reprint of the 1952 ed. published by Faber and
Faber, London.
    Includes index.
    1. Christianity--Philosophy. I. Title.
BR100.J6 1976   201   76-26097
ISBN 0-8371-9022-3

Originally published in 1952 by Faber and Faber Limited, London

Reprinted with the permission of Faber & Faber Ltd.

Reprinted in 1976 by Greenwood Press,
a division of Williamhouse-Regency Inc.

Library of Congress Catalog Card Number   76-26097

ISBN 0-8371-9022-3

Printed in the United States of America

Acknowledgements

My thanks are due to the editors of *The Hibbert Journal* and *The New Statesman* for permission to reprint in Chapter V some passages from an article entitled *The World of Physics and of Plato* which originally appeared in *The Hibbert Journal* and in Chapter IX passages from an article, *The Twilight of the Church*, which originally appeared in *The New Statesman*. I have also to thank Ivor Thomas for reading in manuscript Chapters I, VII and VIII and making a number of valuable suggestions. Mr. Thomas is, however, in no sense responsible for the views here expressed.

C. E. M. Joad

Hampstead, December 1951

Contents

Author's Note

Though the reading of this book is for the most part plain sailing in the sense that it demands nothing from the reader but normal intelligence, reasonable education, patience and good-will, some of the chapters are definitely "stiffer" than others. Chapters IV to VIII treat of matters which belong to philosophy, while Chapter V, which deals also with science, assumes a nodding acquaintance with the conclusions of modern physics. This is not so serious as it sounds since, living as we do in an intellectual climate which science has formed, most educated people, I find, possess this acquaintance, even if they possess no other, while, as to the philosophy, I have long held that any philosopher who takes the trouble to master the art of writing clearly and is at pains to exercise it, can explain most of the things that matter in philosophy to any reader of intelligence and goodwill, provided that the philosopher understands what he is writing about. I ought in fairness to add that this view, which is also that of Socrates, Plato and Hume, is not shared by most contemporary philosophers. In the present instance, the claim which it embodies is chiefly tested in Chapter VIII, in which I endeavour to state my own views.

C.E.M.J.

CHAPTER I

The Plight of the Intellectual

REASON AND FAITH

The following book is an account of some of the reasons which have converted me to the religious view of the universe in its Christian version. They are predominantly arguments designed to appeal to the intellect.

The intellectual approach to religion is out of fashion today and in this introductory chapter I want to explain why in this book I have adopted it.

There are many to whom faith comes easily. These feel no impulse to justify their beliefs since, for them, justification is unnecessary. That God created the world and sent His Son into it at a certain point of time are to them patent truths which it never occurs to them to doubt. I do not think that the number of such persons is as great as it was, at least among educated people; I, at any rate, am not one of them. Until comparatively late in my life the deliverances of reason no less than the weight of the evidence seemed to me to tell heavily against the religious view of the universe, and faith unsupported by reason seemed to me to be no more than a pious propensity to believe in propositions which there was no reason to think true.

It seems so still. While I admit that intellect cannot go all the way, there can, for me, be no believing which the intellect cannot, so far as its writ runs, defend and justify. I must, as a matter of psychological compulsion, adopt the most rational hypothesis, the most rational being that which seems to cover most of the facts and to offer the most plausible explanation

The Plight of the Intellectual

of our experience as a whole. The hypothesis in question is that which is known as the religious view of the world, and the following pages are designed to explain why I find it so.

BELIEF AND WILL

There has been much discussion in my time of the part played by the will in belief. Men have spoken of 'the will to believe', a phrase popularised by William James. But, divorced from reason, the dictates of the will have no authority and carry no conviction. One might just as well will to believe X as will to believe Y. The fact that one does believe X is, on this view, evidence of nothing but the fact that one wills to believe X. The willing of the belief has, then, no bearing upon the truth of that which the belief asserts. Certainly it does not constitute evidence for supposing that the belief is true. Will, in short, neither creates nor destroys the truth of beliefs.

If, in deference to current fashion, I were to try to indicate the part played by will in respect of my own beliefs, I should say that I *will* to believe the hypothesis in whose support the most reasons quantitively and the most cogent reasons qualitatively can be adduced. If to believe because you want to do so constitutes no evidence in favour of religion, to believe in spite of the fact that you would prefer not to do so constitutes no evidence against it. So far from my own religious belief being the result of what the psychologists call wishful thinking, I am disposed to doubt whether, if my wishes had their way, I should to-day be trying to practise Christianity. For while it is true that my intellect is in the main convinced, my wishes— what I suppose Christianity would call 'the natural man'— protest. For the belief that life in this world derives its explanation in the last resort from another cannot but increase the difficulty of living it.

Suppose for a moment that you think that the Christian view of earthly existence as a course of training in moral discipline is correct; then you cannot help but try to act as if you were at school. If the purpose of your existence is not to win

The Plight of the Intellectual

personal happiness but to improve your character, much that you would have light-heartedly done on the former assumption will be forbidden to you on the latter. And though, no doubt, it is a bad thing always to be taking one's moral temperature, one is nevertheless constantly driven to put to oneself the questions: 'Ought I to have acted as I did?' 'Ought I not to resist this desire which I take to be a temptation?' 'Could I not behave better than I am now doing?' Now for most of my life I have cheerfully subscribed to Bentham's maxim that if the word 'ought' means anything at all it *ought* to be excluded from the dictionary. Thus the adoption of the Christian view of the world has not, to put it mildly, made for greater simplicity and ease of living. On the contrary, it has complicated the problem of conduct by adding to the task of securing happiness the task of conforming to moral obligation.

The Disappointments of Christianity

I do not mean that 'duty' has now taken the place of 'happiness' as the motive and the test of conduct. Rather the two run in double harness as first one and then the other takes the bit and directs the course. I say 'first one and then the other', but truthfulness compels the confession that nine times out of ten it is to obtain happiness rather than to do my duty that I aim. Christianity, as I have been taught, insists that this is a false opposition, since, for it, true happiness is to be found only in conformity to the dictates of moral obligation. Bradley's *Ethical Studies*—which, as a teacher of philosophy, it is my business to expound—teaches the same truth. I do not doubt that those who live better lives than I do can testify from their own experience that this truth is indeed true. I can only say that I have not experienced its truth myself. I am disappointed that this should be so. In fact, the whole endeavour to live the Christian life is a series of disappointments. Faith falters, prayer is intermittent, the consolations of religion seem few and doubtful, the sense of disillusion is at times keen. I hoped to become a better person; I do, indeed, at times try. But on the

15

The Plight of the Intellectual

whole, except in so far as the effort, the usually unsuccessful effort, itself has merit, I must confess that I do not often succeed.

(And yet sometimes I think there is a difference. I am told by Christianity that if I pray to God for His help and try to live so as to deserve it, it will be granted. There have been times, as I tell in the Postscript at the end of this book,[1] when I have believed myself to experience the truth of this assertion.)

I do not love God, or I love Him but little even on the rare occasions when I happen to think of Him; I do not love my neighbour as myself, and emphatically I do not do unto others as I would be done by. My character, therefore, is little improved; the main change is in the ever-increasing consciousness of its need for improvement. Yet while Christianity has made little change in my life, my conviction of its truth grows stronger.

If it is not wishful thinking, if it is not the dictate of an arbitrary will to believe that has brought me to Christianity, I see no alternative to the conclusion that the main impulsion is from the intellect. It is because, as I said above, the religious view of the universe seems to me to cover more of the facts of experience than any other that I have been gradually led to embrace it.

ACTION AND BELIEF

And this approach is, after all, in line with that traditionally adopted by Christian thinkers, more particularly in the *philosophia perennis* which has some claim to be regarded as the philosophical background of the Christian creed. Christians are no doubt required to practise the precepts laid down by Christ and enjoined by the Church, but belief cannot affect conduct, unless the belief has an intellectual content, for action always presupposes an attitude of mind from which it springs, an attitude which, explicit when the action is first embarked upon, is unconscious by the time it has become an habitual and well-established course of conduct. When I act in a certain manner towards anything, I recognise by implication that it possesses

[1] See p. 248.

16

those characteristics which make my conduct appropriate. So, too, with my action in regard to God, which implies some sort of knowledge of Him and His relation to the familiar world and to myself as a creature living in that world. If I cannot find good grounds for my beliefs, I shall certainly not persuade myself to act in conformity with them; thus, if I do not accept the attribution of personality to God I shall not succeed in inducing myself to act towards Him as if He were a Person; that is, I shall not seek to know and to love Him, or to pray to Him. Thought, in other words, precedes action in the religious as in other spheres, and the practical significance of the precepts of religion is not separable from the theoretical content from which they derive. It is, then, because my intellect is on the whole convinced that I make such shift as I can to live conformably with its dictates.

I have tried to indicate the relation between the intellect, faith, will and desire as they co-operate to produce religious belief and the endeavour to act conformably with it. If I am right, intellectual conviction must, at least for educated people, come first. Hence the chapters that follow are concerned to indicate the grounds for that conviction and to remove some of the obstacles which in the contemporary world militate against it. I propose to try to argue that the religious hypothesis is the one that covers more of the facts of experience than any other, among which must be included both the fact of the desire to believe and the fact of moral conflict. Due weight must, I suggest, be given to the significance of both these facts.

QUALIFICATIONS

Having proceeded so far, I am constrained to realise that my position is by no means so simple as the foregoing statement suggests. To make it accurate and to make it acceptable even to myself I must introduce three qualifications.

First, I have been taught by psychology that the concept of the personality as a bundle of faculties, reason and emotion, instinct, desire, will and so forth, is untenable. There are, I am told, no

The Plight of the Intellectual

such separate faculties; all shade off, one into another, by imperceptible gradations. Hence to oppose the intellect to will or to intuition, as if they could be separated in fact even if they may be distinguishable in thought, entails a false dichotomy.[1]

Secondly, since it is nevertheless the case that some distinction of faculties must be assumed for purposes of discussion—the nature of my experience when, parched with thirst, I crave for water, being clearly different in kind from the sort of experience that I have when I am doing a sum in my head or trying to solve a chess problem, and it would be, to say the least of it, inconvenient to have no words at my disposal to indicate the fact of this difference, so that I could speak of 'desire' in the first instance and of 'reason' in the second—I propose to say a word on the sense in which I am going to use the words 'reason' and 'intellect'. This is broadly the sense in which Plato in *The Republic* conceives the first, the reasoning, 'part' of the soul.

There is in Plato no hard and fast distinction between reason and desire regarded as psychological faculties. On the contrary, each of his three 'parts' of the soul is informed by its own specific dynamism. I apologise for the vagueness of this word; what I have in mind is that element of passional striving for which psychologists use the term 'conation'. For this element of 'conation' no separate provision is made in the Platonic psychology. Rather each 'part' of the soul is infused with its own conation, which expresses itself in the desires and determines the pattern of the characteristic life of that 'part'. Hence, the distinction which Plato draws between 'parts' is referable not to different faculties but to the different kinds of object upon which the characteristic 'appetition' of each of the three 'parts' is fixed. Thus, the first 'part' of the soul is not intellect; it is the soul or personality as a whole, in so far as its appetition is centred upon the ends appropriate to the intellect; that is to

---

[1] That there is a sense in which a mind, as opposed to a soul, *can* be properly regarded as a bundle, not of faculties but of ideas, I shall argue in a later chapter (see Chapter viii, pp. 203–9).

The Plight of the Intellectual

say, upon knowledge. Plato adds that only the perfectly 'real' can be perfectly known and that in the knowledge of the 'real' what we call the intellect is transcended so that it is the whole personality, albeit a personality transfigured by the nature of its quest, that knows the Forms. It is in this sense, the sense of an aspect of our personalities informed by the desire to pursue and to know certain kinds of 'object' and to 'make after' certain kinds of end, that I wish to use the words 'intellect' and 'reason'.

Thirdly, I am far from wishing to suggest that reason covers all the ground. Much, probably most, of the universe must, I think, remain unknown by the reasons of human beings, at any rate in their present bodily condition. In particular, as I shall argue later, the nature of the spiritual world and, more particularly, the nature of its relation to and intercourse with the familiar order of physical things moving about in space and changing in time must remain unknown by reason. Not only can we not wholly understand—or we understand only formally without realising what it is that we understand—what it means to say that God is a transcendent being, but we cannot understand by what method or by what mode of entry He enters from time to time into relation with the natural order of events which science studies, interrupting them with a series of mighty acts. Intellect, then, can light up only a small area of the universe. For my part, I should subscribe to the familiar paradox that the more we know, the more we are conscious of our ignorance; the further the distance the intellect has travelled, the smaller it seems relatively to the distance still to be travelled.

CLAIMS FOR THE INTELLECT

I wish, then, to put the claims of the intellect no higher than the following: (1) The intellect does, indeed, take us part of the way; (2) we have no other mode of conveyance; and (3) in taking us as far as it does, it justifies us in taking the rest on trust. And this, I suppose, is where faith comes in. If, so far

The Plight of the Intellectual

as your reason takes you, the religious view of the universe seems to afford the most plausible explanation of your experience, then it seems not unreasonable to follow this same view beyond the point at which it leaves reason behind. If it accounts for the things you know and can understand, then it seems to me not unreasonable to hold that it could also offer an explanation of the things that you do not know and cannot understand—always, of course, provided that it is not positively at variance with the findings of any aspect of your experience and does not positively contradict the conclusions of reason in regard to the things that you do believe yourself to know.

Now in following the religious account of the universe beyond the point at which it leaves reason behind, and trusting to it as an explanation of the many things that pass our understanding, we are accepting on faith conclusions which are not demonstrated by reason. In other words, we are acting as if a hypothesis were true which, at the moment at which we act upon it, is still a hypothesis and not a truth. Nevertheless, it is, I suggest, knowledge, the knowledge which we possess already and which reason has won for us, that makes it reasonable to do so. This, in brief, is my own position. I have what I like to believe is a reasonable assurance in regard to the truth of the religious view of the universe, an assurance which, however, never hardens to the point of absolute conviction. I could wish that it did.

The Plight of Contemporary Intellectuals

I think—perhaps because I wish to think—that a belief in religion comes with a quite special degree of difficulty to persons of my training and equipment living in the middle of the twentieth century. We have been taught to take nothing on trust; to bring everything for judgment to the bar of the intellect. Hence faith, which must be taken on trust, and which gives little or no account of itself at the bar of the intellect, runs counter to our training and habits; faith, in a word, is hard for us, while the simple unreflecting faith of uneducated persons is

The Plight of the Intellectual

impossible. But that is only to say that we have the habits and the outlook proper to educated men in all ages who have been trained to rely upon their intellects. If this were all, it would be no great matter, but there is more to it than that. We are the inheritors of a century of religious doubt. This doubt was never so widely spread or so deeply ingrained. In the circles in which I have moved consisting mainly of left wing and left centre politicians, journalists, writers, artists and dons, it is a comparatively rare thing to find an educated man who is also a Christian. It is not merely that only one in ten of the population in contemporary Britain has any continuing connection with any church. More to the point is the fact that the ten per cent includes a very high proportion of elderly persons, particularly of elderly and comparatively uneducated women. Among my own acquaintances I do not think that I number more than half a dozen who are believing Christians. I could, I know, name well over a hundred who are not. In sum, the findings of the contemporary intellect tell heavily against religion. Moreover, the climate of the time is hostile to it, so hostile that many take it for granted that religion does not deserve serious consideration and the traditional religious explanation both of the universe at large and of particular occurrences within the universe is rejected out of hand.

To take a particular example, where I might cite a hundred, consider the implications of the words I have italicised in the following quotation from an address by Professor D. S. M. Watson, delivered to fellow biologists at Cape Town in December 1943: 'Evolution has been accepted by scientists, not because it has been observed to occur or proved by logical coherent evidence to be true, *but because the only alternative, special creation, is clearly unacceptable.*'

I, too, have grown up in this climate and inherit these findings. For most of my life I have been not only an agnostic but a vocal and militant agnostic. I have had all the arguments against the religious hypothesis at my intellectual fingertips, and was ready and apt in their use for the discomfiture of Christian

The Plight of the Intellectual

apologists.[1] The habits of a lifetime cannot quickly be outgrown, and although, as I have said, I now believe that the balance of reasoned considerations tells heavily in favour of the religious, even of the Christian view of the world, it is still in terms of balance and plausibility that my thought proceeds. Where I would testify to certain conviction, I must still speak in terms of plausible hypothesis; when I would rely on the support and enjoy the comfort of a firm faith, I must still confess to moments of disbelief, days of doubt and periods of absolute indifference. Moreover, the questioning intellect will not keep quiet. Constantly, continually, it perceives fresh grounds for doubt and poses new, unanswerable questions.

And since this book will afford no other occasion for their parade, let me here make my one sacrifice to the gods of my past by citing a few examples as evidence of the sort of difficulties with which I must contend.

I will give one example of each kind.

Questions and Doubts

First, as to questions. At the moment of writing there is a great pother about the announcement of a new dogma by the Roman Catholic Church, the dogma of the physical resurrection and present existence in the body of the Virgin Mary. Clergymen of the Church of England complain of another and, as it seems to them, so gratuitous a spoke placed by the Roman Catholics in the wheel of the reunion of the Christian Churches. Nevertheless, they (and I) affirm, in common with all other members of the Anglican Communion, our belief in the Resurrection of the Body. Sunday after Sunday as we do so, I (but not they) wonder what all the fuss is about. For why, I want to know, do we complain so bitterly of the announcement of this new Catholic dogma that the Virgin's body exists and is resurrected at the very moment that we are professing as an article of faith in regard to *all* human beings who would normally be called dead,

---

[1] Many of these I have set out at length in the early chapters of my *God and Evil.*

22

The Plight of the Intellectual

either that their bodies exist now, or that they will sooner or later again come into existence in order that they may be resurrected? Is the element of time so important? Granted that we accept the miracle of the Resurrection of the Body, does it so much matter from the point of view of dogma *when* its Resurrection occurs?

THE PAIN OF ANIMALS

Secondly, as to doubts. I was for years baffled by the problem of pain and evil; in fact, it was this problem that for years denied belief in the Christian religion. Now, I think I see the answer, or at least so much of the answer as will suffice to justify me in taking the rest on trust. God did not wish to create a race of virtuous automata,[1] for of what merit is the virtue, if virtue it can be called, of those who have no choice but to desire, to will and to act as they do? Of what value, then, to be praised or loved by such as these? And what joy or merit can there be in loving them in return, even if it were possible to do so? Hence God created beings possessed of free will in order that they might be in a position to acquire merit by acting rightly *when it was possible for them to act wrongly,* with the result that the amount of virtue in the universe would be increased—of virtue and also of love, since those who acquired virtue by their own efforts as a result of their resistance to temptation and their endurance of suffering would be worthy objects of God's love. Now if they are to be free to choose wrongly, it will follow that some wrong choices will almost certainly be made. The evil in the universe is the consequence of wrong choices or, alternatively, we may say that evil must already be present in the universe in order that it may be chosen. Pain, which is an evil, is also a consequence of wrong choices. Pain, thus comes into the world because men do evil.

So far, so good. The argument is difficult and abstract, but it holds together. Then comes the doubt. What of the pain of

[1] I deal with the significance of human free will more fully in chapter viii, p. 221.

23

the animal kingdom *before* man appeared upon the scene? There has been life upon the planet, according to the biologists, for something like a thousand million years; human life for about a million. During the whole of that vast preliminary period, if the record of the rocks is to be believed, nature was red in tooth and claw. Animals were preying one upon another, going in fear of one another, dying of cold, dying of hunger and wounds. Impossible to believe that they did not suffer; impossible, at least for me, to believe that physical suffering is not evil. Yet this suffering of the animals cannot be explained by the formula to which I have just had resort; it cannot, that is to say, be attributed to the wrong choices of human beings, for human beings did not as yet exist. What, then, are we to say, if we are not to say that God foresaw, permitted and perhaps ordained it? But that, I feel, cannot be. The problem, then—and it is one of many—is for me unresolved. The most familiar way of dealing with it—it is adopted in the writings of N. P. Williams and suggested by C. S. Lewis—is to postulate a cosmic 'Fall' as a result of which the whole of life is infected with sin. I find this doctrine hard to credit on common sense grounds, apart from the fact that it seems to me to have the effect, not so much of solving the problem of the evil of animal pain, as of putting back in point of time the problem of the origin of such evil. Nor are such other solutions as I am acquainted with in the least convincing.

MORE IMMEDIATE DIFFICULTIES

Thirdly, my mind is assailed with more immediate difficulties arising from the acceptance of the Christian religion. For example, there is the danger to mankind from science or, more precisely, from man's use in war of the results of scientific research. Wars have always occurred in the past and will presumably occur again unless—and of this there is no sign—mankind adopts a system of world government with a monopoly of force which makes war impossible, or unless human nature itself changes. At the time of writing, short of such a system or short of such a change, it seems highly probable that the 'cold war'

The Plight of the Intellectual

between the U.S.S.R. and the West will become open warfare, so soon as the U.S.S.R. has a sufficient supply of A- and/or H-bombs to enable the Soviet Government to wage war with what it takes to be a reasonable chance of success.

If the war occurs soon and ends in a decisive victory for one side, some vestiges of civilisation might survive it, but if it is long delayed, so rapid is the rate of scientific invention and advance, that the complete destruction of civilisation and reversion to primitive barbarism seem likely, especially if, when war comes, it is prolonged and indecisive.

THE END OF HUMAN LIFE

There is a further possibility. Famine due to the destruction of crops by radio-active sprays, pestilence resulting from the practice of bacteriological warfare, may cause the disappearance of human life. Radio-active clouds, drifting round the planet, may disintegrate living tissue everywhere. I do not say that these things are certain or even probable; they are at least possible.

What is the bearing of these possibilities on religion? Does God foresee the possible destruction of the human race? Can He prevent it? Does He perhaps even intend it? There is much in Christian literature which might seem to countenance such an eventuality. There are, for example, the talk of Armageddon, the Apocalyptic writings of the Book of Revelation, the persistent belief of the early Christians in the rapidly approaching end of the world and the second coming of Christ—though early Christian writings always speak of these events as if they were to be brought about by the direct intervention of God; not as if they were to be permitted to occur as the result of the unchecked wickedness of man.

Let us suppose for a moment that ours is the only planet anywhere in the universe on which life like our own exists. The question then arises, can God permit this creature, man, whom He has sent into the world in order that, according to the Christian view, he may increase the amount of virtue in the

The Plight of the Intellectual

universe and of objects worthy of God's love—can He, one wonders, permit man to come to so lamentable an end and to destroy himself through misuse of that very gift of intelligence with which God has endowed him? Can God, in other words, permit His experiment to fail? And if not, will He once again intervene with one of His mighty acts to arrest the drift of mankind to self-destruction? May there perhaps be a Second Coming? Certainly the stage seems set for it. Yet how difficult, how almost impossible for a modern intellectual to believe in it as an actually impending historical event.

BIRTH CONTROL AND THE POPULATION PROBLEM

Hard on the heels of this question comes another with its attendant difficulties. One of the most probable causes of war is the pressure of ever-increasing populations upon the world's diminishing food supplies. Throughout most of recorded history the human population of the earth has stood at approximately five hundred millions. Fifty years ago it was just under two thousand millions. In 1950 it was two thousand three hundred millions, and by the end of the century it will be three thousand millions. At the moment it is increasing at the rate of over sixty thousand a day. Thereafter the rate of increase, short of the adoption of birth control over most of the globe, must be very rapid. Science is, once again, the main factor in the situation. Science has improved hygiene, has diminished plague, diminished maternal mortality, diminished infant mortality, so much so that, while a hundred years ago the average age at death of the population of this country was under thirty, today it is over sixty. This new-won ability to protect and lengthen human life has still to be used on behalf of the majority of the world's population. Thus, while the death rate in England is ten per thousand, in India it is nearly thirty per thousand. We may look, then, short of birth control, for a far more rapid increase of the numbers of the human race in the future.

Further, it is science or, rather, the misuse of science's gifts which is reducing the world's potential food supply. It is not

The Plight of the Intellectual

merely that ever-increasing areas of food-producing land are taken for industrial purposes, for spreading suburbs, roads, factories and aerodromes; more to the point is the fact that science has enabled man to farm in such a way as to impoverish the soil and render it unfit for further food cultivation. Civilisation's most obvious need is, then, in the circumstances in which we find ourselves, the need to control the size of the population. Science, having interfered with the laws governing death, should also, one would have supposed, be permitted to interfere with the laws governing birth, and a world population policy prescribing for each nation its optimum population in the light of the available and prospective food supplies is both dictated by the deliverances of reason and demanded by the counsels of prudence. Yet the Churches in general look with disfavour on birth control by artificial methods, and the Roman Catholic Church in particular officially condemns the use of contraceptives on the ground that it is contrary to the teaching of Christ and the will of God. For who, they ask, is man that he should frustrate the life that God intended and prevent the coming into existence of another immortal soul?

Here, then, is a situation in which it would appear *prima facie* that the Roman Catholic Church[1] is deliberately fostering a policy which will tend to promote the destruction of mankind, by positively encouraging the steps which are calculated to make it more likely and by impeding and forbidding the measures which will make it less likely.

Can God, one wonders, will that his creatures should deliberately compass their own destruction through the agency of his Church? Again, I do not know the answer to this question. I mention the matter only because it affords one more example of the conflict between reason and would-be faith by which the contemporary intellect is beset. It is scarcely necessary to add that my own intellect is not immune.

---

[1] I hesitate to speak of the official attitude of the Anglican Church, which is wrapped in its all too familiar obscurity.

27

The Plight of the Intellectual

PRIDE OF THE INTELLECT

Nor are this habit of inconvenient questioning, these re-current doubts and difficulties, all. There is such a thing as the pride of the intellect, a pride in which throughout my life I have been continuously proud. There are certain writers—Shaw is one of them, Swift another and Bertrand Russell another—from whom I derive an enormous intellectual stimulation. Borne aloft on the wings of their intellects, I feel myself raised to an eminence from which I look down upon the past and present of my species, and, as momentarily I perceive through Shaw's eyes or through Russell's, I observe, with amused detachment, its manifold follies, follies from which, while the moment of exaltation lasts, I fondly believe myself exempt. I am suffused with a feeling of immense superiority, as I thank God that I am not as other men. . . .

The above is a summary of some of the reasons which, in my judgment, make religious belief hard for a modern intellectual. At any rate it has not come easily to me. All derive in their degree from pride of the intellect, coupled with the fact that the workings of a contemporary intellect so frequently raise doubts which the Churches cannot allay, suggest questions which they do not answer and point to conclusions which seem to be at variance with their teachings.

What then? I like to comfort myself with the hope that the fact that belief is, for us, difficult means that it will not in us be expected to be certain; that if faith is hard to come by, the fact that but little comes or that it comes but intermittently may not be accounted wholly to our discredit; that circumstances may be permitted to plead in our extenuation.

ANALOGY FROM MORALS

In this connection I find the analogy from morals helpful. We are accustomed to the view that if a man's moral inheritance is bad, if the moral raw material which he brings with him into the world is poor, less in the way of moral performance will be

28

The Plight of the Intellectual

expected of him than of his morally more gifted or more fortunate neighbour. The contrary, at least, seems to be accepted; no one, for example, supposes that the fact that I am habitually sober and abstain from homosexuality is to my credit. I have no temptation either to drunkenness or to sodomy. But if my parents had been dipsomaniacs, if I had been born into a normally drunken household, my occasional lapses after intense moral struggle into sobriety would, it may be hoped, win me some moral marks. Similarly, the congenitally placid man obtains less moral *kudos* from his habitually easy-going good temper than the irritable man who, sensitive to every sound and infuriated by silliness, occasionally succeeds in keeping his temper or at least in concealing the fact that he has not kept it, when compelled to listen to the clack of women's tongues against a background of radio light music in a hotel lounge in which he is trying to write.

This view of morality raises, I know, its own problems. Let me transfer them for a moment to the tennis court. Here are two singles players. A is an easy graceful player, he has a good eye, a lissom body and naturally fluent strokes; with the nonchalance of perfect ease he wins his matches against less gifted opponents. B, on the other hand, has an awkward body and a shambling gait; he moves clumsily and his backhand, evidently cultivated with immense assiduity, is laboured and angular. Imbued, however, with a stubborn determination to win—with what in modern terminology is called 'guts'—he gains his victories against naturally more gifted players by force of will. As we watch him battling in the final of the tournament against A, which of the two do we admire the more, which do we wish to win? Faced with this difficult choice, I would suggest a distinction. Our admiration of A partakes of the aesthetic. He symbolises the Greek ideal, and, for the Greeks, goodness and beauty were not separate, still less opposed as they so often are for us; they were integrated in the single concept denoted by the word κάλος. The condition of A is nearer to that of the divine, since we cannot suppose God to be subject to the

29

necessity of effort and constrained to struggle for His ends. The morality of God, in so far as He is a moral being, is not the morality of man. Now the *moral* superiority is plainly with B. We cannot, it is obvious, count the possession of a good eye at games a *moral* good; it is a natural endowment for which the lucky possessor can take no credit. So, too with the graceful body and its fluent stroke play. But the determination to overcome natural handicaps, the willingness to fight against one's disabilities and to overcome them, and the achievement of victory in spite of one's natural disadvantages—these, surely, are the qualities for which we reserve our specifically *moral* admiration, for these are proper to the limitations of our human condition. I conclude that we are justified in giving more marks, more specifically *moral* marks—if the concept of the specifically and uniquely moral can be accepted—to B rather than to A.

So, too, in life, of those who are handicapped by a naturally meagre moral equipment less in the way of achievement—or so I like to think—is expected. Like batsmen 'going in' on a sticky wicket, fewer runs are required of them than of those who bat with all the conditions in their favour.

CONCLUSION IN REGARD TO THE INTELLECT AND RELIGIOUS
BELIEF

I would like to think that in this matter of religious belief I am in a B-like rather than in an A-like condition. Coming to it late in life, I bring with me all the disabilities of a lifetime of indulged desires and unresisted temptations. Dragging my train of bad habits, I enter the school of morality at the very bottom of the form. Whether this be good theology I do not know. (I suspect that it may not be, since it suggests the conclusion that little in the way of decent behaviour need be expected of me and this is an expectation which, it is obvious, no man is entitled to entertain in regard to himself.) But of the relevance of this concept in its application to the intellect I have fewer doubts. There can be natural intellectual handicaps to the acceptance of religion, just as there are natural moral handicaps to the living of

s to the British Association in 1874, could look for-
to a day when science would be able to envisage and
all that has happened and all that will happen in terms
e ultimately purely natural and inevitable march of
ion from the atoms of the primeval nebula to the pro-
gs of the British Association for the Advancement of
ce', As for life and mind, T. H. Huxley, lecturing to the
h Association, did not hesitate to assert that 'the thoughts
ich I am now giving utterance and your thoughts regarding
are expressions of the molecular changes in the matter of

day that phase has passed and we know too much about
universe to think that we know anything for certain. We
, indeed, entered upon a third phase in which mystery has
rned with a vengeance and the physical universe shows
f to be not only queerer than we understand but, it may
queerer than we can understand. Each fresh advance in
an knowledge reveals a greater unknown. Nor, on reflection,
his surprising. If you think of knowledge as a little glowing
ch, a circle of light, set in an area of environing darkness, the
rkness of the unknown, then the more you enlarge the circle
the known, the more also you enlarge its area of contact with
e unknown.

R. HOYLE'S PICTURE OF THE PHYSICAL WORLD

Such, at any rate, has been the effect of this book of Hoyle's
on myself, nor have the severe strictures to which it has sub-
quently been exposed on the ground that he presents personal
eculations as agreed conclusions and suggests that the sketch
f the universe whose outlines he has drawn is in some sense a
nal picture instead of being a temporary daub, liable to be
uperseded as its many predecessors have been superseded,
ubstantially weakened the impression that it has produced.
or it seems unlikely that any subsequent modifications of Mr.
Hoyle's sketch will have the effect of lessening the magnitude
and mystery of the universe. Whether it is because of a change

a good life; but whereas the moral handicaps partake of the too
little, the intellectual partake rather of the too much. Whereas
in the moral sphere the bad starter is the dunce at the bottom of
the form; in the intellectual, he is the scholarship boy at the
top of it, not because there is any necessary antinomy between
reason and religion—far from it—but because of the intellectual
climate of the age in which we move and the slant which it gives
to the workings of our minds.

I have tried to explain why I have found religious belief
difficult to embrace and faith hard to come by. I believe myself
in this respect to be not untypical. My purpose in so doing is to
justify the somewhat laboured apologetics of the ensuing pages.
For those to whom religion comes easily they will be superfluous.
I can only hope that in offering this explanation I have not been
impelled by exhibitionism and that in concluding it I have not
confessed myself into complacency.

CHAPTER II

Mr. Hoyle and the Physical Universe

The immediate occasion of the writing of this book was the delivery in the summer of 1950 of a series of broadcast talks by Mr. Fred Hoyle, subsequently published in a book entitled *The Nature of the Universe*. They set me pondering again over questions to which I had given little thought since the astronomers gave our laymen's minds their last jolt some twenty years ago. Sir James Jeans and Sir Arthur Eddington possessed great gifts of popular exposition and their books helped us to understand something of the revolution which had taken place since the beginning of the century in man's conception of the nature of the physical universe. The universe was, it seemed, not only much larger but much more complicated than we had believed.

Now, twenty years later, the universe revealed by the astronomers is again different; it is again larger and it is not a whit less mysterious. The presentation of this revised picture should not, I suppose, logically affect our outlook. Physics and astronomy are concerned to accumulate facts; philosophy and religion to interpret them. The discovery that the sun is more likely to explode and roast the earth than to grow cold and freeze it, or the injunction to add a nought or so to our estimates of the size of space or the span of time which were already inconceivably large, even the conception of the continuous creation of matter, have not, as far as I can see, any *necessary* bearing upon our views as to the nature of the universe as a whole, more particularly as regards its origin, purpose, destiny and end. Nevertheless, these things do make a difference—they do, at

any rate, to me—if only because th
mystery of the universe and its a

STAGES IN MAN'S ATTITUDE TO

Man's attitude to the universe see
through three stages. First, there is
set in a world that he is unable to
at the mercy of natural forces whose
and whose workings evade control.
mysterious, but forbidding, and to
diminish the menace, he peoples it wit
his own imagining, gods and goddesses
demons and devils. These, too, for the m
unlike the impersonal forces of nature, t
They can be propitiated, for example, a

Secondly, there are the triumphant a
the apparently limitless possibilities of e
by the scientific method. The first effe
of the sciences was to reduce the importanc
the scale of the known universe, so that
human life in particular seemed no mor
flickering uncertainly in the vast immensiti
and astronomical space. The discoveries
exhibited—or were thought some fifty yea
the universe as essentially material and hun
outside passenger travelling across a fu
environment. Point and purpose, design a
eliminated so effectively that even such a c
of science as H. G. Wells declared in consterna
is a more abundant life before mankind, this sc
time is a bad joke beyond our understanding, a
an empty laugh braying across the mysteries.'

But though they made man small and the
the scientists, during their period of explanatory
reached its climax some seventy years ago, di
prehensible; so much so that Professor Tyndall, in

Mr. Hoyle and the Physical Universe

in myself, a change from the confidence of the young to the hesitations of the older man, or whether the universe has, in fact, come to seem more mysterious, as it has come to be better known, I am impressed by its magnitude and wonder as never before. It was, in the circumstances, natural enough that I should be set thinking again of the mind that planned it.

Mr. Hoyle apparently agrees. 'It is my view,' he writes, 'that man's unguided imagination could never have chanced on such a structure as I have put before you in these talks. No literary genius could have invented a story one hundredth part as fantastic as the sober facts that have been unearthed by astronomical science.' 'I think,' he adds, 'that Newton would have been quite unprepared for any such revelation, and that it would have had a shattering effect on him.'

Particularly striking are the conceptions of the receding galaxies and the continuous creation of matter. As new galaxies condense out of what Mr. Hoyle calls 'inter-stellar gas', they begin to recede. While the nearest are moving at the rate of several million miles an hour, the further they recede the faster they move, so that the most distant observable through our biggest telescope are travelling at the rate of over two hundred million miles an hour. This consideration leads to the concept of the limits of the observable universe. At a sufficient distance from us the galaxies will be moving at the speed of light itself. This means that 'the further a galaxy is away from us the more its distance will increase during the time required by its light to reach us', so that, if it is far enough away, its light will never reach us at all. The limiting distance is, in fact, about two thousand million light years. The largest of our telescopes, which is on Mount Palomar, can penetrate to about half that distance; that is to say, about half the theoretically observable universe is already under our observation. Double that area, and the limit of what the human eye can or could observe is reached. Beyond that limit lies what?

So far as the word of astronomy goes, the answer can only be 'much the same as lies on this side'. 'Theory,' says Mr. Hoyle,

Mr. Hoyle and the Physical Universe

'requires the galaxies to go on for ever, even though we cannot see them. That is to say, the galaxies are expanding out into an infinite space.' It seems likely enough. It would be an odd and very arbitrary coincidence if the limits of the universe coincided with the limits of our possible observation. The universe, then, is not finite as the theory of relativity was at one time thought to suggest, but infinite. Indeed, it is only to one particular system of space and time that Einstein's special theory of relativity applies. But it is far from clear that astronomy is here entitled to have the last word.

THE PHILOSOPHERS ON SPACE AND TIME

For at this point the philosophers put a question: can we, they ask, think of space that extends for ever? I doubt if we can. The concept is not, as it seems to me, one that the mind can grasp. Can we, on the other hand, think of it as coming to an end, as in fact bounded? Again we cannot. For if it is bounded it must be bounded by something; it must, so to say, have an edge. And beyond that edge lies what? Either something or nothing. The 'something', if it is a physical something—and it is difficult to see what else could be a boundary to space—must itself be in space; and 'nothing' is equivalent to empty space. Here, then, is a contradiction.

In this situation philosophers have traditionally made two inferences. Either they have said, space is not wholly real, since it will not in the last resort bear thinking about but leads the mind into contradictions and reality cannot be self-contradictory, or our minds are not capable of fully grasping it.

Similarly with time. Twenty years ago Sir James Jeans presented us with a graphic picture of a universe which was gradually running down in accordance with the second law of thermo-dynamics. Throughout the universe processes of energy diffusion due to the breaking down of the radio-active atoms were everywhere observable. Nowhere was any instance of the contrary process observed. When all the energy originally stored in the radio-active atoms had been equally diffused, there

Mr. Hoyle and the Physical Universe

would be no more happenings of any kind in the universe which would come to rest in a universal stagnation. The process of ubiquitous energy diffusion seemed to entail an act or process of energy concentration. If the contents of a parcel are being continuously and uniformly scattered, somebody must have done the parcel up. Hence Jeans was led to postulate an act or series of acts of creation. 'Everything,' he wrote, 'points with overwhelming force to a definite event or series of events of creation at some time or times not infinitely remote.'

But this picture, too, has changed. A series of ingenious arguments leads Mr. Hoyle to conclude—and the view is apparently widely shared—that what is apparently empty space is not, in fact, empty but contains inter-stellar gas which simply appears. The inter-stellar gas is extremely thinly spread—'the average rate of appearance amounts to no more than the creation of one atom in the course of about a year in a volume equal to St. Paul's Cathedral'. Nevertheless, the total rate of appearance for 'the observable universe alone is about a hundred million million million million million tons per second'. The inter-stellar gas condenses to form galaxies, the galaxies, stars, and from the explosions of the stars are born planets. Thus it is the creation of inter-stellar gas that drives the universe forward. It also invalidates Sir James Jeans's picture. The inter-stellar gas consists of hydrogen atoms. 'Hydrogen is being steadily converted into helium and the other elements throughout the universe and this conversion is a one-way process.' Unless new hydrogen were being continuously created, it would all have been used up long ago. Nevertheless, the matter of the universe today still consists almost entirely of hydrogen. If, Mr. Hoyle notes, 'matter were infinitely old, this would be quite impossible'. (Yet it doesn't seem incompatible with Jeans's notion of the creation of the universe at a time *not* infinitely remote.)

Also if matter were infinitely old, and new matter were *not* constantly being created, all the galaxies would long ago have receded beyond the limits of our possible observation. Hence Mr. Hoyle's conclusion that 'material simply appears—it is created'. This creation, he thinks, has been going on and will go on endlessly. For this reason, if we were to make a film of the universe from any position in space, and the film were run indefinitely, a spectator, however long he watched, would notice a 'general sameness' about it. The universe would also look the same, if the film were run backwards. For 'whether we run the film backwards or forwards, the large-scale features of the universe remain unchanged'. The conclusion is that time, like space, is endless in both directions. And the philosopher's comment is the same: can you, he asks, conceive of endless time? For my part, I do not think that I can. Can you, then, he asks again, think of time coming to an end? Again my answer is that I cannot. For at or after the end of time there would assuredly be either something or nothing. The something would require to be in time and there is no such thing as nothing. Also the ending would itself presumably have to occur *at* a time so that the end of time is also in time which means, presumably, that it is not, after all, the end. Time, in fact, will bear thinking about even less than space.

THE CREATION OF MATTER

Reading Mr. Hoyle, I tried to bring myself to make the imaginative effort required to conceive the nature of matter. The current theory of the ultimate constitution of matter requires us to think of it in terms of atoms. Now the atom is itself a universe in which the planetary electrons in their orbits are relatively as far from the nucleus as the earth is from the sun, while one orbit is—allowing for the difference of scale—as far from another as the orbit of the earth is from that of Pluto. Yet the entire universe of the atom is so small that, in a striking phrase of Ritchie Calder, 'if the entire population of the world were to work in eighty-four hour shifts, counting incessantly day and night, it would take them three years to count a thimble full of atoms'.

Facts of this kind ought not, I know, to impress me, nor, as I remarked above, ought they to make any difference to one's

Mr. Hoyle and the Physical Universe

general concept of the universe. For, what is size that so much should be made of it? It is no more wonderful, it may be said, for God to have made the vastness of the galaxies or the smallness of the atom than to have made the sea, the sky, the earth, the frost or the rain.

Agreed. Yet I *am* impressed, nevertheless, impressed beyond measure by the size and majesty of the universe and by the insignificance of our attempts to comprehend it. What, for example, are we to make of Mr. Hoyle's conception of the continuous creation of inter-stellar gas? The universe, it seems, is being continually furnished with fresh raw material in the shape of hydrogen atoms. Where does this material come from? Apparently from nowhere. It just appears. But if it comes from nowhere it is created and, if created, uncaused. For creation means the appearance of something where there was nothing, or, alternatively, the occurrence of events for which there can be assigned no causes of which the occurrent events can be regarded as the effects. It contradicts, therefore, the assumption upon which physical science, as we have known it, has been built, the assumption, namely, that nature is an orderly scheme in which each event is the determined result of the set of conditions that produced it. If uncaused events can occur, if, indeed, they are occurring all the time, what becomes of the claim of science to enable us to calculate and predict, a claim which, one would suppose, can be sustained only in so far as there are *no* uncaused events, since these must, from the very nature of the case, evade calculation and prediction?

SCIENCE AND EXPLANATION

What, further, becomes of the claim of science to tell us the whole truth about the world? Scientists, you may say, never made such a claim—or at any rate they don't make it now. Perhaps, perhaps not; but what is not doubtful is that the *plain man believes* that science makes it. He believes, that is to say, that though much, nay, most of the universe is still unknown to

Mr. Hoyle and the Physical Universe

science at the present time, much has also been discovered and that what remains is theoretically discoverable by an extension of the same methods as those which have already met with such signal success and will be found amenable to the operation of the same laws as those whose workings have already been mapped. But to revert only to the notions upon which I have briefly touched, to space, to time, and to the continuous creation of matter, so far from being explicable, they are not, so far as I can see, even conceivable in the terms of the concepts which science employs for its thinking.

Moreover, even if science is no longer a stick with which to beat religion, the plain man's indifference to or contempt for religion is largely the effect of science. For he has grown up in an intellectual climate which science has formed for him to accept the criterion of reality with which science has provided him. Not only does he believe the world of matter that science explores to be real, but he believes that whatever else is real must be of the same nature as matter. Now matter is what you can see and touch. Hence to enquire into the nature of the things we see and touch, to analyse them into their elements and atoms, is to deal directly with reality; to apprehend values or to enjoy religious experience—in fact, to enjoy any experience which does not spring from contact with the physical—is to wander in a world of shadows. In sum, to use the eye of the body to view the physical world is to acquaint oneself with what is real; to use that of the soul to see visions is to become the victim of illusion. Such I take to be the instinctive beliefs of contemporary common sense.

Parallel with the belief that the real must be a substance tangible and visible is the belief that it must be subject to the laws which are observed to operate in the physical world—that it must work, in short, like a machine. As Professor Eddington puts it, nineteenth-century science was disposed, as soon as it scented a piece of mechanism, to exclaim: 'Here we are getting to bedrock. This is what things should resolve themselves into. This is ultimate reality.' The implication was that whatever did

Mr. Hoyle and the Physical Universe

not work like a machine—the sense of value, for example, or the feeling of moral obligation, or belief in God—was not quite real, or, even if the sense, the feeling and the belief were admitted to be real since, after all, they really were experienced, that the objects to which they apparently pointed were not. Common sense again agrees.

But to judge from the works and conversation of *contemporary* physicists, there is no longer any basis even in science for these beliefs. Now, it was the growing conviction that the reasons which science was formerly thought to afford, or which most people thought that it afforded, for dismissing the religious view of the universe, were no longer valid, that set me exploring this time-honoured ground once again. For whatever the universe might as a whole, whatever it might at bottom be like, science, I became convinced, could not tell us. Not only were the methods of science far from being exhaustive; when applied to certain kinds of facts with which they were not fitted to deal, they were lamentably unsatisfactory.

A Scientist on the Mind

Reflect, for example, upon the implications of the fact that the correlations which scientists establish are known by a mind. What has science to say about mind? This is a large question and the answer to it cannot be given at the end of a chapter.[1] But that I may bring the chapter to an end by providing one striking illustration of its main contention, let us consider what Mr. Hoyle has to say about the mind.

At the end of his book, Mr. Hoyle, having surveyed first the materialist and then the religious hypothesis, asks the question whether our minds survive bodily death and points out very properly that the answer to the question depends at least in part upon what is meant by a mind. If, he comments, we knew, 'we should be well on the way to getting an answer'. Unfortunately, we don't, he thinks, know what a mind is. But

[1] I return to this question in greater detail in chapters v and viii, pp. 136–44 and 195–210.

Mr. Hoyle and the Physical Universe

one thing he holds to be clear, namely, that 'the mind, if it exists in the religious sense, must have some physical connections', and must, therefore, be 'capable of physical detection'.

Why should it be so capable? Not a scrap of evidence is advanced in favour of this assertion. Of course, *if* the mind is physical, it must have physical connections. But why should it be physical? Why, in short, should it be taken for granted that that in me, whatever it is, that recognises that A^2-B^2 equals $(A-B)$ $(A+B)$, and can follow the chain of reasoning upon which the equation is based, must be a piece of matter analysable into charges of positive and negative electricity? Is it credible that it *could* be a piece of matter, or credible that it could be another piece of matter that finds it credible? Could one piece of matter find another piece either credible or incredible? Can a piece of matter, indeed, do anything at all except move, that is, alter its position in space? But if it cannot —and for my part I find it self-evident that it cannot and regard all such phrases as 'matter become conscious of itself' as mere beggings of the question—the mind cannot either be, or be of the same nature as, a piece of matter. Why, then, must it have 'physical connections' and 'be capable of physical detection'? The answer, such as it is, that Mr. Hoyle gives is that 'survival after death would be meaningless and unthinkable without some interaction with the physical world'. Again, one may ask, *why* should it be meaningless? Because, presumably, our minds, when they animate our bodies, do manifestly often interact with the physical world and Mr. Hoyle takes it for granted that what they often do now they must always do.

But (i) there is absolutely no ground for this assumption. Mind may have pre-existed the body and it may survive it. Shorn of its bodily connection, it may cease to have any contact with the physical world and yet continue *to be*. We do not know that this is so, but we certainly do not know that it is not so.

(ii) There is no ground for supposing that a mind which is *not* at every moment interacting with matter is meaningless and unthinkable. I can think of many kinds of mental activities

42

which certainly do not seem *prima facie* to involve any interaction with the physical world, as, for example, my realisation
of the truth of the algebraic equation given above, the train of
mental activity upon which I engage when I do mental arith-
metic or my recognition of such necessary relations as that, if P
implies Q and Q implies R, then P also implies R.

Mr. Hoyle may, of course, mean merely that in order that
it may engage in these *prima facie* purely mental activities my
mind must interact with my brain upon which, apparently,
he believes it wholly to depend; he may even believe its activities
to be wholly caused by *movements* in the brain. And it may be
the case that this is true. But whether it is true or not, this is not
the point here at issue, which is not whether all the minds we
know anything of now are wholly dependent upon brains, which
is the materialist contention, but whether it is meaningless to
think of minds which do not have any contact with the physical
world. For my part, I am totally unable to see why it should be
meaningless. Even if all those activities of mind with which we
are familiar involved bodily dependence, it would certainly
not be meaningless to suppose that there may be other activities
that do not involve it. And, in fact, we do know of such activities. Telepathy, for example, whose occurrence must, I think,
now be regarded as demonstrated, certainly *seems* to involve
direct communication between minds, that is to say, communication otherwise than through the medium of brains and
bodies. Precognition, again, certainly appears to occur, but pre-
cognition can hardly involve interaction between mind and the
precognised events in the physical world, for if these events are
really in the future, they have not yet occurred and do not,
presumably, exist.

(iii) The view that a mind must have some physical connections is exceedingly ambiguous. If it means that it must interact
with matter or that it must be related to or dependent upon a
brain, then the observations just made apply. But it *may*
mean that it must have physical connections, as it were, tacked
on to it, links or hooks, perhaps, attaching it to the brain, or

Mr. Hoyle and the Physical Universe

perhaps some tail or trail of tenuous matter. Now this view *is*, I think, strictly unthinkable, for if the mind is not material— and to say that it is brings us back to the materialism which Mr. Hoyle explicitly repudiates—there is nothing for the hypothecated physical hooks and links to tack on to. There could only be such a point of attachment if the mind was, in fact, material. What the relation of mind to the brain may be I shall discuss in other chapters.[1]

CONCLUSION IN REGARD TO SCIENTIFIC METHOD

I mentioned Mr. Hoyle's treatment of mind here in order that I might bring out two points. First, in spite of his explicit repudiation of materialism, his thought is still unconsciously dominated by materialist conceptions. (It is rare to meet a scientist whose thought is *not*.) He still thinks of reality in terms of matter, and takes the physical as the standard, the sole standard, of the real. Moreover, matter is still conceived imaginatively after the model of that which we can see and touch, which of course involves the implied assumption that whatever else is real must be of the same nature as that which we can see and touch, and the implied corollary that to appreciate values, to enjoy religious experience, indeed, to enjoy any experience which does not involve interaction with the physical, is to wander in a world of shadows. In effect, then, though he would, I dare say, repudiate the suggestion, Mr. Hoyle has not moved from the position adopted by T. H. Huxley nearly a hundred years ago, as expressed, for example, in the utterance quoted above, 'the thoughts to which I am now giving utterance, and your thoughts regarding them are the expression of molecular changes in the matter of life'. Indeed, he might even subscribe to the grandiose claim of Professor Tyndall.[2]

I conclude that directly scientists leave the domain of science and seek to interpret its findings, they are apt to go astray, if only because of their tendency to import the concepts and modes

[1] See chapters v and viii, pp. 136–44 and 195–210.
[2] See above, p. 34.

Mr. Hoyle and the Physical Universe

of thinking proper to science into spheres to which they are not relevant, as an alternative to denying the existence of such spheres altogether. Having by this means reached startling results, they are apt to take refuge in such purely dogmatic assertions as 'Survival after death would be meaningless and unthinkable without some interaction with the physical world'. Prominent among these spheres is the sphere of religion. The conclusion seems to follow that though science may succeed in increasing our knowledge of the nature of the constitution of the physical world, it can have no contribution to make to the religious interpretation of the universe.

CHAPTER III

The Significance of Evil

To conclude the personal part of this book, I insert here a chapter which partakes of the autobiographical in that it is concerned to describe the influences and to enumerate the factors which led me to reconsider and finally to accept the religious view of the universe. The question may be raised why such a chapter should be worth including. It cannot, it is obvious, be of much interest to those who are already sympathetic to the development it records, most of whom will have reached and passed my stage long ago. Nor is there any reason to suppose that a chapter which partakes of biography rather than of argument will have weight with those who are contemptuous or indifferent. Why, then, include it? Because I believe my case to be not untypical of many of my generation who started from my background. Hence the record of a personal pilgrimage may have more than personal interest.

What I have to record is a changed view of the nature of man, which in due course led to a changed view of the nature of the world.

I. MAN AS INHERENTLY SINFUL

Brought up in a late Victorian Christian household, I went, like nearly all children of the English middle classes, regularly to church (or chapel) and fairly regularly to Sunday-school. Here I was taught that man was born in sin and that the heart of him was desperately wicked. This part of Christian doctrine was not, perhaps, much insisted on, but the Prayer Book was

46

explicit enough. The Confession told me that I had 'left undone those things which' I 'ought to have done', that there was 'no health in' me and that I was a 'miserable offender'. This view of me was further insisted on in the Communion Service in which I was led to 'acknowledge and bewail' my 'manifold sins and wickedness, which' I 'from time to time most grievously' had 'committed, by thought, word and deed against' God's 'divine Majesty, provoking most justly' His 'wrath and indignation against' me.

The Collects reinforced the lesson, pointing out that I had no power of myself to help myself, and adding that without God 'the frailty of man . . . cannot but fall'. For this reason I was encouraged to pray earnestly for God's help. 'O God,' I prayed, 'because through the weakness of' my 'mortal nature' I 'can do no good thing without Thee, grant' me 'the help of Thy grace'— being assured that, if I prayed earnestly enough and earnestly endeavoured to live the kind of life that deserved it, God's grace would in fact be vouchsafed to me.

II. MAN AS INFINITELY PERFECTIBLE

The intellectual climate of the world in which I grew up was utterly antagonistic to the suggestions of the Prayer Book. The early years of the twentieth century were years of achievement and of the hope of yet greater achievement; indeed, the era which came abruptly to an end in 1914 was one of the most confident and successful in the history of mankind. I will speak, first, of the intellectual climate of the time; secondly, of the solid achievements by which it was sustained; and, thirdly, of certain specific doctrines in which it was expressed.

(a) CREATIVE EVOLUTION AND ITS IMPLICATIONS

The dominating philosophy of these years was that of creative evolution, a philosophy which found expression in various forms in the works of Shaw and Bergson and, subsequently, of Alexander. What all these writers had in common was the conviction

The Significance of Evil

that man was master of his fate. The world was his for the making; the future was dependent on his will; his destiny was in his own hands.

Of the metaphysical implications of this view I shall speak in a later chapter.[1] Here I am concerned only with its practical implications. These derive chiefly from the absence of what might be called any limiting factor to human aspiration and achievement. Grant the existence of a supernatural world, and it is not unreasonable to suppose that it might constitute a framework by which the conditions of man's life would be set, such a framework, for example, as might in certain circumstances act as a check upon his aspirations and a limit to his achievements. The form which such a framework had traditionally taken was that of a moral law. The universe, religion had taught, is governed no less by moral than by physical laws. Hence, if you behave in such and such a way, such and such results will follow more or less automatically as a result of the workings of cosmic morality. Thus, the Greeks taught that if man grew too big for his boots and aspired to a status beyond his station, the gods would grow jealous and cast him down. Pride, in fact, goes before a fall or, more precisely, there is a Nemesis in things as the result of which *hubris* will be followed by disaster. Doctrines of oriental fatalism often give expression to the same idea and in Christian thought man's power is always limited by the will of the Creator to whom he is subject.

Now the outstanding characteristic of the views to which I have referred is the clean sweep that they made of this conception of a limiting supernatural. For them there was no force other than man, or other than that expressed in man, to bar his path, to punish his transgressions, to limit his aspirations, to cramp, in a word, his style.

Moreover, the force that was expressed in man, the sole spiritual force—if the word 'spiritual' is no misnomer—in the universe was dynamic. Shaw's Life Force, for example, was creative; it had, in particular, creative power over matter.

[1] See chapter vi, pp. 156–63.

The Significance of Evil

'Vitality with a direction' he called it, expressing itself in the will to create matter or to mould the matter which it finds ready for its moulding. 'Evolution shows us this direction of vitality doing all sorts of things.' Thus 'the will to do anything can and does at a certain pitch of intensity, set up by conviction of its necessity, create and organise new tissue to do it with.'

Bergson's *élan vital*, which is at once the thrusting force that drives evolution forward and the inner reality of ourselves, is a creative impulsion of endless duration, while matter, sometimes conceived as a creation of our own intellects, is on other occasions represented as an occasional interruption of the impulsion. Alexander's Space-Time, the matrix from which the cosmos as we know it has evolved, develops by the inner necessity of its own being ever higher stages of consciousness. It has developed us and it will develop beyond us, will, in fact, develop God.

To sum up the general implications of these philosophies as they bear upon the status and prospects of human life: (i) There is nothing in the universe other than man to which man is subject, by whom or which he is controlled and to whom or which he owes obligation, worship, reverence or love. (ii) There is nothing intractable in man himself, nothing which is not the product of the evolutionary process, and which, since man is himself a creature in continuous development, cannot be improved through the continuance of that same process. For just as the universe is man's for the making, so man himself is in the making. Whatever in man seems imperfect and regrettable, whatever flaws of character or deficiencies of mind he may exhibit, can be bred out of him by a further instalment of the process that produced him. Indeed, he himself can learn consciously to direct that process in whatever direction seems good to him, can, therefore, if he so wills, direct it to the betterment of himself.

To quote from the philosopher who most perfectly expresses this not untypical late-Victorian view, 'the ultimate development of the ideal man', wrote Herbert Spencer, 'is certain—as certain as any conclusion in which we place the most implicit faith, for instance that all men die'. For 'progress', Spencer

The Significance of Evil

maintained, 'is not an accident but a necessity. What we call evil and immorality', he continued, 'must disappear'. 'It is certain', he triumphantly concluded, 'that man must become perfect.'

Nor was this view confined to the materialists and agnostics of the nineteenth century. It infected its poets, even its religious poets. The hymns of the country church which I attend are taken from a volume, *Songs of Praise*, first published in 1925 by the Oxford University Press as 'a collection that should be national in character'. Two are included by the Victorian poet J. Addington Symonds. The following selection is taken from one of them.

> *These things shall be! A loftier race*
> *Than e'er the world hath known, shall rise*
> *With flame of freedom in their souls*
> *And light of science [sic] in their eyes.*
>
> *They shall be gentle, brave and strong,*
> *To spill no drop of blood, but dare*
> *All that may plant man's lordship firm*
> *On earth and fire and sea and air.*
>
> *Nation with nation, land with land,*
> *Inarmed shall live as comrades free;*
> *In every heart and brain shall throb*
> *The pulse of one fraternity.*
>
> *New arts shall bloom of loftier mould,*
> *And mightier music thrill the skies,*
> *And every life shall be a song,*
> *When all the earth is paradise.*

Perfection, in short, however it be conceived, is achievable by man upon earth. Indeed, it will be achieved.

(b) THE ACHIEVEMENT OF SCIENCE

It was chiefly upon the achievements of science that these remarkable predictions were founded. So rapid and unprecedented had been the advance of science, that to give plausibility

The Significance of Evil

to the belief in a continuous and indefinite improvement both of man and of man's universe, it was enough to point to the solid achievements of the last hundred years.

The record of progress effected by science during the period which ended with the first decade of the twentieth century was, indeed, very impressive. Through its agency most of the external enemies by which man's life had been hitherto oppressed seemed in a fair way to being overcome. To those who look back over the past existence of man upon the earth it wears a squalid and fear-ridden aspect. The record of history shows man's life at the mercy of forces that he could neither control nor understand, forces of fire, of flood, of earthquake, of pestilence and famine; his communities have been oppressed by want and disease; in the sweat of his brow he has earned a meagre living from nature; his manual strength has been exploited in ruthless servitude to other men.

By the beginning of the nineteenth century most of these external enemies to man's welfare had either disappeared or been substantially diminished. The nineteenth century saw an enormous increase in man's power over nature. Coal was dug from the depths of the earth; iron and steel were forged into instruments for the achievement of human purposes; first steam and then electricity were harnessed to man's use, and, as a result, there was a great increase in the amenities of living. Cotton, for example, became cheap, and as a consequence human beings became clean; for cheap cotton gave women clothes that could be worn in place of the leather stays and wadded petticoats in which their bodies had hitherto been encased for months at a time owing to the difficulty of changing them. Even the greatest ladies of the seventeenth and eighteenth centuries tended to wear their clothes until they rotted to pieces on their bodies. Hence cheap cotton meant a diminution in human stink. As late as the middle of the nineteenth century sweeps were washing three times a year, while many of the poorer classes did not wash at all. . . . Again, man's increased power over matter enabled the streets to be paved and 'gas-lighted' and so reduced both

51

The Significance of Evil

crime and disease. Behind the streets of eighteenth-century London was hidden a squalid confusion of buildings, courts, rents and closes, often the disputed property of several claimants and all of them ramshackle. These provided harbourage for all the beggars and criminals of the city, as well as for those more or less permanent residents, typhus and smallpox. This is not to be wondered at when we read that Londoners drank water from the same source into which they poured their sewage. Gas lighting, paved streets and new houses thus meant less crime and better health.

As a consequence the length of human life was substantially increased. A child born in the eighteenth century had every prospect of dying; three out of four children born in London did, in fact, die before they reached the age of five, the population of the capital being only maintained by continual immigration from the country. The chances of a son of Charles II surviving were about a quarter of those of a baby born in a twentieth-century London slum. Here are some figures: whereas in 1840 the Englishman's average age was twenty-nine years, in 1870 it was thirty-five, in 1901 forty-eight and a half, in 1935 fifty-nine, and in 1949 sixty-six. In the space of twenty years between 1911 and 1931 the infant mortality rate alone dropped by 40 per cent. The houses in which people live are healthier and more comfortable than they have ever been and fewer people live in them. As recently as 1881 there were on an average $5\frac{1}{2}$ persons living in every house in England and Wales. In 1950, in spite of shortages caused by the war and the increase of population, there were $4\frac{1}{2}$. Men do not work so hard nor do they work for so long as they have done in the past. The Englishman's working week in 1932 was, on an average, just over six hours shorter than it was in 1914, and twelve hours shorter than it was in 1880. Although men do less work, they get paid more for what they do. Thus, when all allowance is made for the increased cost of living, the real wages of the working-class population were in 1951 about 30 per cent higher than they were in 1914.

The Significance of Evil

Human beings die less frequently from unpleasant diseases. Thus the mortality from measles is now 23 per cent, from diphtheria 10 per cent, from typhoid fever 9 per cent, and from scarlet fever 3 per cent less than it was in 1877. Epidemics such as typhoid, which used to be regarded as natural catastrophes, are now treated as preventable scandals for which those who are considered to be responsible should be arraigned in court.

More important than the fact that men suffer less from diseases is the fact that they suffer less from pain. There is a time-honoured controversy as to the most important single discovery in the history of the human race. Some opt for fire; some for the invention of the wheel; some for the growing of corn. For my part, I would give my vote to the invention of anaesthetics. It came late—as recently as the eighteenth century men were knocked unconscious, or made roaring drunk on gin before undergoing an operation—and when it came, it met with considerable opposition. Inevitably it was preached against from the pulpit—what new inventions, one wonders, from forks for table to lightning conductors, have not been preached against from the pulpit?—special exception being taken to the use of anaesthetics to relieve the pain of women in childbirth. God, it was obvious, had intended women to suffer; otherwise He would not have made childbirth painful. Therefore, to mitigate their pain was to thwart His intentions, which was impious. The same difficulty was not, however, raised in the case of men, for God had not manifested the same indifference in regard to male suffering—had He not taken care to put Adam into a deep sleep before extracting the rib which was to become Eve? In spite of the displeasure of the pulpit, the use of anaesthetics to mitigate suffering increased throughout the nineteenth century.

The above are only a few examples of the manifest benefits which man's increased knowledge of matter and increased ability to use his knowledge in furtherance of his ends have conferred upon our race. All are due to science.

In consequence there has been engendered a new attitude to the universe and to the status of human life within it. Before the age of science reality was conceived as something given and unchangeable, and the fundamental human problem had been how to subdue man's life to the dictates of this reality, and to conform to the conditions that it imposed. The problem is *now* how to subdue reality to man's desires and to make it conformable to his aspirations. Thus, for a problem of morals, a problem of discipline and control—how to govern the human soul—there has been substituted a problem of technique—how to alter reality in ways which are agreeable to man.

Nor is this the only change. Hitherto men had pursued philosophy and science out of curiosity, because they wanted to understand the world. Now they tend to pursue science from love of power, because they wish to change it. Hence pure science for the sake of knowledge has tended increasingly to give way to applied science for the sake of power. Both changes presuppose a changed attitude to the cosmos and a revised estimate of man's position and prospects within it. As a result, man's life is no longer conceived as being enclosed within a given non-human framework which lies outside his control and sets a necessary limit to his power and his aspirations. Man is the master both of his environment and his fate. His task is to arrive at such an understanding of the nature of that environment as will enable him to achieve the mastery he desires. Thus, for the problem of how to achieve wisdom which will enable man to control himself, is substituted the problem of how to acquire the 'know-how' which will enable him to control his environment. It will be seen that the scientific achievements of the early twentieth century were at once the prop and the mirror of its philosophy.

THE IMPROVEMENT OF HUMAN NATURE

Nor were the achievements confined to the material sphere. In many ways it must have seemed, indeed, it did seem to those of us who were adult before the First World War—and the appearance was maintained until at any rate well into the 'twenties—that man's nature was being steadily altered for the

The Significance of Evil

better. The crudities and savageries of the past were disappearing. As civilisation advanced, life grew easier and human beings more human.

Consider for a moment the evils that had disappeared from the lives of men—witchcraft and cholera, gladiatorial games and slavery. Each of these evils must at the time of its prevalence have seemed—as war seems today—to be irremediable. Human nature being what it is, men must have said—men did, in fact, say—it was impossible to abolish slavery. But by repeated appeals to men's sense of justice, to their reason, to their compassion, slavery was over large parts of the earth abolished. Even torture, it seemed, was largely a thing of the past and would in due course disappear from the few comparatively barbarous areas of the world that still resorted to it. And there was a growth—indeed, in some respects there is still a growth—in considerateness and gentleness in man's dealings with his fellow men. Consider, for example, the implications of such a play as Ben Jonson's *Volpone*. Volpone is attended by three permanent servitors, a eunuch, a hermaphrodite and a dwarf, whose business it is to amuse and divert him. When I saw this play I was first shocked by their gambols, and then bored. Why? Not, I think, because the actors did not do them justice, but because physical deformity no longer seems to twentieth-century man to be in itself funny. The sixteenth-century audience, presumably, laughed at the eunuch, the hermaphrodite, and the dwarf because they were deformed men, or were not fully men. In me and, I think, in most of the audience present, the spectacle roused a feeling of pity tinged with repulsion.

In his *Voyage to Lisbon* Fielding writes as if he takes it for granted that, being old and dropsical, he will have to endure for some hours the jeers and laughter of the crowd by the riverside before embarking on board ship. I do not think that he would now have to dread the results of a similar exposure. Taking us by and large, we should be prepared to be compassionate, where once we jeered.

The Significance of Evil

OPTIMISM OF THE EARLY TWENTIETH CENTURY

Be this as it may, the prevailing hopefulness of the era that ended with the First World War cannot, I submit, be seriously doubted. The age, at any rate, *seemed* hopeful to most of those who were living in it. I possess a published copy of a lecture on *Decadence* delivered by the late Lord Balfour to the students of Newnham College, Cambridge, early in 1908. In this lecture Balfour looks forward to a continuation of the great period of progress which had characterised the western world for the last two thousand years. Here are his concluding words: 'Whatever be the perils in front of us, there are, so far, no symptoms either of pause or regression in the onward movement which for more than a thousand years has been a characteristic of western civilisation.'

It was in 1913 that Professor Bury contributed to the Home University Library a book, *A History of Freedom of Thought*, which subsequently became a minor classic. At the conclusion of his record of man's struggle to achieve the right to think freely, to express his thoughts freely in writing and to read what fancy or inclination suggested, a struggle whose development he had traced for some two thousand years, he ended with this remarkable judgment: 'The struggle of reason against authority has ended in what appears now to be a decisive and permanent victory for liberty. In the most civilised and progressive countries freedom of discussion is recognised as a fundamental principle.'

(c) TWO CHARACTERISTIC DOCTRINES

Buttressed as it was by the achievements of science, the dominant philosophy of the time gave rise to two characteristic doctrines which, however much they might differ in other respects, had this in common, they both maintained the infinite malleability and, therefore, by implication, the infinite perfectibility of man.

One of these doctrines maintained that evil and imperfection

The Significance of Evil

were due to bad external conditions and relied, therefore, chiefly upon science's new-won mastery over matter, resulting in its ability to harness the forces of nature in man's service, to improve the conditions of his life. The other aimed more directly at the control of human nature itself, partly by eugenics and scientific breeding, designed to produce a desired type of human being, partly by an education designed to cause men to think, to will, to desire and to value in desirable ways, partly by a direct assault upon unregenerate elements in the psyche by means of psychological techniques. I will say something of each doctrine in turn.

(1) MAN'S IMPROVEMENT THROUGH EXTERNAL CONDITIONS

This, I take it, is the essence of the Marxist creed. Man's psychological, moral and 'spiritual' life—the word 'spiritual' is placed in quotes to indicate the ambiguous status accorded to the spirit in the Marxist analysis of human nature—is, for the philosophy of Marxism, a reflection of the social structure of the society to which he belongs and, more particularly, of the social and economic class to which he belongs within that structure. The social structure is itself regarded as the product of material circumstances, being, in fact, determined by the way in which at any given period men satisfy their fundamental needs. Thus the relation between man and man is determined by the relation between man and things; and the individual's psychological consciousness, including, therefore, his moral consciousness, is determined by the relations prevailing in society between man and man. In the past man's moral condition has been bad because the social structure has been bad. It has been a class social structure within which the great mass of mankind has been able to exist only on condition that men sold their labour to the owners of the means of production. The owners of the means of production have exploited the masses' necessity, returning to the worker only so much of the proceeds of his work as was necessary to keep him alive and reasonably fit and appropriating the surplus for their own use.

The Significance of Evil

Such is the essence of capitalism under which the great mass of mankind is and is of necessity poor, ill-educated and oppressed.

But capitalism is only the last of a series of social phases which—though the relations between the classes, reflecting, as they did, the different methods which man has from time to time adopted for satisfying his fundamental needs, have varied —all had this in common, they all entailed the exploitation of a property-less by a property-owning class. Thus the moral outlook and consciousness of mankind have not at any time been much better than they are under capitalism.

The object of Marxist Communism is to abolish the two-class structure of society and to establish a classless structure. The change will have two important results. First, all those vicious effects which spring from the class system—ostentation, arrogance, selfishness, and pride on the one hand, and snobbery, humility, servility and degradation on the other—will disappear. Secondly, the poverty and ignorance of the masses which are directly due to the class system will also disappear. At the same time, the application of science to productive processes in the interests of society as a whole, unfettered by the restrictions and competition which are inherent factors in the capitalist system, will lead to a great increase of wealth and ultimately of leisure. Hence, under a fully established Communist régime the level of morality and happiness of most human beings will be immeasurably higher than it is now or has been at any time in the past, owing to the abolition of the conditions which have kept the mass of men starved, brutish, backward, ignorant and poor. Given the continued existence of a classless society, the process of moral betterment may itself be expected to continue indefinitely, to continue, indeed, *ad infinitum* to perfection, if the term 'perfection' can be said to have any meaning in the terminology of the Marxist philosophy.

I have purposely kept this sketch of the doctrines or, rather, of the bearing upon man's moral life of the doctrines of Marxism brief to the point of inadequacy, since I assume that the doctrines

The Significance of Evil

in question are too familiar to require elaboration. The precise form in which their teaching, that whatever in man is regrettable is due to external circumstances, was brought home to me was the form given to it by Bernard Shaw.

Shaw on Poverty. It was under the influence of Shaw, whom I hero-worshipped, that I had become a Socialist, and his most lightly conceived doctrines had for me the authority of gospel. One was precisely this doctrine that evil was due to the external circumstances of men's lives and, in particular, to the circumstance of poverty. This doctrine was being urged with unmatched eloquence in one of the great passages of English prose in the preface to *Major Barbara*. Shaw's indictment of capitalist society is based on its acquiescence in the poverty of most of its members. 'Let him', he represents the capitalist as saying, 'be poor':

'Now what does this Let Him Be Poor mean? It means let him be weak. Let him be ignorant. Let him become a nucleus of disease. Let him be a standing exhibition and example of ugliness and dirt. Let him have rickety children. Let him be cheap and let him drag his fellows down to his price by selling himself to do their work. Let his habitations turn our cities into poisonous congeries of slums. Let his daughters infect our young men with the diseases of the streets and his sons revenge him by turning the nation's manhood into scrofula, cowardice, cruelty, hypocrisy, political imbecility, and all the other fruits of oppression and malnutrition. Let the undeserving become still less deserving; and let the deserving lay up for himself not treasures in heaven, but horrors in hell upon earth. . . .

'The evil to be attacked,' then, 'is not sin, suffering, greed, priestcraft, kingcraft, demagogy, monopoly, ignorance, drink, war, pestilence, nor any other of the scapegoats which reformers sacrifice, but simply poverty.' What, in short, is the matter with the poor is their poverty.

And the remedy? The remedy for evil is the remedy for the poverty that engenders it—namely, money.

The Significance of Evil

'Money is the most important thing in the world. It represents health, strength, honour, generosity and beauty as conspicuously and undeniably as the want of it represents illness, weakness, disgrace, meanness and ugliness. Not the least of its virtues is that it destroys base people as certainly as it fortifies and dignifies noble people. . . .'

'The crying need of the nation,' Shaw concludes, 'is not for better morals, cheaper bread, temperance, liberty, culture, redemption of fallen sisters and erring brothers, nor the grace, love and fellowship of the Trinity, but simply for enough money.'

I dare say Shaw would not accept this as a full account of his view, for there is nothing here about the distinctive vices of the rich, luxury and arrogance, ostentation and cruelty and pride, vices which in other connections he has censured with the eloquence of a Swift or a Bunyan. Nevertheless, the ethical implications of the doctrine explicitly stated in the preface to *Major Barbara* and drawn intermittently throughout the course of his work are sufficiently clear. Evil is neither endemic nor ineradicable in man; it is the product of circumstances. Remove the circumstances, give everybody, for example, an equal and an adequate income irrespective of work done, and the evils due to poverty will disappear together with the evils of snobbery and patronage which are poverty's by-products. For the vices of the rich may be expected to disappear when our social system has been so remodelled as no longer to put a premium upon wealth. (It is worth noting that the 'great man' as Shaw conceives him, Caesar, for example, or St. Joan, is wholly without the characteristic vices of the rich; so, too, are the Long-Livers in the fourth play of *Back to Methuselah*.)

(II) Man's Improvement Through Psychological Adjustment

The second view put forward in various forms in the works of Freud, Jung and Adler, and now constituting the common stock-in-trade of most psychologists, treated evil as a form of maladjustment to life or as one of the consequences of maladjustment.

The Significance of Evil

Man has certain basic instincts which in themselves are neither good nor bad. Owing to unfavourable environment or unsuitable handling in early childhood, these are thwarted and distorted in various ways; or the child is oppressed by his parents and stores up hatred in his unconscious; or he develops a sense of guilt in respect of the performance of purely natural functions and represses into the unconscious the desires and cravings in respect of which he is caused to feel guilty; or he is humiliated or snubbed and spends the rest of his life trying to compensate for the resultant sense of inferiority of which he may well be unconscious. The consequences of maladjustment are as numerous as the formulae which different psychologists have adopted for their description. All, however, concur in taking a negative view of evil. Evil, that is to say, is not, for them, a positive and distinctive force, endemic in the heart of man. The behaviour and the desires which have been traditionally regarded as evil or as sinful or as wicked—it should be noted that words like 'evil', 'sinful', 'wicked', are sedulously avoided; instead we hear of 'ill-adjusted behaviour' or 'aggressive instincts'—are interpreted as being due to the pressure upon consciousness or to the outcropping in consciousness of elements in the psyche which have been thwarted or repressed by the circumstances of early life. The moral is the same as that of the view just described; change the circumstances, place the child in an approved environment, give him love and freedom, make him feel important but not too important, refrain from oppressing or restricting him, carefully avoid inculcating feelings of guilt or inferiority, and he will grow up into a psychologically healthy, cheerful, effective, balanced and fearless adult.

This view is so pervasive in modern thought, particularly in America, that it is hardly necessary to give examples. I confine myself to one afforded by the utterances of an official holding an eminent position in the contemporary world, Dr. Brock Chisholm, Director of the World Health Organisation appointed under U.N.O.

In the passage which I have selected Dr. Chisholm is discussing the overriding problem of our time, the problem of war.

The Significance of Evil

How, he wants to know, is mankind to obtain secure and enduring peace? He rightly sees that the source of war is in the human heart. It is because men desire wrongly, will wrongly and have unregenerate instincts that there is war. The problem, then, is to correct or at any rate to redirect these undesirable tendencies in human nature. Now this problem is treated by Dr. Chisholm exactly as if it were a problem of science, the science in question being that of psychiatry. A pamphlet entitled *The Psychiatry of Enduring Peace and Social Progress*, which is a reprint of a lecture[1] delivered by Dr. Chisholm when Deputy Minister of Health for Canada, begins with the customary tribute to the knowledge and authority of science: 'Scientists of this generation have no obligation to admit superiority of knowledge or of wisdom [*sic*] in any body of traditional belief or authority.' In the light of their knowledge and wisdom, Dr. Chisholm exhorts them to 'accept our own responsibility to remodel the world in bolder, clearer, more honest lines'. For human nature is limitlessly malleable and 'within the possible expressions of human nature are the personalities of a Caligula or a Franklin Roosevelt, a female guard at Belsen camp or a Florence Nightingale, a Hitler or, almost, a Christ'. Dr. Chisholm proceeds to argue that it depends upon the psychological and physical environment in which children grow up which of these various possibilities will be realised. It is the task of psychiatry to devise the right environment, for the art of life is something that psychology and psychology alone can teach. 'Psychiatrists', in fact, '. . . must become specialists in living'.

Dr. Chisholm's pamphlet provoked much discussion and comment among the distinguished audience. However sharply they might differ on other points, the commentators all agreed in thinking that the correction of whatever may be regrettable in human nature is a job for science. Pavlov, for example, was quoted with approval. 'Only science,' he wrote, 'exact science about human nature itself, and the most sincere approach to it

[1] The William Alanson White Memorial Lecture delivered at Washington at the William Alanson White Psychiatric Foundation in 1946.

by the aid of the omnipotent scientific method will deliver man from his present gloom and will purge him from his contemporary shame in the sphere of inter-human relations.' Again and again the same note is struck. Psychologists and therapeutists, 'the custodians of knowledge and those skilled in human techniques', are the people to whom we must look for the improvement of human nature. For it is 'accepted universally by psychiatrists', said Henry Wallace, at that time Secretary of Commerce in the United States Government, 'that the sad state of the recent generations of mankind is due to a sense of inferiority and guilt and fear'. Somewhere, it is intimated, a formula exists for removing that sense. We have only to discover and apply the formula and all will be well.

I have referred to this pamphlet and the comments it evoked because it is typical of much of the thought of our time, particularly of that which is called advanced.

III. RETURN TO TRADITIONAL VIEW

THE RECORD OF HISTORY

This view of human evil which I adopted unthinkingly as a young man I have come fundamentally to disbelieve. Plausible, perhaps, during the first fourteen years of this century when, as I have tried to show, the state of mankind seemed to be improving—though even then the most cursory reading of human history should have been sufficient to dispose of it—it has been rendered utterly unplausible by the events of the last forty years. To me, at any rate, the view of evil implied by Marxism, expressed by Shaw and maintained by modern psychotherapy, a view which regards evil as the by-product of circumstances, which circumstances can, therefore, alter and even eliminate, has come to seem intolerably shallow and the contrary view of it as endemic in man, more particularly in its Christian form, the doctrine of original sin, to express a deep and essential insight into human nature.

63

The Significance of Evil

For am I really to believe that the passions, the rages, the callous indifference to human suffering, the unbridled lust for domination and display exhibited by the men of restless energy and dominating will who have fought their way to power during the last forty years, are adequately to be explained as the by-products of a feeling of inferiority engendered by neglect in school? That every guard who has taken delight in the beating and torturing of helpless prisoners in concentration camps was imbued by suppressed feelings of guilt, or that the horrors of, let us say, the Russian Revolution, the Russian purges or the Nazi invasion of and retreat from Russia can be adequately accounted for as the inevitable by-products of revolution and war brought about by a change in the methods which human beings adopt to satisfy their fundamental needs? Is it not obvious that human arrogance and love of power, that human brutality and cruelty, that, in a word, man's inhumanity to man, are responsible for these happenings; obvious, too, that it is precisely these characteristics that have written their melancholy record upon every page of human history?

The foregoing is, as I am well aware, in no sense entitled to rank as argument. Nor, indeed, will the remainder of this chapter consist of argument. For I am not arguing so much as trying to describe a new way of looking at things, the truth of which was insistently borne in upon me by the events of the times. It was only later that it struck me that this new way of looking at things was only a very old way; was, in fact, the way which I had been taught in my childhood, namely, the Christian way. And with the conviction that mankind is in part evil—I am giving here the sequence of the stages of this conversion, if conversion it may be called, as they actually occurred—came a conviction of the evil in myself.

Up to that time I had been, I think, agreeably immune from the sense of sin. I had offended in many ways, perhaps more than most, against the moral law, but I had suffered very little from any sense of guilt. I was in particular a stranger to the struggle between duty and temptation, being preserved from the conflict between 'ought' and 'want' by the happy (or unhappy) circumstance of not supposing that there could be for me a sense of 'ought' other than that imposed by 'want'.

This book is not the aftermath of an Oxford Group House Party, and I am not proposing to indulge in the luxury of personal confession. Let it, then, suffice to say that my eyes were gradually opened to the extent of my own sinfulness in thought, word and deed; so that, finding that it was only with great difficulty and effort that I could constrain myself to even the most modest degree of virtue, and that very rarely, I came whole-heartedly to endorse the account of me given in the English Book of Common Prayer.

Life a Mixture of Good and Evil

I am not, of course, suggesting either that I or that people in general are wholly wicked. Far from it; merely that all of us are wicked in some degree, all of us wicked on occasion, and that we are so because strands of evil are inextricably woven into our fundamental make-up.

I have come to see life itself in these terms. That here on earth perfection is not to be found; that good and evil are always mixed and never pure; that every cloud has a silver lining; that the darkest hour comes before the dawn; and that equally there is always a fly in the ointment, a canker at the heart of the rose —these opinions and sentiments are the stock-in-trade of the secular as well as of the religious wisdom of the ages. Today the thought which they enshrine colours my attitude to life in practice as well as in theory. I have come, that is to say, to see life in terms of a challenge, a challenge to effort and endeavour, a challenge to sacrifice and self-denial, a challenge, above all, in my own particular case to the voluntary submission of myself to and voluntary endurance of boredom. For I have found by experience that unless the effort and endeavour have been expended, the pleasures of tranquil enjoyment cannot be tasted. The pot of tea and the anchovy toast, the boiled egg and the home-made strawberry jam, never taste so well, the enjoyment

The Significance of Evil

of the armchair by the blazing fire is never so consciously savoured as after a day's climb in the hills in sleet and mist. And when was a hot bath ever so grateful as when one had come home wet through after a day's hunting? Or—to take an example from another sphere—when .was the half-hour with the novel ever so pleasant as after a couple of hours reading or writing philosophy?

Unless, again, the self-denial had first been practised that which should have brought enjoyment only too quickly brought satiety. For me it was literally true that unless I first fasted I had no pleasure in the feast. Moreover I had long ago discovered that if one is to avoid satiety it is wise to abandon one's pleasure before it has been fully savoured—to stop, in fact, while one still wants to go on. As to the boredom against which so much of my life has been a constant campaign, I have found by experience that the best way to invest my London life with its meetings, its committees, its lunches, its parties, its receptions, its chance gatherings with acquaintances, even its intimacies with friends, I will not say tolerable—for I am at all times able to tolerate it very well—but significant with a keen edge of interest and excitement to it, is to intersperse it with tracts of time spent in the country where conversation is limited to the practical and immediate. If you have too much of them, even the best talkers are a bore, and the round of meetings, lectures, conferences, discussions, interviews, in which so much of my life has been spent, a weariness of the spirit. I do not wish to suggest that I live in the country merely in order to escape from London; or that metropolitan occasions are always brilliant and conversational exchanges in the country always flat. I live in the country as much as I can, because I like living in the country and enjoy taking part in the activities and pursuits of a country—in my case—of a farming life. I know, too, that there is a sense in which the life of the countryside goes deeper than the life of the town. The art of conversation is a metropolitan art, and I take a keen pleasure in it when it is good; but it is not good so often that it is worth the sacrifice

The Significance of Evil

of those regional conversations, never recorded, which have gone on through all the centuries of human history and which go on still to-day, though it is not always easy for a sophisticated townsman to graduate for admission to them.

These observations are, I dare say, commonplace enough. At any rate the truth that they illustrate is sufficiently familiar. Indeed, my excuse for setting it in these personal terms is no more than a desire to avoid the charge of retailing platitudes, a charge which a more general statement might have justified. To put in summary form a conclusion which I might endlessly illustrate, I came to see that there was no activity or pursuit without its specific drawback, no way of life without its specific disadvantage, no excellence of character without its correlative vice, and that these things, the drawbacks, the disadvantages, the vices, are not just accidental opposites, but are bound up with and brought into being by the pursuit and enjoyment of the goods to which they are opposed.

To take one example where a hundred might be cited, consider the condition usually regarded as fortunate, the condition, namely, of being in easy circumstances, possessed of both wealth and leisure. Obvious in life and notorious in literature, its drawbacks are the necessary by-products of its advantages. Abundance of worldly goods diminishes our pleasure in using and enjoying them, while too much liberty of choice in regard to occupation, precisely because it is the off-spring of wealth and leisure, makes choice difficult and complicated. Thus the man called 'fortunate' is perpetually perplexed with the questions: What shall I do that will give me most satisfaction? How shall I occupy my leisure? And if this be true of the so-called fortunate man, fortunate in respect of his wealth and leisure, it is ten times truer of the fortunate woman.

PLATO ON PURE AND IMPURE PLEASURES

There is, I repeat, nothing new in all this. The doctrine has, indeed, been the commonplace of moralists in all ages. For my part, I had met it first in Plato's *Philebus* in the form of the

The Significance of Evil

distinction between 'pure' and 'impure' pleasures. But though I had uncritically taken its truth for granted, it was not until comparatively late in life that I recognised in terms of my own experience that it was, indeed, for me, true. Let me briefly recapitulate the doctrine.

Pure pleasures are distinguished from impure by reason of the fact that they contain no admixture of pain. Many pleasures, Plato points out, are dependent for their pleasantness upon the degree of the preceding dissatisfaction to which they are relative. Thus the pleasure of the convalescent is dependent upon the fact of his preceding illness; of the resting man upon his preceding fatigue; of the water-drinking man upon his preceding thirst. These states and activities, convalescing, resting, water-drinking, are characterised by the sort of pleasure whose nature, when it is experienced in its crudest form, as, for example, in the form of relief from long and wearing pain, we all recognise for what it is. We recognise, that is to say, that the pleasure experienced on relief from pain owes its pleasantness solely to the fact that we are no longer suffering the pain which we formerly suffered. These, then, are impure pleasures.

There are, however, other pleasures which, Plato points out, are not dependent on want or need. Pre-eminent in the class of pure pleasures Plato places the pleasures of intellectual and aesthetic activity. And it is, I think, obvious that the pleasures of listening to good music, of looking at good pictures, of solving a difficult problem, of carrying on an abstract discussion, of pursuing a difficult but fruitful line of research, are in no sense determined by, or dependent upon, a preceding state of need, or a preceding experience of pain. We are not made miserable because we are *not* listening to music, however intense our enjoyment when we are.

Plato's recommendation of the pleasures of the mind and the spirit is, then, based on their immunity from the drawbacks both of the craving that comes before satisfaction and the satiety that succeeds it. In principle, I dare say that Plato is right. I am prepared to believe that the lives of the scholar and the scientist, the artist and the saint, are among the best that life has to offer, but I have not the temperament for the life of scholarship and research, the gifts of the artist, or the strength of character of the saint. Though I am on the whole happy when reading and writing, I am too restless to sit stationary at my desk for long hours together. Thus most of the satisfactions that I have known in life have belonged, I fear, to the class of Plato's 'impure' pleasures. Only in music and in nature have I found a pleasure which is comparatively 'pure' and which, I am thankful to say, has grown with the years, so that these two have come to afford the major satisfactions of my life.

Thus I have come fully to subscribe to the truth of Plato's strictures upon most of the things that men call pleasant; yet, being unable to cure myself of my all too human addiction to them, I have accepted, too, his verdict upon the life of *l'homme moyen sensuel* as a chequered life of satisfactions and dissatisfactions. I have learned, too, that the latter on the whole, and especially as one grows older, are predominant.

I have come, then, to accept the conclusion that we must not expect to be very happy here on earth or—to put the same conclusion rather differently—that it is only a certain amount of happiness, and that not very great, that our natures are capable of sustaining.

THE PESSIMISM OF THE SAGES

And again I find the conclusion endorsed by the general experience of mankind. It is, for example, an interesting exercise to put to yourself the question whether in the whole body of literature with which you are acquainted you can find a single really happy day. The nearest approach to such a day that I have been able to call to mind is that on which Nicholas and Natasha Rostov go hunting with Ilagin and the 'Little Uncle' in the second volume of Tolstoy's *War and Peace*. It is a record of a day spent by young, vigorous people in the full bloom of youthful health and strength in the excitements of competition and the chase. In the evening there is a supper with music on the

The Significance of Evil

guitar and dancing and then a drive home in a droshky through the starlight over the snow, when the spirits of brother and sister are drawn nearer than ever before, than ever again. It is as good a day as falls to the lot of any of us, yet even this day is chequered with frustrated hopes and fierce disappointments.

Turning from literature to legend, I am reminded of the Arab prince of the tenth century whose reign marked the climax of the Caliphate of Cordova, and who, preparing his last will and testament, wrote as follows:

'I have now reigned more than fifty years, always victorious, always fortunate: cherished by my subjects, feared by their enemies, and surrounded by general reverence. All that men desire has been lavished on me by Heaven; glory, science, honours, treasure, riches, pleasures, and love; I have enjoyed all, I have exhausted all!

'And now, on the threshold of Death, recalling to remembrance all the past hours in this long period of seeming felicity, I have counted the days in which I have been truly happy: I have been able to find only eleven!

'Mortals, appraise by my example the exact value of life on earth!'

I cannot resist adding a comment on the Caliph's testament taken from a book, *From the Unconscious to the Conscious*, which deserves to be better known than it is, by Gustave Geley, Director of the International Metapsychical Institute in Paris:

'It will suffice,' writes Geley, 'to take an average normal human life, that of a man placed in ordinary circumstances and of ordinary understanding, and to consider it coolly.

'What does his existence consist in?

'During one quarter of a century he works to acquire the means of livelihood; for another quarter he struggles amid perpetual anxieties to make these means of life give a sufficient return; then he dies without knowing exactly why he has lived at all. "To will without motive, always suffering, always struggling, then to die, and so without end, century after century, until the crust of the planet breaks into pieces!" cries Schopenhauer.

The Significance of Evil

'What pains and sorrows, what anxieties and disappointments during the short quarter century during which the man "enjoys" his gains; ephemeral youth with its short-lived illusions; a life worn down by preparation for living; hopes always disappointed and always renewed; a few flowers culled by the wayside of life and soon faded; a few instants of repose, and then the weary march forward again. Personal anxieties; family worries; heavy and ceaseless work; vexations, disillusions, and deceptions; such is the common lot of mortals. For those who have an ideal it is even worse; some intoxication in the pursuit of illusions and heartbreaking discovery of impotence to attain them. Where is the man who, like the great Caliph, on reckoning up his days of complete happiness could count on finding eleven? Who is he who could find one single day of undiluted happiness?'

I have chosen two comparatively unknown expressions of a pessimism in regard to the quality and nature of man's life in support of which more famous testimony could be cited. I might, for example, have quoted Sophocles', 'Not to be born is past all prizing best; easily the next best is to return as soon as possible whence we came'; or Homer's 'No more piteous breed than man creeps or breathes on earth'; or Burton's 'No fiend could so torment, tyrannise over, vex as one man doth another'; or Gibbon's 'History is a record of the crimes, follies and misfortunes of mankind'; or John Stuart Mill's, 'The mass of the human race live a life of drudgery and imprisonment'; or Gissing's 'History is the lurid record of woes unutterable'. All these various remarks constitute a comment upon human life with which, as the years have gone by, I have found myself increasingly in sympathy.

I chose the Caliph and Gustave Geley because their mood tallies most closely with that in which this chapter is written, and runs more closely parallel with the particular strand of my own experience that I want to throw into relief.

What, then, of the doctrines which I learned in my youth, and in particular the doctrine of human well-being continually advancing towards perfectibility?

71

The Significance of Evil

INADEQUACY OF THE MARXIST ACCOUNT OF EVIL

By the light of this new and, as it seemed to me, deeper insight into the nature of human experience, they stood revealed as not only trivial but as false. The philosophy of Marxism in particular, with its implication that what men call evil will disappear with the establishment of a classless society, seemed hopelessly wide of the moral mark. Can it really be the case— I venture to repeat the question—that all the evils which have oppressed human life are of economic and political origin, that the parent who whips his helpless child, the owner who keeps his dog permanently on a chain, or the man who revenges himself by pouring vitriol on the face of the girl who has jilted him, are adequately to be explained as the by-products of an economic system based on the monopoly of the ownership of the means of production resulting in the exploitation of the labour of one class by another? The thing had only to be stated for the irrelevance of the alleged cause to the so-called effect, which it was invoked to explain, to become glaringly obvious.

As to the Shavian diagnosis of wickedness as the by-product of poverty, it was only too obvious that it neglected the distinctive vices of the rich—arrogance and pride, luxury and vulgarity and ostentatious display. Above all, it failed to make provision for what has come to seem to me, if not the greatest of human vices, the most potent source of human misery: man's lust for power over his fellow men. Was it, indeed, any more credible that power-loving and power-exercising could be explained in terms of compensation for the lack of the satisfactions of wealth, than that they should be explained in terms of compensation for the lack of the satisfactions of sex?

INADEQUACY OF THE PSYCHOLOGICAL ACCOUNT

The mention of sex leads to a consideration of the psychological explanation of evil in terms of thwarted *libido*, sense of inferiority unconsciously felt, or lack of integration of the elements of the personality—at least it should do so, if I had the

The Significance of Evil

knowledge or, indeed, the patience to do justice to it. But in this case the *argumentum ad hominem* seems to be sufficient and conclusive. For this pre-eminently is a sphere in which the proof of the pudding is most relevantly to be found in the eating. There is a natural reluctance to use this argument except in cases where its applicability is glaring. But the claim of psychology to improve human nature is assuredly such a case. Take a look, then, at psychologists, men who presumably possess the 'know-how'—the use of this distinctively modern expression seems appropriate here—of human nature and of the methods by which its deficiencies may be remedied; who have, moreover, in so far as they are practising therapeutists, undergone in their own persons thorough courses of the treatment they prescribe for others, whose complexes have, then, presumably been dispelled, whose feelings of guilt and inferiority eradicated, whose instinctive 'aggression' directed into socially harmless channels. Are they notably better than, are they even characteristically different from, their fellows who, innocent of psychology, get along as best they can by the light of their own unaided common sense and moral insight? Are they, in particular, less aggressive? I do not think that they would themselves claim that they are. Yet while the conduct of the expert in psychology is not specifically differentiated by reason of his professional knowledge from that of the rest of us, we all of us know a *good* man when we meet one—at least, I am pretty sure that I do.

Psychological treatment is, no doubt, of great value in remedying certain specific neural and mental disorders; it may even help in the mitigation of emotional imbalances. I am far from wishing to belittle its competence in these spheres; but as an explanation of the common or garden wickedness of the ordinary man, of his pride, his unscrupulousness, his temper and his cruelty, it is hopelessly inadequate.

THE LIMITATIONS OF SCIENCE AS AN IMPROVER

As with psychology, so with science in general. When I was young people looked to science to control not only matter but

The Significance of Evil

life. By means of eugenics we looked forward to the breeding of socially desirable types; by sterilisation or compulsory birth control, to breeding out undesirable ones. Suitable human material having been provided, it was hoped by means of a scientifically designed training and education to produce the kind of personality which was both useful and creditable to the community. Meanwhile, the control of matter had already gone some way to diminish and would ultimately eliminate all the external enemies to man's happiness.

The claim that science has conquered or at least reduced many of the factors that have oppressed man's life[1] in the past is, I have conceded, justified. Yet as we look out upon the contemporary world, it is hard to believe that man's lot is better than it has ever been. In spite of the multiplication of machines to save us from dull and drudging toil, many of us in the west work harder than we have ever done. Indeed, it is only by enlisting the labour of women that we can get our work done at all. Although we are always saving time, most of us never had so little time to spare. In many parts of the world science has been used to imprison man's mind and to hand to the government or to the party or dictator who has won control of the government the keys of its cell. Above all, science has so increased our powers of destruction that the next war bids fair to put paid to our civilisation altogether.

As science has continued to develop, it has become increasingly clear that it is not an end but a means, a means to the furtherance of man's desires. Science is not in itself a good thing or a bad; it is ethically neutral. What it does is to satisfy men's desires and to help them to fulfil their purposes. If the desires and purposes are on the whole good and make for human welfare, this added power of satisfaction and fulfilment is itself a good; if bad, then it, too, is bad. But the purposes themselves science seems impotent to change, still less to improve. Nor can it alter men's desires or—if it be maintained that in certain circumstances it can—it can do so only in pursuance of the pur-

[1] See above, pp. 51–4.

The Significance of Evil

poses of other men, those, namely, who wish men's desires to be such as are agreeable to themselves and to conduce to the maintenance of their power.

There, indeed, is the 'rub'. Let us suppose that science were to give us direct power over human nature. Who would wield that power and in the interests of what? *Quis*, in other words, *custodiet ipsos custodes*? Until this consummation is reached, it is relevant to point out that, in so far as science has sought to obtain *direct* control over human nature, the results have not been impressive. So far from the so-called science of eugenics being applied to the breeding of socially desirable types—and what, incidentally, are socially desirable types, those desired by governments because they are apt to receive instruction, intellectually malleable and amenable to discipline?—the selective use of birth-control by the upper, middle and upper working classes has led to a general lowering of the quality of the human material from which society is recruited. The best stocks fail to keep up their numbers, while society is increasingly recruited from its lowest strata. The effects of this lowering are temporarily masked by improvements in hygiene, social welfare and the raising of economic standards by means of which we have hitherto more than made good the deterioration in the quality of the human beings who are the new material of our society. But you cannot indefinitely continue to grow figs on thistles, and it is hard to believe that the level of human intelligence and character can be maintained in face of the dysgenically selective application of science to the production of human beings. Indeed, the effects are already beginning to be felt in a continuous increase in the number of mental defectives and a general decline of literacy. (In 1950 there were over three million illiterates in Great Britain alone.)

The elimination of some diseases has been accompanied by an increase in others—cancer, for example, duodenal ulcers and coronary thrombosis—while as the age-average goes continually up as the result of science's success in holding life in ageing and decaying bodies, society is found to be carrying the burden of

The Significance of Evil

increasing numbers of socially useless people whom every previous civilisation had the sense to allow to die.

I am citing these examples, not in disparagement of the results of science, but in illustration of the two theses here urged: the first, that all good is shot through with correlative evil and that in particular all human advancements and improvements are double-edged; and the second, that to improve man's science, which means increasing his power without increasing his wisdom and his virtue, without, that is to say, improving his knowledge of how to use it, is to bring our world to destruction.

THE SUPERNATURAL SIGNIFICANCE OF MORALITY

I have already drawn attention to the frequency with which the considerations upon which I have here laid stress appear and reappear in the secular wisdom of mankind. They are testified no less by its religions. That this should be so, that there should, in other words, be a natural transition from ethics to theology, from the facts of moral experience to the need for religious interpretation, appeared from my new point of view inevitable.

With my thought permeated by the conviction of the necessary imperfection of human life, I have dwelt in the foregoing passage chiefly on the natural unhappiness of man. It is only the platitudinousness of the observations I should have had to offer which led me to refrain from dwelling on the hackneyed theme of his natural sinfulness.

I have spoken above of my newly awakened realisation of the evil which is inherent in human nature and, more particularly, of the evil inherent in myself. I have tried to show how this realisation arose from a determination to take the fact of evil seriously, coupled with a refusal to accept any of the contemporary devices for writing it off as a deviation from, a derivative from, or a lack of, something else. To take the fact of evil seriously is also to take the fact of morality seriously, since the conviction that some things and states of mind are positively evil carries with it

The Significance of Evil

the consciousness that the things *ought* not to be done, the states of mind *ought* not to occur, and the consciousness of *ought* carries with it in its turn, as I think Kant conclusively showed, the consciousness of freedom. Is it not, indeed, meaningless to say that something *ought* not to happen or *ought* not to be if, in fact, it could not have happened or could not have been otherwise?

Again, following Kant, I am unable to see how the facts of the moral consciousness and, in particular, the fact of the opposition between 'is' and 'ought', between desire and duty, can be explained in terms of purely *natural* causation. Natural causation, in which conception I include psychological determinism, can account for what *is*, explaining it by causal laws as the determined effect of what *was*. But when a complete analysis has been given of all the determining factors, biological, anthropological, physiological, cultural, psychological and biographical, when due regard has been paid to the influence of training, education, environment and so forth, all of which contribute to make a man's consciousness what at any given moment it is and which determine what at any given moment he *wants*, the notions of *ought* and *should* seem to me to slip through the meshes of the causally determining net whose strands the various sciences weave. 'I am this'; 'I want to do this'—so much may well be explained by the determination of causal factors, but 'I ought to be *that*,' 'I ought to do *that*'—how are these to be explained in terms of the same factors?

Hence the consciousness of being evil, carrying with it, as it did and must inevitably do, the conviction that I ought not to continue in my evil but ought to try and rectify the elements in my character which were responsible for it and which, therefore, I deplored, came to have a significance which extended beyond the sphere of ethics proper.

For why, after all, should one *mind* about being what, on the purely natural interpretation of morality, one could not help being?

So, too, with the experience of moral obligation, more particularly as it expressed itself in the feeling that one ought on

77

The Significance of Evil

occasion to help other people, even at the expense of one's own comfort and pocket. Was not this just another case of the opposition between convenience and obligation, between want and ought, and if one sometimes, however rarely, did something that one did not *want* to do, something which it was clearly against one's interests to do, was not *that* also a fact that slipped through the meshes of the network of natural causation?

I am aware of the inconclusiveness of these considerations; conscious that they are controversial and that the significance I am attributing to them can be, and has on good grounds been called in question; nor without an excursus into moral philosophy which cannot be undertaken here[1] can they be further supported. Let me, then, bring them to a point by saying that I am citing them in order to illustrate my conviction that (i) the realisation of my own sinfulness; (ii) the fact of minding about my sinfulness; (iii) the endeavour, however feeble and intermittent, to correct it at the cost of comfort and convenience; (iv) the feeling that one ought sometimes to try to help others at the expense of comfort and convenience, and (v) the opposition between *want* and *ought*, desire and duty, which considerations (i) to (iv) exemplify, are *not* to be explained purely in terms of natural causation. If they are not, then they are significant in the sense of requiring interpretation in terms of some other, that is, some non-natural origin. To put this positively, they can be explained only on the assumption that in addition to the natural there is also a non-natural order of the universe which is immanent in and on occasion intrudes actively into the natural. I am saying, then, that the only satisfactory basis for the facts of moral experience, *if they are taken seriously*, is a supernatural one.

That the explanation of the phenomena of the natural world does not lie within the natural world and that science which describes these phenomena, telling us *how* they occur, cannot tell us why they occur as they do—these are familiar considerations

[1] I have done my best to make it elsewhere. See *Decadence: A Philosophical Enquiry*, chapter vii.

78

The Significance of Evil

upon which I shall touch in another chapter.[1] I am here suggesting that just as the explanation of the facts of the natural world must lie outside it, so, too, must the explanation of the facts of moral experience lie beyond it, since, while modes of explanation which rely purely on natural causation may explain how things behave according to their nature, how tigers tear their prey and stones roll down hill, they cannot explain why creatures should go against the dictates of their nature, as man does when he opposes duty to desire and recognises the imperative of the concept of 'ought'.

Now the demand for a supernatural explanation brings us face to face with the claims of religion. Hence it is no accident that, as I observed above, the religions of mankind have both testified to the significance of morality and sought to explain it.

THE TEACHING OF RELIGION

In the preceding pages I have put forward two contentions: first, that man cannot in this life achieve great or continuous happiness; secondly, that it is his nature, as, indeed, it is the nature of all his earthly experience, to be at least in part evil. These characteristics of man's life, belong, if I am right, to the condition of his earthly existence. They are, then, irremediable. What has religion to say about them?

I can call in witness only the two religions with which I am acquainted; the religion of classical Greece and the religion of Christianity. The Greeks were so conscious of the force of the considerations I have urged, more particularly in their bearing upon man's happiness, that they may be said to constitute the distinctive characteristic of Greek religious thought. There was, the Greeks held, a fate, conceived as an impersonal, moral law operative in the universe such that if man transgressed its ordinances he would suffer. He does, in fact, transgress them by aspiring above his proper station, and aspiring in particular to obtain too much happiness, too much knowledge or too much power.

[1] See chapter v, pp. 135–52.

The Significance of Evil

More precisely, the gods are jealous and are constantly on the look-out for behaviour on the part of man which suggests an endeavour to make himself equal to them by the acquisition of powers which are in excess of those proper to his nature. *Hubris* (insolent arrogance) and *pleonexia* (trying to get more than your own fair share) are the characteristically Greek vices, for signs of which the gods are constantly vigilant. When they occur they are visited with condign punishment. In other and more colloquial language, men have a constant tendency to grow too big for their boots. When they do so, the gods 'take them down a peg'.

Nor is it only excess of power or wealth that is censured. Too much good fortune, too much happiness are also dangerous. When a man has had a long run of good luck, then he should be more than usually on his guard. Solon's admonition to Croesus, 'Call no man happy until he is dead', is constantly illustrated in Greek history or, rather, it is illustrated in all history, but the Greeks were constantly drawing attention to the illustrations.

THE CHRISTIAN TEACHING

But it is from Christianity that the attitude to life I have tried to describe receives its fullest endorsement. Christianity teaches that man is born in sin, that this world is a vale of tears and suffering, that we can do no good thing without God's help, that great or continuous happiness is not to be looked for, and that we should be thankful for what little is vouchsafed to us. These doctrines go to the very heart of the condition of man. It is a tragic condition, having been made what it is by the mystery of the 'Fall'. It is because of this event that men are by nature wicked and, being wicked, are bidden to try to become better. Our life here is, then, to be looked upon as a period of training and discipline designed to teach us, if we are willing to learn, how to become better, and, since it is mainly through suffering that men learn, suffering is to be expected. We cannot, then, expect to be very happy here on earth, and we cannot expect to be very good. Indeed, neither complete happiness nor complete virtue is obtainable on the purely human level.

The Significance of Evil

These doctrines seem to me to cover more of the facts of life than any others with which I am acquainted. They make sense of experience and in particular they make sense of its pain and frustration, as no others do. If they are right in what they assert, man's condition here is governed by certain inescapable limitations which put a limit to his progress and his aspirations. We should try to adapt ourselves to these limitations rather than to make changes which ignore them.

RESIGNATION RATHER THAN REFORM

There is a book by C. S. Lewis, *The Abolition of Man,* which played no small part in preparing my change of view and in precipitating the new outlook which it involved, while it was still, as it were, in solution. A passage in this book puts what I am trying here to express better than I can hope to do.

'For the wise man of old, the cardinal problem had been how to conform the soul to reality and the solution had been knowledge, self-discipline and virtue. For magic and applied science alike the problem is how to subdue reality to the wishes of men: the solution is a technique; and both, in the practice of the technique, are ready to do things hitherto regarded as disgusting and impious (such as digging up and mutilating the dead).'

When I was young and under the influence of the outlook of the generation in which I grew up, I sought, like the rest, to change the world to suit my wishes; now I am content if I can conform my wishes to the world. I look to Christianity as a discipline which will help me to do so.

THE DISAPPOINTMENTS OF THE OPTIMISTS

It is because the efforts of the generation of my youth, the generation of optimists that flourished before 1914, sprang from a misconception of the nature of man's lot, that they have been so largely unsuccessful. To put it more specifically, to reject the doctrine of original sin, as so many of those whose outlook was formed in the atmosphere of Left-wing politics and rationalist philosophy rejected it, was to fall victim to a shallow optimism

F 81

The Significance of Evil

in regard to human nature which led men to think that the millennium was just round the corner waiting to be introduced by a society of adequately psycho-analysed, prosperous Socialists. It is because we rejected the doctrine of original sin that we on the Left were always being disappointed; disappointed by the refusal of people to be reasonable, by the subservience of intellect to emotion, by the failure of true Socialism to arrive, by the behaviour of nations and politicians, by the masses' preference for Hollywood to Shakespeare and for Mr. Sinatra to Beethoven; above all, by the recurrent fact of war.

To end on the personal note on which I began—and let me here repeat that what I have written in this chapter belongs to the nature of personal explanation rather than of argument—to believe, as I have grown to believe, in the fundamental and in this life ineradicable nature of human sinfulness is intolerable, unless there is some source of guidance and assistance outside ourselves to which we can turn for comfort and assurance. Presently the facts of sin and evil came to present themselves with such overwhelming strength that unless one were able to seek assistance, if not for the overcoming of them, at least for the not succumbing to them, one would give way to despair. The more I knew of it, the more Christianity seemed to offer just that strengthening and assistance. And with that the rationalist-optimist philosophy, by the light of which I had hitherto done my best to live, came to seem intolerably trivial and superficial—a shallow-rooted plant which, growing to maturity amid the lush and leisured optimism of the nineteenth century, was quite unfitted to withstand the bleaker winds that blow through ours. I abandoned it, and in abandoning it found myself a Christian.

CHAPTER IV

That Religion is Merely Subjective. The View Examined and Rejected

I. STATEMENT OF THE SUBJECTIVE VIEW

I propose in this chapter to consider the grounds—perhaps the commonest and most widely advanced at the present time—for dismissing religion on the score of its *mere* subjectivity. There are, it is pointed out, certain human experiences, emotions, sentiments, cravings, needs, desires, which have traditionally been regarded as specifically connected with religion. There is the sense of awe and reverence commonly interpreted as man's response to the vaguely felt presence of a Divine Person, the author of his being; there is the sense of need, the need for some factor, whether power or person, in the universe to worship, since here on earth we can find nothing which is worthy of our whole-hearted worship; there is the need, thrown into relief by the very size of the scientists' world, for someone to comfort our loneliness, to succour our weakness, to mitigate our feelings of unwantedness and friendlessness in an alien universe, to provide, in short, the confidence which is born of the assurance that at the heart of things there is something akin to ourselves, and there is the sense of purpose, the conviction which most men feel, however vaguely, that there must be *some* kind of meaning and purpose in the universe in general and in human life in particular, since it is intolerable to us to suppose that our existence is without significance, our aspirations meaningless, our suffering without avail. Now the subjectivist contention

That Religion is Merely Subjective

is, in effect, that man is impelled by these feelings to invent the notion of a being greater than himself to comfort his need, to assuage his loneliness, to serve as a focus for his emotions of reverence and worship and awe and to invest his life with purpose and significance—to invent him and then to project him upon the canvas of an empty and meaningless universe, there to worship, as an objective and independent being, the product of his own creativity. Having invented and projected, he then proceeds to devise and elaborate myths about the creature of his invention; the development and elaboration of these myths are what we know as religion.

Such in general is the line of thought which represents religion, not as the response of the soul to something which is given as objective, but as the expression of the soul's own creativity. Religion, then, gives information, not about the external universe, but about the nature of human need. It belongs to the domain, not of metaphysics, but of psychology.

Such is the account of religion which I propose in this chapter to examine. Let us look at it in a little more detail: first, in its relation to the sense of need, and, secondly, to that of purpose.

RELIGION AS A PRODUCT OF HUMAN NEED

I begin with the sense of need. We are asked to think of primitive man as a stranger in an alien world, ignorant alike of his origin and his destiny. His life is at the mercy of forces he can neither control nor understand, forces of fire and flood, of earthquake, storm and drought. His crops fail, his communities are assailed by famine and decimated by recurrent outbreaks of plague. Worst of all, he is oppressed by his fellow men; hostile tribes raid his villages, burn his houses, carry off his women. How helpless, then, is primitive man, how hostile the environment that surrounds him, how numerous the dangers by which he is beset. So intolerable is his sense of helplessness that he is driven to adopt any and every device to mitigate the starkness of reality. One of the worst features of that reality is the impersonality and consequent inaccessibility of the natural forces

The View Examined and Rejected

that oppress him. And so he invents semi-human creatures, gods and goddesses, demons and spirits, and projects them into this impersonal environment. There are spirits of fire, storm and flood; there are gods of fertility and demons of disease. The advantage of the substitution of these semi-human for non-human agencies is obvious; while the latter are inaccessible, the former can be approached, interceded with, prayed to, propitiated, bribed, even threatened. Hence, the whole apparatus of ritual and ceremony and sacrifice designed to curry favour with the gods, to keep them well-disposed and to appease them when they are angry. Is a long drought harming the crops? A sacrifice is offered to the rain god. Is there reason to apprehend the assault of a neighbouring tribe? One sacrifices a prisoner to propitiate the god of *the* tribe, one's own, so that he may be persuaded to give victory in battle over the assailants. A regular scale of sacrifices is drawn up appropriate to different occasions; as the importance of the occasion grows, so does the eminence of the sacrifice. Virgins are very eminent. . . .

Thus in fear and bribery religion begins. The argument from origins—there is not essentially more in the mature condition of a growing and developing thing than there was in the origin from which it developed; what it was in germ, that in essence it still is—is then invoked to demonstrate that what religion *began as*, that *in essence* is what it *is now*, a rationalisation of man's innate need, and a projection into the outside world of the 'father figures', as Freud would call them, which meet the need, assuage the fear and comfort the helplessness.

Nor, indeed, is the account given of contemporary religion and of the need which *it* satisfies very different. Consider the universe revealed by science. How unimaginably vast are the tracts of space, how inconceivably long the periods of time which astronomy and geology ask us to contemplate. Nowhere in time, save for a brief period of a few hundred thousand years, is anything remotely approaching the human discernible. There *may* be beings like ourselves upon other planets, but there is no indication that there are. For the rest, the universe appears to be

85

That Religion is Merely Subjective

lifeless and mindless. So far as the reports of the sciences run, it certainly would not appear to have been designed for life. Most of it is empty space, most of the rest radio-active matter, most of the rest stars. Thus, in the vast immensities of geological time and astronomical space, life in general and human life in particular seems like a tiny glow, flickering uncertainly for a brief space, and, when the conditions which brought it into existence no longer obtain, destined to be extinguished in the one corner of the cosmos that has known it.

THE SENSE OF PURPOSE

I turn to the significance of the sense of purpose. The pointlessness of human life in the universe revealed by science is no less intolerable than its insignificance. We did not ask for life— it just happened to us. We are pitch-forked into it without so much as a 'by your leave'. Nor do we choose the conditions under which we live; we do not choose our age, our country or our social status. Presented with life on these arbitrary terms, we have to make the best of it and manage as well as we can, much as though we were required to give a public performance on the violin, while learning the instrument, as we go along. We grow up, mate, bring children into the world, satisfy our desires, pursue our careers, gratify, so far as we are able, our ambitions, and then we die without knowing why we have lived. What, we wonder, has been the point of it all? Why was life given us? Has the whole affair, which has meant so much to us, been of no cosmic account, been, in fact, an accident without point or purpose, of no significance to anything or anybody? But that, surely, is intolerable.

As with *our* lives in particular, so with human life in general. Science, invoking the second law of thermo-dynamics, tells us that life will one day disappear from the only corner of the universe that has known it. Thereafter presumably time will continue indefinitely to unfold itself without any occurrence of any kind to break the eternal monotony. Or if by chance there are fluctuations in matter which will ultimately bring life again into the universe, it will have no more cosmic significance than the life which has been blotted out.

And this thought, too, is intolerable to us. We cannot bear to think that there is nothing behind and beyond the visible appearance which science studies. . . .

And so we insist that there must be something behind and beyond, must, in fact, be a Being and that that Being has a purpose. In the fulfilment of that purpose we have a part to play; in fact, we have been created precisely in order that we may play it. Thus we invest ourselves with importance by making ourselves of interest to a Personage who is Himself of overwhelming importance, and our lives with significance by casting them for a part in the drama of some cosmic design. Now the notion of cosmic design implies a Mind, the Mind of the Designer.

THE DEMAND FOR AN EXPLANATION

A variant of the same theme is afforded by our demand for an explanation. We cannot bear to understand that the universe is itself without understanding, that it has no meaning, that, in fact, it just *is* without explanation of *why* it is. There must, we hold, be some reason why things are as they are; we may even go to Leibniz's length and insist that the reason is that they *are for the best.* The most natural expression of the conviction that the universe is rational in the sense of having an explanation is the view that it was created by a Mind and had, therefore, a beginning in time.

Now it is obvious that the explanation of material happenings cannot lie in matter itself. It cannot, then, be discovered by an examination, however intensive, of material happenings, a truth upon which Socrates insisted when he pointed out that, while science can explain how things happen, by tracing their causation back in time, it cannot explain why they happen as they do. If there must be an explanation, and no explanation is to be found in the familiar world which consists, after all, of nothing but material things moving in space, some of which *may*

87

be animated by minds, it must lie outside the familiar world. There must, then, be a supernatural order which affords an explanation of the natural and what more likely than that this supernatural order is or contains a Mind? Mind, we know, as a fact of personal experience, can control the movements of matter. A mind may even create material structures, as when the mind of an engineer plans and builds a machine, or the weight-lifter causes a roll of muscle to appear upon his arm by performing appropriate exercises. What more natural, then, than to invoke a Divine Mind to plan the universe and build the structures of which *it* is composed. And looking at the universe with these presuppositions, looking at it, then, in the expectancy of finding evidences of design, we duly find them and present our findings in such books as Paley's *Evidences*.

PURPOSELESS LIVES

Nor are these theoretical considerations all. There is also the question of practical need, for it cannot be doubted that most of us feel the need of a purpose in our lives. Whatever rule of life we may embrace in theory, few of us succeed in being hedonists. Many of us, indeed, try when we are young, but the unsatisfying results of a life of consistent pleasure-seeking are notorious. They have been the stock-in-trade of the moralists since moralising began, and most of us finding ultimately that the attempt to secure happiness by means of a succession of pleasures is as unsatisfying as the attempt to get a light at night by striking a succession of matches, give up the attempt in despair at our lack of success.

As with pleasure, so with the other classical objects of pursuit, ambition, wealth and power. Considered as goals, overriding purposes in the interests of which we are bidden to forgo immediate satisfactions and to thwart subordinate, interfering purposes, these are subject to two disadvantages. First, very few of us achieve them. There is a reason for this since, as Plato pointed out, most of them are limited goods in the sense that the achievement of any one of them by A precludes

The View Examined and Rejected

the achievement of that same one by B—the extent to which I acquire money or exercise power being *ipso facto* the extent to which you do not. Secondly, when achieved, they are found to be profoundly unsatisfying for reasons upon which the moralists have again (and rightly) laid stress. The main objection to them is to be found in the consideration that the appetite for them grows with what it feeds on, so that however much wealth, fame or power you may have, you never think you have enough.

I do not propose to develop this theme here; to do so would take me too far from the main subject of this chapter. I propose, then, to take it for granted that most of the purposes which men set before themselves for achievement in this world are for one reason or another found to be unsatisfying. But how if there were a purpose which extended beyond it—for example, a moral purpose realised in the pursuit of duty and resulting in the strengthening of character, or a religious purpose to be fulfilled in the long run by the achievement of salvation? These would surely be exempt from the strictures which purely worldly ends have provoked, if only because they are never wholly realised.

Moreover, there are certain impulses in human nature—in speaking of impulses I am deliberately using a non-committal word—which are not satisfied by a life of self-seeking. There is the impulse to serve a creed or a cause, the impulse to do good to other people, the impulse to help those who are in trouble—to do these things even at the cost of our own comfort and convenience.[1] What account are we to give of these? Can *they* be justified by any worldly standard? They cannot; indeed, judged by the criteria of prudence, profit and expediency, they stand revealed as pure folly. For why, after all, *should* I help other people? Why *should* I prefer duty to pleasure. Why *should* I sacrifice myself in any way *unless* there is some standard other than the hedonic and the prudential, *unless* worldly goods are not the only goods to be taken into account, *unless* the explana-

[1] See the last chapter (chapter iii, pp. 76-9) for a development of the notion of the significance of morality.

tion of our life here is to be found in another life elsewhere, in terms of which this life receives its meaning and from which it derives its justification? Moral experience seems, then, to imply the presence of some purpose, which is also a moral purpose, in the scheme of things in terms of which alone the scheme makes sense, just as *some* at least of the needs which seem to be universally implanted in the heart of man appear to demand for their satisfaction the admission of ideals and purposes which are at once more continuing and more imperative than the gratification of the appetites or the pursuit of expediency. Yet what account are we to give of the purposes and the standards they imply, of the need and the impulses it generates in purely *this*-worldly terms? To recognise such a purpose, to pay attention to such a need, to observe such a standard is patent folly if this is the only world, since no justification can be found for them here.

And seeing that it is, indeed, folly, we hasten to provide the required justification by insisting that there is another world which makes sense of our altruistic impulses and explains and justifies our occasional preference for duty over expediency. What is more, so far from success in this life constituting a passport to success there, it is, we insist, a definite disqualification. It is better, then, in the long run, to be poor, humble and lowly; better *not* to succeed; better to do good to others and to sacrifice the self; better, that is to say, not by the ephemeral standard of the here and the now, but better in the long run by the standard of the lasting satisfactions of eternity. Here, then, is another stimulus to man's imaginative capacity, the stimulus to invest our existence with a purpose and to make sense of the impulses which lack justification in this life by providing for them justification in another.

II. ANSWER TO SUBJECTIVISM

I propose to divide the answer to the formidable case just outlined into three parts.

The View Examined and Rejected

(1) The Mind Viewed in the Context of its Situation

Let us consider for a moment the nature of the needs which, according to the argument just considered, religion is designed to meet. Inevitably they are subjective, since they are needs that men's minds feel. But are they adequately to be regarded as *merely* subjective in the sense of having no reference beyond themselves?

An argument which I first met in the works of Fechner seems to me to have relevance here. Briefly, it runs as follows: if the objects that satisfy religious need did not exist, it is hard to see how the existence of the need itself is to be explained. Granted that man has made the belief in the objects affirmed by religion because he needs it, he did not create the circumstances in which he needs the belief, the circumstances which obliged him to invent it. Hence, the demand for a religious faith by human beings must be based on the same real nature of things as that which produced the human beings who make the demand. It is hard to credit in practice and it leads to self-contradiction in theory to suppose that nature has constituted man in such a way that he can only survive and prosper if he holds a belief in something which is not.

Let me try to express this important argument of Fechner's in my own way. The premises which underly the charge that religion is *merely* subjective are commonly those of naturalism and determinism. These I take to be as follows. There is only one form of being, namely, the being that belongs to the things that we can see and touch; there is only one order of reality, the natural, spatio-temporal order; every event which occurs on this plane obeys the laws of physics and is, therefore, subject to the law of cause and effect; it does not, that is to say, occur spontaneously and in theory a complete explanation for the occurrence of any given state of affairs can be found in the state of affairs which immediately precedes it in time. Assuming that we accept these postulates, how are we to explain the occurrence and developments of human needs? In particular, how are we

91

to explain the emergence of the needs and wishes of which, on this view, religion is a rationalisation?

Man's needs and wishes are the expressions of man's nature; they are what they are because he is what he is. How, then, did man come to be what he is? To this question those who take the naturalist view give a quite definite answer. Man, they say, has evolved in and through interaction with his environment. This is a non-committal statement to which, I imagine, all biologists would subscribe. Materialists go further and exhibit life as a mere function of its environment, a by-product of the workings of purely natural forces; while the mind of the living organism they represent as an emanation from or an epiphenomenon upon its body and brain. Thus, a chain of causation is established which begins in the external environment, stretches across the living body of the organism via the stimulus-response linkage, and ends in the mind of the organism via the nerves-brain-mind linkage. Events in the mind of man must, then, in the last resort be regarded as the end products of a chain of causation stretching back to events in the physical world of nature.

We must suppose that this process has continued over a very long period. Throughout the whole of this period everything that has occurred in a mind or consciousness is the indirect result of something which has first occurred in the world external to the mind or consciousness. Are we not, then, entitled to look upon mind as a reflection or register of the outside world, reproducing its features and taking its shape, as the bust reproduces the features and takes the shape of the mould in which it is cast? But if it *is* a reflection, the characteristics of a mind will reproduce at least in part the characteristics of the environment in which they have evolved and which they reflect. The needs and wishes of a mind are among its characteristics. Hence its needs and wishes are not arbitrary, but reflect features in the external world which generate the needs and provoke the wishes. But if they generate and provoke, must they not also fulfil and satisfy, or at least be capable of satisfying?

92

The View Examined and Rejected

I do not wish to suggest that this materialist account of the origin and nature of human beings and their wishes is true; I do not think that it is. I am only concerned to point out that, *if it is true*, then the needs and wishes which religion seeks to fulfil and to satisfy must point to some factor in the external world which has generated them, and which guarantees the possibility of their satisfaction, in which event religion cannot be *merely* subjective.

THE 'TU QUOQUE' ARGUMENT

But let us suppose that the feelings from which religion takes its rise and the judgments in which they find expressions *are merely subjective*, in the sense that they convey information only about the psychology of the person feeling and judging. What account, on this basis, are we to give of the laws that rule the *mind's* reasoning? When the mind reasons about the natural world, it makes continuous use of the law of induction. Induction, indeed, is pre-eminently the method of science. Induction proceeds from the particular to the general; *because* the sun has been observed to rise on a great many occasions in the east and on no single occasion in the west, north or south, *therefore*, we say, the sun *always* rises in the east. In other words, we formulate a law by induction. Here is a statement of the law of induction which I take from Bertrand Russell. 'When a thing of a certain sort, A, has been found to be associated with a thing of a certain sort, B, and has never been found dissociated from a thing of the sort B, the greater the number of cases in which the things A and B have been associated, the greater is the probability that they will be associated in a fresh case in which one of them is known to be present.' The greater the number of these cases, Russell continues, the more probable it is that A is *always* associated with B.

But how is this law itself to be validated? Certainly not by observation, since it purports to apply to cases not observed; also to cases in the future—the sun, we say, will rise *tomorrow* in the east. Nor yet by reasoning, since any process of reasoning

93

which sought to establish it would need to assume it in order that the process might be performed.

How, then, is the law validated? The answer is that in the last resort it is not validated. The mind, in fact, simply assumes it or, if you prefer to put it that way, the mind simply sees that it is true. But how if this process of 'assuming' or 'seeing' itself be *merely* subjective? How if it *merely* gives information about the way the mind works and not information about a world external to ourselves?

So, too, with the law of causation. This is commonly supposed to be a law regulating the behaviour of external events. It presupposes a causal tie between events such that because one of them, the cause, has occurred, the other, the effect, is bound to follow. It asserts, then, a *necessary* connection. Hume sought to show that the idea of necessary connection was based upon nothing but custom. The mind, accustomed to observe regular conjunctions of events, came to believe that there must be a connection between them to account for the conjunction; but this belief, said Hume, is illusory. Hence for the necessary connection between events, Hume substituted a disposition of the mind to believe in it. Now such a disposition is subjective. But how, if it, too, is subjective in the sense of being *merely* subjective, if, giving information about the disposition of the mind, it gives none about the external world to which it purports to refer?

Now most philosophers would agree that Hume's criticism has not been satisfactorily answered. If it is not answered, then causation goes the way of induction as a mere disposition of the mind to believe in certain ways.

The extent to which the orderly scheme of nature which science explores and affirms relies upon causation is too obvious to require elaboration, but if causation, like induction, is a belief which neither observation nor reason can justify, what ground have we for assuming such a scheme? Moreover, if as Professor Whitehead has pointed out, 'nature within any period does not refer to nature at any other period'—and,

The View Examined and Rejected

indeed, it does not if there is no causal tie—memory goes the way of induction and causation.

Finally, there are certain values whose authority scientific procedure implicitly invokes, among which order, consistency and coherence are the most eminent. There is also the law of cosmic economy, first announced by Occam, according to which if two alternative explanations can be given of any phenomenon of which one is the more economical in the matter of hypotheses than the other, then the more economical is to be preferred. There is also, I believe, a value, elegance, which mathematicians acknowledge. If of two solutions to a problem one is more elegant, that is, presumably, more pleasing to the mind, the more elegant is to be preferred. (Speaking from experience I can vouch for the acknowledgment of a similar canon in its application to the chess problem.)

THE DILEMMA

Now the question which I wish to raise is this. Either induction, causation and what I have called the 'values' of science are subjective or they are not. (By the use of the word 'subjective' in this connection I mean that they are creations or inventions of the human mind which have no reference outside it, or that they are laws which govern the workings of the human mind, or that they are descriptions of the way in which the human mind behaves.) If they are, what answer can be offered to the charge that they are *merely* subjective in the sense that they give us no information about the nature of a world external to the human mind which conceives them or, alternatively, whose behaviour they record? If they are not, then, presumably, they are to be interpreted as the mind's awareness of and response to features of the universe which are presented for its apprehension and understanding. They record man's findings about the nature and the working of that universe.

It seems to me that the situation here is logically on all fours with the situation in regard to religion. For in regard to the feelings, beliefs and judgments which constitute the body of

95

That Religion is Merely Subjective

what is called religious knowledge, the same question may be asked, the same dilemma put. If the first alternative is taken in regard to religion, then its application must also be pressed in regard to thinking about the universe in general and to that kind of thinking which is called scientific in particular. (Yet it is chiefly from the side of science, that is, by those whose intellectual outlook has been formed by science, that the charge against religion that it is *merely* subjective is brought.) In this event, no argument about the external world can be said to have objective validity in the sense of having reference beyond the human mind which conceives it and the arguments urged by scientists and others against religion have no objective validity.

If the second alternative is taken, then its application must be pressed in regard to the feelings, beliefs and judgments which make up the body of what is called religious knowledge. They, too, must be interpreted as the response of the human mind to features of the universe presented to it; they, too, convey the mind's findings about that universe. This is not, of course, to say that the findings are correct. The mind may make mistakes, especially when the data which it seeks to interpret, conveyed, as they are, at one level of reality, purport to originate in and to serve as clues to another. It is sufficient to establish the point that it is at least *possible* for them to give us information about the nature of a universe which is external to our own minds, information which may be clarified and increased as the study of religion deepens and what is called the religious consciousness develops. In either event, science conceived as a stick with which to beat religion is a stick which breaks in the hands.

(2) THE NATURE OF THE RELIGIOUS CONSCIOUSNESS

It is relevant to consider more precisely what is the nature of the faculty or faculties which are involved in religion and of the experiences which constitute what is called the religious consciousness.

Under the influence of the romantic movement, the element of pure feeling in religion has been emphasised—I should be

The View Examined and Rejected

inclined to say, over-emphasised. Schleiermacher, for instance, finds the origin of faith in an undifferentiated feeling of the Infinite and the Eternal, Otto in what he calls the feeling of the 'numinous'. Now in emphasising religion as feeling, these theologians, as it seems to me, play into the hands of the sceptics; for, in so doing, they make it a purely private and personal possession of the human consciousness, having no necessary reference outside the consciousness which entertains it.

For what, after all, is the nature of the distinction between knowledge and feeling? It is that knowledge is essentially communicable, while feeling is not, precisely because knowledge is of the intellect, and reason is public and common whereas feeling is personal and private. Thus, given good will and a normal intelligence, on the side of the learner, I can undertake to convince him that the angles at the base of an isosceles triangle are equal and to show him why they are equal, because his reason to which the exposition is addressed is of the same kind as my reason from which the argument proceeds—at any rate both reasons contain elements in common. If, on the other hand, having the toothache I try to explain to him what the toothache is like, my exposition will be meaningless unless he has himself experienced the feeling whose nature I am seeking to convey. More precisely, if he has experienced *some* pain, then it will not be wholly meaningless, since he will know what pain is and can be made to understand that toothache is a particular variety of it, though the nature of that variety will remain uncomprehended and, therefore, unknown. If, however, he had never experienced any pain of any kind, then my statement that I have toothache would be strictly meaningless, in the sense that he would not know what it was that I was talking about. It is for precisely this reason that the testimony of mystical experience in religion carries so little weight with non-mystics, for the mystics, in seeking to convey the nature of the reality which their experience reports to them, are conveying something which is strictly meaningless to those who have not themselves had experience of that reality. Thus, the phrases in which they seek to communicate their vision—'a delicious desert', 'a dazzling darkness', 'the drop in the ocean and the ocean in the drop'—merely baffle and irritate, unless those to whom they are addressed have enjoyed some tincture, however faint, of the experience which they are designed to report.

Now the reason why knowledge is communicable and feeling is not is to be found in the fact that knowledge is of something other than and external to itself, whereas feeling reports nothing but the fact of the feeling. Knowledge, in short, involves a reference to something else, namely, that which is known; feeling does not. It is, then, important to consider further the question whether religion is ever adequately described as pure feeling.

FEELING AND COGNITION

It seems to me that some at least of the experiences associated with religion cannot be satisfactorily relegated to the category of pure feeling. Let me cite an example of what I take to be pure feeling arising from the senses of taste, smell and sight. I happen intensely to dislike the taste, the smell and the sight of beetroot. Three characteristics of this experience of mine are relevant to the question at issue. First, it is not cognitive; I do not, that is to say, think that my feeling of dislike gives me a kind of *knowledge*, a knowledge, for example, of some objective quality of disagreeableness belonging to the beetroot which the feeling registers. I doubt if the beetroot possesses an objective disagreeableness. My feeling of dislike is, therefore, adequately described as an occurrence in my consciousness. It communicates no information to others and purports to give none. Secondly, the experience is not an experience of my whole personality, nor is my whole personality in any way brought into play by it. Certain specific constituents of my personality alone are involved, namely, the senses of taste, smell and sight. When I say that I dislike beetroot, though the dislike is veritably

98

The View Examined and Rejected

mine, I have no disposition to go on to say that my personality as a whole was engaged or involved in the experience of disliking. Thirdly, the feeling is not communicable. Not only can I not communicate my dislike to others, I cannot make them understand what my feeling in regard to beetroot is, unless they share it.

Let me now contrast the 'feeling'—I put the word designedly in quotes to draw attention to the fact that more than feeling is involved; it is part of my contention that the religious consciousness is never adequately described as just feeling—involved in the experiences associated with religion. The religious consciousness seems to me to possess three outstanding characteristics.

CHARACTERISTICS OF THE RELIGIOUS CONSCIOUSNESS

First, it certainly *purports* to give me knowledge. This knowledge can be formulated in a series of propositions in which religion demands belief. The belief demanded is not always reasonable in the sense of being a belief for which reason can give completely satisfactory grounds, but it is always reasonable in the sense that it is never repugnant to reason.

Examples of the propositions which the believer would be said to know are that God created the world and loves it; that the universe is governed by a moral law, God's law, and that to break it is to incur His displeasure; that—though this belief is, presumably, confined to Christians—at a particular moment in history God became incarnate and participated as a man in human life; that as a Being so incarnate He died and then after a certain period of time rose from the dead. These propositions may, like any other propositions, be true or they may be false, but they do purport to give information about occurrences external to ourselves which may be true or false; they do, then, claim to be known. Moreover, the faculty by which I know them is the cognitive faculty, the faculty that asserts that something is the case, however this faculty be defined.

99

That Religion is Merely Subjective

DEGREES OF KNOWLEDGE AND REALITY

Secondly, not only is the faculty cognitive, but it is never *merely* cognitive. I have said above that the religious consciousness is never adequately described as merely feeling; I now add that it may, and on occasion does, involve the whole personality. I hold—though the view, which is in essence Plato's, cannot be defended in detail here—that reality reveals itself in a number of different grades or orders which are correlated with ascending degrees of wholeness on the part of the knower. Thus at the bottom of the scale there are the simple feelings of pleasure or pain associated with, say, the drinking of water when thirsty or the putting of the hand inadvertently upon hot metal, experiences in which the element of cognition, though present, is reduced to a minimum. Lust is pure feeling, but as it deepens into love more elements of our nature are, as we say, involved: tenderness, for example, trust and self-sacrifice. On the same plane of wholeness as love—or it may be on a higher—is aesthetic experience. I see a flower as a splash of colour and the visual sense only is involved. I see it as a botanist and the sense of vision touches off, as it were, a background of technical knowledge which is involved in its apprehension. I see it as an artist, and besides the sensory experience, besides knowledge, there is now also an experience of the spirit. For though I say I *see* it as beautiful, it is with the eye of the soul rather than with that of the body that its beauty is perceived, if only because beauty is not a visual quality which stimulates the senses in the sense in which colour and shape are.

Similarly, while the sense of hearing alone may be aroused by the ticking of a clock, and hearing plus emotion, the emotion of irritation, by the repeated sound of a yapping dog or a motor horn, in the experience of listening to great music all the faculties of my being are caught up and fused. For, so long as the experience lasts, I *am* the listener not only in the sense that it is I who listen, but in the sense that there is no part of me which is not gathered into the experience of listening.

The View Examined and Rejected

The difficulty of finding words to describe psychical experiences presents itself prominently here, and I am seeking only to illustrate by examples a position which I do not here attempt to defend. Briefly, the position is that of Plato. It is to the effect that as grades of knowledge are set over against and correlated with grades of reality, so it is only the completely real that can be completely known; also that perfect knowledge is never adequately described as a purely intellectual process, but involves an integration and results in an enhancement of the whole personality, the knower being enlarged and enriched by the nature of that upon which his cognition is directed.

Thirdly, the religious consciousness, even if it is not, like rational knowledge, wholly communicable, is not, like pure feeling, incommunicable. From the standpoint of communicability, it stands midway between our knowledge of the equality of the angles at the base of an isosceles triangle and the pain of the toothache or the dislike of beetroot. I cannot convince a person who has had no religious experience that there is such a thing. In this sense the religious approximates to the toothache and the beetroot cases. But just because and just in so far as there is no mind without *some* tincture of religious experience, I can feel a reasonable assurance that the great majority of people will in fact share my feeling of awe and reverence in a great cathedral, or of wonder at a sunset, or of fear in certain sacred places—will, in short, experience Otto's feeling of the 'numinous'.

Perhaps the most commonly shared element of the complex of feelings which go to make the experiences which we call religious is a sense of dependence. Schleiermacher speaks of an immediate consciousness of *absolute dependence*. This, I think, if it is taken as an assertion of what all or most men feel, asserts more than the evidence warrants. Dependence implies, after all, a relationship between two things, between that which depends and that upon which there is dependence, and both must presumably be conceived, however vaguely, if the sense of dependence is to be felt. Now, it seems to me unlikely that all or even most contemporary men have a definite conception of God.

101

That Religion is Merely Subjective

Most contemporary men in the west are agnostic. Nevertheless, there are certain moments in our lives, moments of peril, when we have reason to believe that at any moment our lives may be cut short, when most or all of us seem to feel pretty much the same emotion. The atheist who starts to pray as the ship sinks, the agnostic who feels impelled to fall on his knees and beseech the clemency of an unknown Power at his wife's child-bed—these are phenomena too familiar to call for comment. They are examples of feelings, notably the feeling of dependence, which all or most of us share, irrespective of our beliefs. At a lower level of shared experience is the feeling of awe and mystery which most of us have when, for example, we attend midnight mass on Christmas Eve in a great cathedral. Even in the case of those of us who do not believe with our minds, the awe, the mystery, is in our bones and we believe with our hearts.

These, then, are examples of experiences which, because they are shared, belong to the category of the communicable. If I am right in calling them religious—and whether we do so or not is, after all, a question of belief—it would seem to follow that the feelings commonly associated with religion are at least in part communicable. The religious consciousness, then, falls in this sense and to this extent on the side of my geometrical illustration rather than on the side of the pain of the toothache and the dislike of the beetroot and may, therefore, be held to be a consciousness of objectivity.

(3) RELIGION AS THE FORMULATION OF EXPERIENCE

It is, I think, significant that, though the starting point of religion may lie in feeling, it is a feeling which we have a need to formulate, a need which is not felt in the beetroot class of case. The feeling associated with religion is conveyed with the addendum—it may be a quality or a constituent of the feeling—that that to which it relates is in principle both comprehensible and explicable, even if we can never wholly comprehend or adequately explain it. That which challenges comprehension and explanation is an experience, the essence of which is that it

The View Examined and Rejected

is felt to be not purely subjective. And because it is felt not to be purely subjective, it demands to be mediated, that is to say, placed in some kind of framework by reason. The result is the composite whole that we know as religion. Religion, then, in so far as it is an assertion of propositions which claim to be true, is reason's formulation of what man feels and has always felt intuitively about the nature of the universe. It is the formulation by the intellect of man's instinctive experience of objectivity.

Now, reason's formulation of experience can increase in fullness and in subtlety just as man's knowledge of the nature of the physical world grows with increasing experience and through his knowledge of the results of the experiences of others. Just as each generation of scientists and mathematicians, instead of starting from scratch, begins where its predecessors left off, inheriting the knowledge which they have accumulated and taking it as the point of departure for further developments of their own, so, too, I suggest, man's knowledge of the spiritual world builds upon the experience of his predecessors. Thus we can trace an increase both in the fullness and in the subtlety of man's religious knowledge from the crude fertility cults and mystery religions of the remote past to the elaborate refinements of Christianity and Buddhism, which are obviously seeking to convey—whether they convey truly or falsely is not here the point at issue—experiences of greater range and subtlety than those of primitive man.

This is not to say that the progress of religious knowledge is either continuous or necessary. There are setbacks and recoils and there may be 'Dark Ages' in religious no less than in scientific and cultural knowledge. I am suggesting merely that if one considers human history as a whole, it shows a clear growth both in the range and complexity of those formulations of spiritual experience which we call religious creeds, which matches a growth in the subtlety and penetration of the insight whose revelations the formulations seek to express in intellectual terms.

That Religion is Merely Subjective

This, again, is not to say that faith is its own evidence or that insight guarantees the objectivity of that which it professes to find. We cannot argue, 'I pray; therefore God exists' as Descartes argued, '*Cogito ergo sum*'. What in the light of history we are entitled to say is that the life of devotion carries its own evidence with it in the sense that, if we live in a certain way and, in particular, practice, the virtues which religion enjoins, the evidence grows stronger, the conviction more assured.

The case of religion from this point of view is not other than that of any experience of value. While neither my pleasure in chocolate peppermint creams nor my dislike of beetroot expands and develops with increasing experience, my appreciation of beauty in nature and in music, my perception and appreciation of unselfish sacrifice in others, above all my consciousness of the presence of Deity in contemplation and of His response in prayer, most emphatically does; or, rather—for I do not wish to claim more than is justified by putting this in personal terms —the experience of mankind is to the effect that it emphatically does.

THE SIGNIFICANCE OF MYSTICISM

This leads me to say a word on what appears to be the culmination of the development of religious knowledge in mystical experience. To this I myself lay no claim. I have, however, read a certain amount of the literature of mysticism and am acquainted with the kind of criticism which interprets the mystical state as *merely* subjective in its significance, a phase in the biography of the mystic not in essence dissimilar to the states of exaltation which may be brought on by fasting, solitude and the use of drugs, destitute of any significance save the purely psychological. Or the mystics are classed with epileptics and hysterics. . . .

In the accounts given by the mystics of their experiences and in the descriptions of them written by others, four points have struck me as significant. (i) Mystics, unlike epileptics and unlike those in whom a special psychological condition has been induced by opium, hashish or other drugs, do claim a kind of

104

The View Examined and Rejected

knowledge. Mystical experience constitutes the outstanding expression of the cognitive element in religious experience upon which I have sought to dwell. It is that element raised to its highest pitch of intensity as directly and immediately revelatory. The mystic seeks to report something that has been revealed.

(ii) About the mystics' reports there is a certain unanimity. Whether they are Christian, Buddhist, Sufi, Brahmin or Mohammedan, mystics living in different ages and countries tend to concur in regard to the following points: (a) The reality with which they make contact is some kind of consciousness, though whether this is termed personal or super-personal depends upon the nature of the mystic's religious background. For the Christians it is usually personal. (b) This consciousness is of a One in which the incorrigible plurality of ordinary existence is transcended and disappears. (c) The One is never merely known but also loved—the mystical experience is usually described in terms of ecstatic delight which in passing leaves behind a feeling of poignant regret. (d) In mystical knowledge the gulf between the subject and object is transcended and the being of the knower is temporarily taken up into and merged with that which is known. (e) As recollected, the mystical vision gives a meaning to ordinary life which it lacked before and provides a perspective within which its values may be more truly assessed.

(iii) Thirdly, the mystics are whole men and women. So far, at least, as the western mystics are concerned, they conduct their practical lives with not less than normal efficiency. Some have been skilled in the conduct of public affairs. This day-to-day normality, this practical efficiency, distinguishes them from the visionaries, the epileptics and the drug addicts with whose experiences the mystical state has certain superficial affinities.

(iv) Men can deliberately cultivate a way of life which will increase the number of these experiences and enlarge the range and the content of their revelation. Once again, there is agreement as to what this way of life is. Though asceticism, fasting and sleeplessness have been practised, they are in no sense necessary. What is necessary is a certain degree of non-attach-

That Religion is Merely Subjective

ment to the ordinary goods of life, abstention from violent emotion and a refusal to satisfy the more violent desires. On the positive side there is the practice of certain religious exercises, notably meditation and recollection, designed to produce concentration and above all frequent and systematic prayer.

The way of life which is prescribed is, finally, that which would normally be called moral. The mystics are good men who live lives of service to their fellows. Indeed, there is a definite suggestion to the effect that the content of their vision requires them to return—as Plato would put it—to the cave and devote their lives to the service of struggling humanity.

The above constitutes a list—it is no more—of the considerations which seem to me to distinguish the mystical from allied psychological states to which the mystical state has often been likened by those who wish to throw doubt upon the validity of its testimony. The importance of the distinction lies, for me, in this. It seems reasonably certain that the so-called visions of the epileptic and the drug addict have purely subjective relevance. They give no information about any object, person or situation other than the psychological condition of the visionary. Unless the mystical is distinguished from these states it, too, falls under the suspicion of possessing a purely subjective reference. If it can be successfully distinguished, then this particular reason for doubting its revelatory character disappears. If it is revelatory, it does indeed tell us something of the nature of the reality which underlies the familiar world. It is, therefore, religious testimony of the highest importance.

CHAPTER V

Science and Religion

I propose to devote this chapter to a consideration of the relations between science and religion.

A. INTRODUCTORY—THE ALLEGED INCONGRUITY BETWEEN SCIENCE AND RELIGION

It has often been represented that the conclusions of science are hostile to the tenets of religion. Whatever grounds there may have been for such a view in the past, it is hard to see with what good reason such a contention could be sustained today. The points at issue are so familiar that a cursory treatment in what is intended to be no more than an introductory section to the main argument of this chapter must suffice.

EVOLUTION

Take, first, evolution. The doctrine of evolution has been held to lend countenance to a philosophy of cosmic progress. But does it, in fact, lend countenance to any philosophy at all, except to a form of Pragmatism which, I should urge, is no philosophy at all? Let us suppose that we reject all the variants from and glosses upon the doctrine which Darwin first enunciated, and take our stand on the strict Darwinian formulae. Natural Selection and the Survival of the Fittest may, then, be regarded as established beyond reasonable doubt as the *methods* by means of which the series of changes in species which are referred to as evolution takes place. What conclusion touching

Science and Religion

the issues raised in this book are we entitled to draw? First, negative, the species of creatures that are successively evolved countenance no doctrine of progress in the sense of a discerned development towards an end or goal. Nor, indeed, could they do so, for the notion of goal implies a standard by reference to which the goal is assessed and seen to be desirable. Suppose, for example, we say, as many have done in the past, that natural selection promotes the survival of 'better' or 'more desirable' stocks. The observation, if it is to have meaning, must entail the acceptance of some agreed concept of 'better' and 'more desirable'. Now the words 'better' and 'more desirable' suggest an ethical criterion. But what sort of ethical criterion could the process of evolution itself provide? The so-called science of evolution records a number of successive changes. It tells us, in fact, what has occurred but it does not tell us, nor could it do so, what *ought* to have occurred. In informing us that certain events have taken place, it cannot and does not assure us that it is *desirable* that they should have taken place. Science, in a word, is concerned with facts, not with their valuation. Of Natural Selection we are entitled to say no more than that it serves as a sieve through which those forms of life, which happen to be adjusted to their environment, pass. Hence, the types which survive are deemed to be valuable by no criterion other than that of the fact of their survival. As F. H. Bradley put it: 'The one criterion for Darwinism is the abstract success or prevalence of whatever happens to prevail, without any regard to its character. And this leaves us in the end with no criterion at all.'

As with creatures, so with ideas. In the world of thought the analogue of 'the strongest must be best' is that the ideas which prevail must be true. More precisely, the ideas by means of which humanity has so far survived and developed get called true. By continuing to entertain and act upon the same ideas, there is a large probability that we shall continue to develop in the same direction in the future. In other words, that which 'works' is true. This, as I remarked above, is the doctrine of Pragmatism. It is no part of my plan to criticise Pragmatism.

Science and Religion

Such criticism should, indeed, be by now unnecessary. It is, however, relevant to point out that on the assumption that the methods of science are exclusive and the account that it gives of the universe exhaustive no other philosophy is possible.

To sum up, evolution is a piece of cosmic machinery, the machinery by means of which living things perpetuate their species, introduce gradual changes into it and illustrate them. What has this machinery to do with religion or the religious view of the universe? What is there to preclude us from saying that *this* is the machinery that God devised and through which He works in order to people the planet with various and changing forms of life? That life should over millions of years have evolved slowly by a succession of very gradual changes, punctuated by occasional abrupt mutations is just as compatible, neither more nor less, with the hypothesis that it was originally created and that its development is guided by a Divine Mind, as the view that it was created fixed and unchangeable by a series of sudden successive acts.

THE SIZE OF THE UNIVERSE AND ITS UNIFORMITY

The size of the universe and its uniformity are sometimes regarded as affording grounds for conclusions hostile to religion. It is difficult to see why. On the point of size, science, it is true, has enormously extended the scope and scale of the non-living. In the vast immensities of geological time and astronomical space, life appears as a tiny glow, flickering insecurely and doomed to destruction so soon as the conditions which favour its emergence cease to obtain; so soon, in any event, as the operations of the second law of thermo-dynamics work to their predestined conclusion. Such is the picture that recent science suggests.[1] But the size of the universe and its duration are in no sense relevant to its religious interpretation. For of two things, one:—either vastness, loneliness, majesty and impressiveness are characteristics present in and belonging to the nature of things, characteristics, then, which are given to and discerned

[1] But there are still more recent variants. See chapter ii, pp. 35-9.

by the human mind, or they are not. In the former event, vastness and majesty are, surely, precisely what we should expect to find as characteristics of God's creation. In the latter, these are nothing in themselves; they are merely testimonies to the creative imagination of the human mind. Pascal's observation—'Man is only a reed, the weakest thing in nature, but he is a thinking reed'—applies, and it is our minds that demonstrate their superiority by their ability to invest the universe with qualities which *we* find formidable.

There is a touch of vulgarity[1] in these immensities of time and space or, rather, in the fact of being impressed by them. If any conclusion is justly to be based upon them, it is surely that drawn by Pascal in his passage, The Two Infinites, that man occupies a unique position in nature in that he stands at the midway point between the infinitely large and the infinitely small, stands, in fact, on a bridge that spans two abysses. In sum, if the contrast in scale between man and the galaxies has any significance, it is not to diminish but rather to exalt mind as embodied in man in comparison with the matter of the physical world.

So, too, with the uniformity and regularity of natural law. If natural law had been devised by a Divine Mind to regulate the behaviour of the physical universe—and what is there in science to show that it has not?—are not these precisely the characteristics that one would expect it to exhibit? Scientists have often expatiated upon the majesty of nature and upon the imposing regularity of natural processes. Precisely what one would expect of processes that God ordained!

THE INERRANCY OF THE BIBLE

This is not to say that a rigid adherence to the literal inerrancy of Biblical statements on the subject of history and geography will not involve discrepancy with the conclusions of science. The chronology of Genesis, with its account of creation

[1] Or is this feeling that it is vulgar to be impressed one's own feeble comeback—a pathetic assertion of the self—in the face of the facts that one cannot help but find impressive? See chapter ii, p. 39.

as a series of abrupt and successive acts, the doctrine of the solid heaven and the fixed earth, the view that asses speak, the notion that if you go below the earth you will find first waters and then hell, even, it may be, that hell conceived as a place in space to which Christ descended and in which He is said to have spent seventy-two hours—none of these doctrines could, I imagine, be endorsed by science, and, if taken literally, most of them would be at variance with what science has shown to be the case. But is it really necessary to the truth of religion that such assertions should be taken at their literal face value? Are they not relative to and to be read in the context of the historical and geographical knowledge of the age in which they were conceived? This does not mean that the myths and legends of the Old Testament are without value. Religion is first and foremost a statement of belief; it is a creed. But it is never merely a creed, but a creed charged with emotion and hallowed by its associations. Without the assistance of creeds, religion cannot develop. Religion from this point of view is like ivy; it requires a support and clings to whatever extraneous supports are offered to it. Even if the supports grow old and are seen to be insecure in their foundations, this does not mean that they can be excised without damage to the plant that has climbed by their means and is now inextricably entangled with them.

Myths and legends may come in the course of centuries to serve as symbols. Now, symbols may acquire value, a value which is sacramental; nor can their place be taken and their office performed by another symbol manufactured for the purpose to conform with the existing state of scientific knowledge. As Dean Inge has put it in a remarkable phrase: 'Pieces of obsolete science, imprisoned, like a fly in amber, in the solid mass of religious creed, may have become the casket in which the soul keeps her most valued treasures.'

CONCLUSION

The general conclusion of the above lines of thought is as follows.

111

Science and Religion

Not only is there not, but there cannot be any *necessary* conflict between science and religion. Let us suppose that God created the world and set it going. The celebrated Paley simile of the watch and the watchmaker is, on this hypothesis, not inappropriate. For the watchmaker does not only make a watch; he prescribes certain laws which determine its mode of working, so that it shall function automatically without his continuous intervention. God, on this hypothesis, prescribed the laws of the universe's working, not only the laws of physics and chemistry which regulate the behaviour of matter, but the laws of biology according to which life, which He also created, evolves and develops. The so-called laws of evolution, then, are to be regarded as constituting the *method* which God chose to adopt for, among other things, the creation of man. Science investigates these laws and records their mode of operation. This process of investigation and recording will, it is obvious, continue. Modifications will be introduced as further discoveries are made, but the fact of their introduction will not require a corresponding modification in the general conception here suggested, nor will it afford grounds for revising the hypothesis from which the suggestion proceeds. Since, however, the laws are on this hypothesis prescribed by the mind of an Infinite Being, it is highly doubtful whether all that there is to be known about them will ever be known by us, although it is conceivable that our minds may ultimately know all that is *knowable* by us. (I have suggested in the last section of this chapter that there are certain aspects of the universe, even of the natural universe, which science not only does not know, but will never know.)

From this point of view the contrast in scale between man and the solar universe has little significance either for philosophy or for religion. In so far as it may be supposed to have any, its tendency is to exalt mind as compared with matter and to conduce to the greatness of God, since mind understands the material universe and, reflecting upon its vastness, is naturally led to draw conclusions in regard to the mind that made it vast.

Science and Religion

A word may be added on the much discussed question of the so-called 'conflict' of faculties. Is it, for example, true, as has been so often asserted, that science is the product of reason and that its conclusions are susceptible of proof, while religion belongs to the sphere of a vaguely conceived faculty known sometimes as 'intuition', sometimes as 'spiritual insight', a faculty frequently presented as divorced from, even if it is not actually opposed to, reason.

There is no ground for this alleged opposition. In the first place, the type of psychology which it presupposes, the psychology which represents the human mind or *psyche* as a bundle of faculties of which one can be singled out and termed 'reason', another 'intuition', is outmoded and cannot be sustained.[1]

In the second place, the supposed opposition is invalidated by the fact that there are few, if any, characteristics that can be attributed to reason that cannot with equal plausibility be attributed to other faculties. Reason, for example, can err; but so can such a traditionally intuitive faculty as conscience. Thus, while it has often been said that it is wrong for a man to act against his conscience, he is in no sense blameworthy for the kind of conscience that he has. Instinct and intuition can also err. To illustrate by an example given by Bertrand Russell, the hens who have been daily fed by the farmer's wife are instinctively moved to run towards her approaching figure, until the day comes on which the hand that fed them wrings their necks. Had they not trusted to instinct, they would not have been led to their deaths.

Again, it has been said that instinct and intuition are innate and that their authority is, therefore, unquestionable; but reason is also innate, as integral a part of our natures as are intuition and instinct.

I do not propose here to develop a thesis which should not

---

[1] I have suggested elsewhere (see chapter viii, pp. 203–10), that the mind may be a bundle of *ideas*.

now need re-stating. Indeed, the convergence on this point of the testimony of contemporary thinkers who on other matters differ radically, does not require reinforcement from me. It is not the identity of reason and intuition that is asserted, merely their universal and inextricable interweaving in the textures of those two departments of thought which are called respectively scientific and religious.

In illustration of my contention, that on this issue at least there is a widespread agreement, I venture to quote a number of representative opinions. Here is Benjamin Whichcote, a seventeenth century divine: 'I oppose not rational to spiritual, for spiritual is most rational. Where reason speaks, it is the voice of our Guide, a natural voice we cannot but hear; it is according to the very voice of our nature. It is also true in Religion, to follow God and to follow right Reason, is all one.'

Butler in the *Analogy* takes the same line. 'I express myself with caution lest I should be mistaken to vilify reason, which is indeed the only faculty we have wherewith to judge concerning anything, even revelation itself.'

In our own time, Dean Inge has criticised 'the notion that faith is fundamentally irrational and its dogmas exempt from being brought to the bar of ordinary evidence'.

The following quotation from a representative of a different religion, Sir S. Radhakrishnan, expresses the same view. 'In order,' he writes, 'to be able to say that religious experience reveals reality, in order to be able to transform religious certitude into logical certainty, we are obliged to give an intellectual account of the experience. Hindu thought has no mistrust of reason. There can be no final breach between the two powers of the human mind, reason and intuition.'

I conclude with a passage from Bertrand Russell's essay, *Mysticism and Logic*, which seems to me to put briefly and cogently all that is worth saying on this issue.

'But in fact the opposition of instinct and reason is mainly illusory. Instinct, intuition, or insight is what first leads to the beliefs which subsequent reason confirms or confutes; but the confirmation, where it is possible, consists, in the last analysis, of agreement with other beliefs no less instinctive. Reason is a harmonising, controlling force rather than a creative one. Even in the most purely logical realm, it is insight that first arrives at what is new.

'Where instinct and reason do sometimes conflict is in regard to single beliefs, held instinctively, and held with such determination that no degree of inconsistency with other beliefs leads to their abandonment. Instinct, like all human faculties, is liable to error. Those in whom reason is weak are often unwilling to admit this as regards themselves, though all admit it in regard to others. Where instinct is least liable to error is in practical matters as to which right judgment is a help to survival; friendship and hostility in others, for instance, are often felt with extraordinary discrimination through very careful disguises. But even in such matters a wrong impression may be given by reserve or flattery; and in matters less directly practical, such as philosophy deals with, very strong instinctive beliefs are sometimes wholly mistaken, as we may come to know through their perceived inconsistency with other equally strong beliefs. It is such considerations that necessitate the harmonising mediation of reason, which tests our beliefs by their mutual compatibility, and examines, in doubtful cases, the possible sources of error on the one side and on the other. In this there is no opposition to instinct as a whole, but only to blind reliance upon some one interesting aspect of instinct to the exclusion of other more commonplace but not less trustworthy aspects. It is such one-sidedness, not instinct itself, that reason aims at correcting.'

In the light of this weight of authority we may, I think, confidently conclude that religion, in common with all the other high activities of the human mind, is a product of a combination of reason and intuition, and that it is an error to regard reason as the special province of science, while relegating religion to that of intuition.

Science and Religion

B. THE WORLD OF SCIENCE AS AN IMAGINATIVE PICTURE OF THE REAL

It is instructive to consider in a little more detail the nature of the account of the world that science—and more particularly the sciences of chemistry and physics—provides and the ontological status of the world which the account purports to describe. The account of the world given by physics and chemistry has, I suggest, the status of an imaginative picture suggested by the behaviour of a something which is unknown. For, whatever else it may or may not be, that which so behaves is not that which is known. Two questions arise; what is the relation of the world whose behaviour the scientist purports to describe (*a*) to the familiar world which he observes and (*b*) to the 'reality' which so behaves?

FLAW IN THE PROCEDURE OF PHYSICS

I begin by making the obvious point that science calls in question the familiar world. There is a celebrated passage in Eddington's writing in which he describes how the physicist, when he wishes to establish contact with his world, is required to divest himself one by one of his sense-organs. Divested of ears, nose, palate and skin, he is, it is true, permitted an eye, but since everything that he observes is through a microscope or a telescope, only one. Nor is it difficult to see why the physicist's sense organs may be dispensed with; for the qualities which in our ordinary daily life the sense-organs seem to reveal to us— colour, solidity, sound, smell, temperature—are, in the physicist's world, simply not there.

Take, for example, heat. A gas, we are told, consists of molecules of about a hundred-millionth of an inch across, with comparatively large spaces between them, moving about in all directions with an average speed measured in hundreds of yards a second. The molecules meet and collide, and in consequence of their collision the gas has a certain temperature. If the gas is placed in a flame or hot body, the molecules of which it is composed will gain in energy, moving more rapidly and colliding more violently. Imperceptibly the temperature of the gas goes up; heat, as we say, is generated. But the cause of this heat is the greater energy of motion of the molecules; or, as a textbook on physics would put it, heat is nothing but the energy of motion of molecules.

Similarly, sound is said to be caused by, or alternatively to be, waves in the atmosphere. These waves vary in length, in frequency of vibration, and in mode of vibration. Variations in length determine the loudness, in frequency of vibration the pitch, and in mode of vibration the quality of the sound. Sound, then, is produced by atmospheric waves. Atmospheric waves are described as regions of pressure and rarification in the atmosphere moving forward with a certain velocity; and the movement of such a region of atmosphere is the cause of, or simply *is*, sound. Thus the properties of the atmospheric waves which the sounding body gives out determine the character of the sounds which are heard. But the waves are not noisy; sound, in fact, for physics is the movement of *soundless* waves.

Most significant of all is the case of colour. Modern physics deals with immense numbers of electro-magnetic waves, which, so far as their intrinsic characteristics are concerned, differ from each other only in point of speed, wave-length and frequency. In terms of their wave-lengths and frequencies they are graded in the electro-magnetic spectrum. The rays which are called 'light rays' occupy only a small part of this spectrum, at one end of which are located the so-called cosmic rays, and, at the other, wireless waves whose wave-length is measured in hundreds of yards. We may express this by saying that in the scale of wave-lengths and frequencies, according to which waves are arranged in the electro-magnetic spectrum, there is a certain section of waves which are—or which have effects which are—visible; these are called light-waves.

Light, therefore, is, or is caused by, a certain set of wave-lengths of varying frequencies in the electro-magnetic spectrum. Within this section of wave-lengths which are, or which cause, light, certain subsections are earmarked for the different colours. Thus, just as light-waves constitute a section of the waves graded by the electro-magnetic spectrum, most of which are not visible, so each colour is constituted by a sub-section of waves of particular frequency and wave-length falling within the light section.

But these sub-sections of waves are not themselves coloured.

It may, then, be safely asserted that the world which the scientist describes and which he takes as real is not the world with which our senses appear to acquaint us. Now there is, of course, no slightest reason why the appearance presented by the familiar world should be regarded as sacrosanct. Anyone who has a small acquaintance with philosophy will be cognisant of the variety of ways in which the claim of the familiar world to be, or to be equivalent to, reality can be impugned. Although philosophers cannot demonstrate to one another's satisfaction what the actual world is like, they can demonstrate to the point of conviction that it is not like the familiar world which common-sense believes itself to observe and which it takes as real.

But to admit this is not to accept the scientist's picture of the world without cavil. For there is assuredly a flaw in the procedure by means of which he establishes it. This is clearly brought out in a passage in Lowes Dickinson's book *After Two Thousand Years* in which Plato, evoked for the purpose from the Shades, is interviewed and interrogated by a representative young man of our own age. Plato and Philalethes, the modern, are discussing the notions of 'bodies' and of atoms, into combinations of which physical science asserts that 'bodies' are analysable.

The dialogue proceeds as follows:

'*Philalethes*. Indeed, they are improperly called bodies. We prefer to call them energies.

'*Plato*. Does not that make rather strange that confidence in the deliverance of the senses which was the starting point of this discussion? For, as I gather, whatever energies may be, they cannot be seen, or touched, nor smelt nor tasted.

Science and Religion

'*Ph.* Naturally not. We have much discussion about that, and much disagreement. Some say that only these ultimate energies are real; others that they are not real at all, but figments of our minds enabling us to predict the movements and operations of things seen and felt and heard, which latter alone are real.

'*Pl.* It seems, then, that this reality of sense is more uncertain than you led me to suppose.

'*Ph.* You must remember that the whole conception of invisible energies is derived from the perceptions of the senses, so that if they are not valid, neither is it. The foundation of all is therefore always sense, whatever else sense may lead us to infer.'[1]

Philalethes, then, is arguing that, *unless* sensory observations are 'valid' the atomic picture of the physical world would not be 'valid' either, but that since the former are apparently 'valid', or at any rate are taken by him to be so, we are entitled to assume that the latter is 'valid' also. The conclusion seems far from necessitated. One might just as plausibly argue that if the latter is 'valid', the former cannot be, in which case since, as Philalethes says, the latter is based upon and derived from the former, the latter cannot be either.

To put the point more precisely, let us call the world perceived by our senses X and the world whose existence physics asserts and whose characteristics it describes, Y. X has qualities; it is, for example, noisy and coloured. Now if the Y picture of the universe is correct, the observation which reveals it as X must be incorrect; X, in fact, is not what the world is *really* like. But if the observations which reveal the world as X are delusive, the process of inference, which, taking them as its premises, proceeds to infer Y, must be faulty; therefore, the conclusion of the inference, namely, Y, is invalid.

In sum, physics, starting from a world which appears to be noisy and coloured, reduces it to a world which is neither. The process may or may not be justified; but what I fail to see is how

[1] Lowes Dickinson, *After Two Thousand Years*, Allen & Unwin (1930), p. 168.

you can perform the reverse process, how, that is to say, from ingredients that are neither noisy nor coloured you can educe or derive a world which contains noise and colour. You cannot get out of a given set of ingredients what is not contained in them.

There is, then, as it seems to me, a flaw in the procedure of many physicists. In so far as they impugn the validity of the familiar world which they observe, they impugn also the conclusions which they reach by process of inference from their observations.

STATUS OF THE SCIENTIST'S WORLD

What account, then, are we to give of the status of this world of atoms and electrons that the physicist infers but does not observe? It may help us in the attempt to determine its status and its relation to the familiar world, if we consider in detail the procedure by means of which the physicist excises the familiar world's characteristics. For this purpose let us return to the case of sound. What, then, according to the physicists, happens when, as we say, we hear something? Waves of specified velocity and length travel through the atmosphere, waves which are not, as we have seen, noisy. They impinge upon the eardrums in the middle ear and impulses are then transmitted *via* the cochlea and cilia of the inner ear to the brain, where complicated neural disturbances result. None of the pulsing waves of air postulated by physics, none of the events in the body described by physiology, neither the vibrating membranes of the eardrum, the movement of fluid in the cochlea, the swaying of the cilia, nor the disturbance of nerve cells in the brain is, presumably, noisy. So far, then, as the physicist's and physiologist's account of the matter goes, non-noisy events occurring outside the body impinge upon the non-noisy substance of the body—or, more precisely—are causally linked with non-noisy events inside the body, as a result of which we hear a sound. Now, from the impact of non-noisy events upon a non-noisy substance, or, more precisely, from the holding of a causal relation between two sets

120

of non-noisy events, I do not see how noise could be generated. Yet noise is what we hear.

Is noise, then, something which is added by the mind or something which exists only in and for a mind? If so, some form of Idealism is true and neither version X nor version Y gives the correct account of the external world. But if this is the case, if, as Plato puts it in the dialogue referred to,[1] 'sense is a misappearance to us of some reality different from sense', it is clear that scientific knowledge can never be purely empirical, since the world of which science purports to give us knowledge is other than that which appears to our senses. But, again, if this *is* the case, why do scientists so persistently scout even the possibility that the real world may be mental or spiritual or even such as Plato describes? The view implicitly held by most scientists seems to be that the familiar world is a misleading appearance of a non-sensed reality, some, at least, of whose characteristics—for example, that it consists of moving particles of electricity—physical science purports to enumerate. Are we, then, to believe that eyes and brains consisting, as they do, of uncoloured, noiseless, particles of electricity, convert into colour and noise other non-coloured, noiseless particles? It seems highly unlikely. Whatever may be the true account of the matter, this is, I suggest, strictly incredible. If such a process of conversion really takes place, is it not necessary to postulate a mind to do the converting?

These are some of the difficulties which beset the attempt to give a satisfactory account of the status of the physicist's world. On what lines are they to be resolved? There seem to be broadly two possibilities.

(1) THE IDEALIST HYPOTHESIS

The first, as I have just hinted, is the idealist. Since the qualities which we observe in the familiar world are not to be found in the world of physics, one obvious recourse is to say that our minds, stimulated by the external world, the reality

[1] See p. 118.

affirmed and described by physics, invent them, project them, into the physicist's world and then proceed to acknowledge and recognise them as features of the familiar world. The familiar world is thus a compound of the physicist's world and the qualities which our minds have projected into it. This is the view which I suppose most philosophers have taken, and constitutes one of the many forms of the philosophy of Idealism.

The idealist position can be argued from many points of view. We can, for example, take a Kantian view of Space and Time and permit ourselves to be convinced by the reasons, the many highly plausible reasons, which Kant gives for thinking Space and Time to be ideal. But if Space and Time are mental constructions or, to adopt a somewhat more precise simile, a pair of mental spectacles through which we look out upon the world, then, one would have supposed, the world of which we say, that it is *in* Space and *in* Time must be ideal also. For it is hard to see how a space and time which are ideal can relate and bind or, indeed, affect in any way events which are themselves not ideal but *given*. Moreover, why—supposing that we waive this difficulty and hold the relating and binding to be possible— should they relate the events in the ways in which they do, in fact, relate them? If, for example, it is my mind which constructs the spatio-temporal relations between things and events which are not themselves constructed by my mind, why should I deliberately construct the temporal relation which I describe as a missed train or the spatial relation which I know as a missed catch at cricket?

Kant's *noumena* must, in short, as his successors saw, be sacrificed on the altar of a logical Idealism. But if they, too, are subtracted from the world that is given, then no independent reality is left and the world is ideal through and through.

THE DILEMMA

This is not except incidentally a book on philosophy, and I do not propose to develop the views of the idealists nor, though I do not myself hold them, do I here propose to criticise them. I

Science and Religion

mention them only because they enable me to throw into relief the difficulty which the point I have sought to bring out offers to the classical scientific view of the universe. This difficulty may be put in the form of a dilemma. Either the spatio-temporal relations which bind events and the laws which the events appear to obey are *constructed* by the mind or they are *discovered* by it. In the first event, the world is ideal through and through and the difficulty with which science has been thought to confront the traditional religious view disappears. In the latter, both the laws and the spatio-temporal relations which obey them being *discovered* are presumably *given* to the mind which discovers them. If given, they are contained in the world which confronts the mind just as truly as the physical events which conform to the laws and are presented to us in a spatio-temporal matrix. The 'real', then, contains non-material facts; it contains laws and it contains spatio-temporal relations. It is hard to conceive of laws existing in their own right as so many arbitrary pieces of cosmic furniture. Laws point inevitably to a mind which prescribes them, to, in fact, a lawgiver. Hence, whichever horn of the dilemma is accepted, science regarded as a stick with which to beat religion breaks in the hand, for, whichever line we take, the results of science seem to demand the sort of interpretation which religion would accept as congenial.

But this, I repeat, is not primarily a treatise on philosophy, and I return to the argument from which I have momentarily digressed, the argument touching the idealist implications of modern physics.

EDDINGTON'S IDEALISM

In this connection it is worth pointing out that, uncertain as the implications of contemporary physics must be recognised to be, one at least of the implications most commonly drawn by physicists themselves is the idealist. Take, for example, the considerations upon which Sir Arthur Eddington lays stress. These are familiar enough, and I need do no more than refer to them.

Science and Religion

Eddington draws attention to the fact that the phenomena with which physics deals and upon which its conclusions are based are not *things*, as they exist in themselves, but things only in so far as they are measurable.

Physics, then, is an account of the universe in terms of the quantitive aspects of things, since only the quantitive aspects are measurable. It follows that physics is a science of abstractions. The concrete things which have been quantitively measured and from which abstractions have been made slip through the meshes of its net. Physics, again, deals not with things but with symbols. Readers may remember the well-known passage in which Eddington shows how physics replaces actual concrete things and the relations between them—an elephant sliding down a grassy hillside, for example—with sets of pointer readings and the relations between *them*. We define A in terms of its relations to B, B in terms of its relations to C, and so on. Emphasising that A, B and C are themselves symbols, Eddington draws the same conclusion, namely, that physics does not deal with, in the sense of giving an account of, the actuality of real things; it is concerned only with a set of abstracted appearances and the relations between them, those appearances, namely, which they present to and which are, therefore, registered by clocks and scales in terms of pointer readings.

But perhaps the most important of his arguments is that which is derived from a consideration of the *nature* of the evidence upon which the physicist bases his assertions and the way in which that evidence reaches him. The evidence is the evidence of his senses; it is derived from observation. What, then, is involved in observation by means of the senses? The passage in which Professor Eddington answers this question is so relevant to my argument that I take the liberty of quoting from it. 'We all share the strange delusion that a lump of matter is something whose general nature is easily comprehensible whereas the nature of the human spirit is unfathomable. But consider how our supposed acquaintance with the lump of matter is attained. Some influence emanating from it plays on the extremity of a nerve, starting a series of physical and chemical changes which are propagated along the nerve to a brain cell; there a mystery happens, and an image or sensation arises in the mind which cannot purport to resemble the stimulus which excites it. Everything known about the material world must in one way or another have been inferred from these stimuli transmitted along the nerves. It is an astonishing feat of deciphering that we should have been able to infer an orderly scheme of natural knowledge from such indirect communication. The mind as a central receiving station reads the dots and dashes of the incoming nerve-signals. By frequent repetition of their call-signals the various transmitting stations of the outside world become familiar. We begin to feel quite a homely acquaintance with 2LO and 5XX. But a broadcasting station is not *like* its call signal; there is no commensurability in their nature. So too the chairs and tables around us which broadcast to us incessantly those signals which affect our sight and touch cannot in their nature be like unto the signals or to the sensations which the signals awake at the end of their journey.'[1]

Eddington draws the characteristic idealist conclusion. There is one thing and one thing only of which, he says, the knowledge does *not* come to us by this roundabout method of communication, a thing which we know directly and not by means of a set of precarious inferences. This is the thing that lies at the hither end of the line of communication and is, in fact, our own mind. 'Mind,' he concludes, 'is the first and most direct thing in our experience; all else is remote inference.'

The world of physics is, then, for Eddington, the result of a series of mental inferences from what are presumably, for him, mental data.

Idealist Philosophy Not Favourable to Religion

I do not myself subscribe to Eddington's analysis of the process of perception and of its results; nor do most philosophers.

[1] Sir Arthur Eddington, *Science and the Unseen World*, pp. 21, 22.

Science and Religion

It is, indeed, exposed to criticisms which will immediately occur to anyone who is acquainted with modern theories of perception. But this, I repeat, is not a book on philosophy and I do not propose to detail these criticisms here. I proceed, rather, to indicate the relevance to the theme of this chapter of the idealist tendencies in contemporary physics of which I have given examples. This relevance is three-fold.

First, the condition of physics and chemistry at the present time points as plausibly in the direction of an idealist interpretation of the subject matter studied as fifty years ago it seemed to require a materialist and determinist interpretation. Secondly, an idealist interpretation is at least in one respect favourable to, even if it does not entail, a religious interpretation, for in asserting the primacy of mind and representing the material world as secondary, an appearance to a mind of something which is in its essential nature either unknown or mental in character, it affirms some part of what many of the religions have claimed. Thirdly, it is clear that, whatever view we take of the matter, science, as I remarked above, no longer affords grounds for discrediting religion. Admittedly, it does not show the religious view of the universe to be true, but equally it no longer provides the grounds which it was once thought to provide for holding that the religious view of the universe must be untrue.

Nevertheless, I do not myself believe that the idealist view of the world, even though it is at first sight more congenial to religion than is the materialist, can be rendered easily compatible with the demands of religion. It is not merely that Idealism is inconsistent with the whole Christian tradition which insists that God created *something*, and set in train a procession of events into which from time to time He has intruded in a series of mighty acts; that in ascribing all the many and varied qualities of the featured world to the creative capacity of the human mind—readers will remember Professor Whitehead's celebrated observation: 'Thus nature gets credit which should in truth be reserved for ourselves; the rose for its scent; the

Science and Religion

nightingale for his song; and the sun for his radiance. The poets
are entirely mistaken. They should address their lyrics to themselves and should turn them into odes of self-congratulation on
the excellency of the human mind. Nature is a dull affair,
scentless, soundless, colourless; merely the hurrying of material
endlessly, meaninglessly'[1]—it savours of cosmic impiety: that
in reducing all to mind and eliminating any factor of brute intractable stuff in the universe, Idealism renders the problem of
error and evil even more insoluble than it was before; that it
finds difficulty in emancipating itself from the purely immanentist pantheism which is criticised elsewhere in this book[2]—it is
not any of these considerations, important though I think some
of them to be, that weigh with me in rejecting Idealism, so
much as the conviction that the attempt to resolve away the
element of what may be called 'brute-given' in the universe
which in their different ways all idealist philosophies undertake
fails and must fail. In a word, the universe seems to me to be
dualistic though not, in the last resort, irreducibly dualistic.
I deal with this question below and in a later chapter[3] and here
refer to it only in so far as it bears upon the theme of this one,
which is the relation of science to religion.

THE ELEMENT OF 'BRUTE-GIVEN'

Its relevance in this connection seems to me to be as follows.
The outstanding difficulty of the idealist mode of interpretation is the difficulty of setting limits to its application. We have
been taught by Berkeley and Hume to recognise that the considerations which, in so far as they are valid, point to the mental
origination of secondary qualities can and should be extended
to apply to primary qualities also. What is there in the spatial
location of the atom, what, even, in the velocity of atomic movement, to resist the analysis which disposes of noise and colour as
constituents of the external world, present in it independently

[1] *Science and the Modern World* by A. N. Whitehead, pp. 68, 69.
[2] See chapter vi, pp. 156–76.
[3] See p. 131, and chapter viii, pp. 221–4.

of our consciousness? As for material 'substance', philosophy had disposed of *that* long before physics threw doubts on the 'lumpiness' of matter. Hence, once the idealist mode of interpretation is pronounced legitimate, nothing is left in the external world which is entitled to resist its application. Yet if the physicists' account of the world is to have meaning, there must, I submit, be something for the account to apply to.

The procedure of science is to take the given phenomena of the sensible world, and to analyse and correlate them with a view to exhibiting an apparently chaotic diversity of happenings as exemplifying the workings of law. Success in this undertaking enables us to understand and to predict. The understanding is of the immediate causes of the phenomena; the prediction is of their recurrence, given the same causes, in the future. As it advances, science succeeds in bringing an ever greater area of that which is initially given to the senses under the aegis of an ever-diminishing number of laws. As its researches are pushed farther and farther back, what was formerly accepted as 'brute-given' is shown to be amenable to law and brought within the scientific fold. But science will never succeed in dispensing with the necessity for postulating a something which is regarded as that to which at any given moment its laws are applicable, and this something, from the very fact that it is *its workings and consequences* which scientific law maps and predicts, must itself be other than the operations of law. It must, that is to say, itself be unamenable to and unreachable by the operations of law at the particular stage which science happens then to have reached. Granted that it may subsequently become amenable, yet it can only do so by giving place to a new something which assumes the *rôle* of 'brute-given' in its place. The following quotations from Professor A. E. Taylor put the point clearly:

'We have to appeal in all our explanations of the actual not only to "laws" but to "collocations". Science, which hates to accept anything whatever as mere bare "given fact", is always trying with much success to reduce the "collocations" with which

128

it starts as given to mere consequences of "laws".' It reduces the 'collocation' which appears as brute-matter to elements; the 'collocation' of elements to atoms; the 'collocation' of atoms to charges of positive or negative electricity.

'But every success in such reduction is achieved at the price of acquiescence in some assumption of an earlier and more ultimate "collocation". Without "collocations" which have to be taken as "brute fact", as *there*, we do not know how or why, the functional dependences we call "laws" would reduce to functions without any arguments, and would thus become as insignificant as the symbol ϕ before a blank. Here we clearly come upon an inevitable limit to the whole work of scientific explanation.'[1]

Science, then, analyses the world into a comparatively featureless and, therefore, unknown X, collocations, stuff, matter—the name we give to it is immaterial—and the laws which govern its behaviour. Increasingly, all positive statements that can be made about the world belong to the category of law. Yet there must be something for the statements to be statements about, for the laws to apply to. It is this irreducible something that I have called the element of 'brute-given'.

(2) THE PLATONIC HYPOTHESIS

The necessity to make provision for such a 'something' brings me to the second hypothesis which is broadly that of Plato. Plato's view, as it is generally understood, envisages the presence in the universe of a substance or stuff as the medium in which the Forms manifest themselves. This medium is in general referred to as wholly featureless, all the qualities we perceive in the sensible world being due to the manifestation in it of the Forms. Its main function is to serve merely as a medium for the manifestation of the Forms, just as the main function of the 'matter' of modern physics seems to be to serve as a 'something' for the laws which physics formulates to apply to. There are, however, one or two passages in Plato wherein this stuff is

[1] A. E. Taylor, *Contemporary British Philosophy*, vol. ii, p. 298.

Science and Religion

thought of as obscuring or resisting the full manifestation of the Forms, as the raw material in which the ideas of the artist seek to express themselves may be intractable, resisting the full realisation of the conception which is in the artist's mind.[1] It is, I hope, not too fanciful to suggest that the celebrated indeterminacy, i.e. the unamenability to law, of some of the fundamental particles of modern physics may be evidence of the existence of a similar intractability in the stuff, the study of whose behaviour must, I am suggesting, be regarded as the subject matter of physics. But I am well aware that this suggestion may declare me an ignoramus in regard to these deep matters, and I had better drop it before fancy takes me further.

If we accept the Platonic hypothesis according to which the features of the observed world are due, not to the creative capacity of the human mind, but to the manifestation in it of immaterial Forms, we shall find it hard to resist his further view that a metaphysic so conceived requires, nay demands, the activity of a mind, of, in fact, God. Plato's God can, indeed, scarcely be described as creative. His relation to the familiar world is that of a midwife rather than of a creator in that, while creating neither Forms not stuff, both of which Plato regards as given, God mediates, as it were, between them, bringing the Forms to birth in the stuff or—another suggestion of Plato's—moulding the stuff on the model of the Forms which he takes as archetypes, and using the concepts of mathematics and, in particular, space and time as the instruments by means of which the modelling is accomplished.

It is a commonplace that the climate of Plato's thought is more congenial to the spirit of Christianity than that of any of the other pre-Christian philosophers. Plato can be read as a forerunner of what is to come, and where his thought varies from the Christian teaching, the variation can generally be adjusted without essential change of principle. This is the case in regard to the present issue, for a God whose function is

[1] This notion is developed in a later chapter. See chapter viii, pp. 222, 223.

Science and Religion

restricted to those of the midwife and the modeller is in no sense necessitated by the acceptance of the two principles of Forms and stuff; the Platonic ontology, in other words, does not necessitate the Platonic view of origins. Granted that on other grounds we accept the need for a creative God, He might just as well have *created* a world composed of the Platonic constituents of Forms and stuff, first creating Forms and stuff to be its fundamental constituents. Indeed, the notion of uncreated stuff and uncreated Forms which just happened to be lying about in the world, arbitrarily given pieces of metaphysical furniture, without maker or designer, is hard to credit.

As regards the stuff, the element of what I have called 'brute-given', if this was created as, I suppose, on the Christian view it must have been, its creation must be regarded as logically prior—it may even have been chronologically prior—to the divine creativity which works in and upon it, stamping it with the impress of Form. To put this in terms of the wording of Genesis, 'the dust of the ground' from which 'the Lord God formed man', was also a creation of the Lord God. Thus the universe of forms and stuff, though dualistic, is not irreducibly dualistic. Similarly, in regard to the Forms. Form seems to demand a conceiver, just as stuff seems to demand a maker. And the Christian view, according to which those Forms, *which are also Forms of value*, namely, Truth, Goodness and Beauty, are revelations of a more fundamental unity, does not conflict with the essential requirements of the Platonic metaphysic. Just as Forms demand a Form-conceiver, and stuff a stuff-maker, so natural laws—laws to which the events of the world conform, which constitute what used to be called the uniformity of nature—if we take them, as I have argued above we should, as given and not as imposed by the human mind, demand a law-giver. It is these laws which, as I take it, science explores and maps. The laws of evolution constitute one example, being the laws in accordance with which God caused living things to develop; the laws of physics and chemistry constitute another, being the laws according to which the stuff of the world behaves.

131

Science and Religion

To put this in Platonic language, the Forms of Beauty, Goodness and Truth are modes of God's revelation in the world, the ways in which he permits himself to be known by man. Man studies and seeks to manifest in himself God's revelation as Goodness in morals and religion; he studies and seeks to realise God's revelation as Beauty in art; and he studies and uses for his own purposes God's revelation as Truth in science and mathematics. Scientific and mathematical knowledge is thus the record of what man has discovered about God under the attribute of Truth, just as the body of the world's art is the record of what man has discovered about Him under the attribute of Beauty.

THE WORLD OF SCIENCE AS AN APPEARANCE

I do not, of course, wish to press these suggestions which the reader will dismiss, if he so pleases, as metaphysical fancies inspired by Plato. I mention them only to throw into relief the argument of this section which is to the effect that what science has discovered about the world is in no sense an enemy to its religious interpretation. For so far from being the world of solid fact which the man of common-sense believes himself to observe, the scientist's world is on any showing largely inferred and constructed. Science, in fact, does not—and this is the gist of the whole matter—give us knowledge of the empirical world, if we interpret the words 'empirical world' in what I suppose to be their correct sense, that is to say, the world revealed to sensory observation. To realise that this is so, it is not necessary to have either a knowledge of science or even an acquaintance with philosophy. It is sufficient to reflect upon the significance of the familiar difference between how things are and how they look. The stick in water looks bent but, we say, *is* straight; the polished surface feels smooth, but examination through a microscope discloses that it *is* uneven; the earth's surface may look flat, but we know that it *is* curved, and so on.

Now, when we formulate scientific laws we intend them to apply to the behaviour of natural objects, to natural objects, that is to say, not as they appear to be, but as we know them to be, *natural objects as we know them to be* being other than natural objects as we actually experience them. Take, for example, a square block of wood. I never *see* it as square simply because I cannot *see* all its sides at once; nor do I *feel* it as square. Again, I never *see* the molecules, atoms, protons and electrons of which, if I am a physicist, I know the block of wood to be composed. What, then, is the relation of the information yielded by my sense-experience to the order of nature that science explores and describes?

If I may again invoke Plato, I should say that our visual impressions are taken as clues to an order of reality of which they supply evidence, but which is other than they. It follows that the order of my actual experiences is different from the order of objects and events which science describes.

It is, of course, true that when we say that the stick seen in water *is* straight, we correct our visual impressions by evidence derived from touch, and that when we say that the surface *is* uneven, we correct our tactile impressions by evidence derived from sight. But the inference is, once again, forced upon us that the order of things about which science gives us information is neither the same as the order of our visual impressions nor the same as the order of our tactile impressions. Both are clues to what is other than they, but clues of varying degrees of accuracy. In the first instance, the tactile, in the second, the visual clue is taken to be the more accurate. The conclusion is that the kind of knowledge that science gives is not empirical; for it is not sense-experience that assures me that the stick is straight, the surface uneven, the earth curved and the block square. I know these things as the result of a process of reasoning which is based upon an *interpretation* of my sense-experience.

The fact that we make a distinction between what seems crooked and is straight, seems two-dimensional but is a cube, seems flat but is curved, taking the contents of our sensory experiences as clues to something else of which these are an appearance, has an important bearing upon the fashionable contemporary analysis of perception known as phenomenalism. For what the fact implies is not only that we take our perceptions—and I am here using the word 'perception' in what I take to be its original and correct sense to denote our acts of sensing or perceiving—as revelatory of what is other than ourselves, but that we take the immediate content of what they reveal to us to be a clue to something other than the content. We know, then, that the physical world is other than it seems to the perceiver to be. But if this is so, no analysis of the physical world in terms purely of sensory experience can ever be exhaustive, since sensory experience gives us information only about what seems and, as Plato insists, we cannot have *knowledge* of what *seems*; nor, indeed, if I am right, does science purport to give us such knowledge.

CONCLUSIONS

I have sought to show that the scheme with which science presents us is not a transcript or copy of reality in some sense in which the scheme with which religion presents us is an invention about reality. Neither scheme belongs to the realm of empirical knowledge, for in neither case can the features which the scheme asserts be observed. Each scheme is a picture of the world *suggested* by direct experience, a picture to which that experience is taken as a clue. The scheme of science is a picture suggested by the behaviour of we know not what, which in some way that we do not understand gives rise to the experiences that we receive through our senses; it is to this 'we know not what' that the experiences are taken as a clue.

The religious scheme is a scheme to which the experiences of the spirit, and, more particularly, the experience which is a feeling of dependence, be taken as a clue. Both schemes are, therefore, from this point of view logically on all fours. If religion is an abstraction and its 'truths' are symbolic, so are those of science. If religion is subjective in the sense of being *merely* subjective, so is science. If, on the other hand, science may claim to give us knowledge, suggesting or even revealing

134

to us the nature of that to which it is taken as a clue, so may religion.

If the foregoing is correct, the sphere of natural science, though it may and, as I have said, does give us information about the nature of what is, does not give us exhaustive or exclusive information. It concerns itself only with a single aspect of reality, that aspect, namely, which may be made the subject of exact observation and experiment and which can be measured.

Other disciplines, other experiences, other modes of thought and study, will give us information about other aspects. In particular, since the universe to which science introduces us is not self-created—for to postulate self-creation is to offend against science's own causal principle—nor self-explanatory— for pieces of matter moving about in space are not, nor do they carry with them, the explanation of why they are and move— something else must exist to perform the office of creation and explanation, this something lying outside the scope of science. Thus, science does not exclude but rather demands the existence of other spheres of reality, known to us by different methods and evoking different kinds of experience, to explain the existence and the workings of the world which science itself studies.

What, then, are the spheres of reality which elude the scientific method of approach? *Prima facie*, they are the spheres of ethics, aesthetics and religion. The point at which our enquiry brings us to these spheres is also the point at which we catch sight of those problems which have notoriously proved intractable to scientific method. I propose, then, in concluding this chapter, to give some account of them.

C. THE LIMITATIONS OF SCIENCE

There is a number of problems which science is unfitted to solve; there are areas of experience of which it is unable to afford any reasonably plausible account, areas belonging, as it were, to a different dimension from that in which science moves. I will say something of these problems.

THE BODY-MIND PROBLEM

Prominent among them is the problem of the relation of the mind to the body. This is not the place for a full-dress discussion of this problem. Broadly, there are two alternatives; either the mind is part of the body or it is not. If it is not, then the presumption is that it is not material and we not only do not know but cannot conceive how it interacts with, in the sense of affecting and being affected by, the body. The mode of mind-body interaction is, in fact, a mystery.

Grant the religious view of the universe; grant that God made man in His own image, breathing the breath of life into his nostrils and this mystery is precisely what we should expect. We should not, after all, as I remark elsewhere, expect to understand the mode of God's working.

Now man, on the religious view, is a member of two orders of being; he has one foot in each of two camps. The relation between these two modes of being a relation which, as I argue in another chapter,[1] involves the mystery of transcendence and immanence, is not one that we are likely to be able to comprehend. But that this should be so is intolerable to science which is driven by the nature of its procedure, a procedure which rests on the assumption of the universality of the causal relation, to treat the mind *as if* it were part of the body. It is natural, then, that the philosophies congenial to science should be those of materialism and behaviourism, if philosophies they can be called. It is also inevitable that the tendency of science should be determinist and that scientists should implicitly reject, even if they do not in so many words deny the possibility of free will.

IMPLICATIONS OF THE ADMISSION OF FREE WILL

For consider some of the implications of the admission of freedom which make nonsense of that universal scheme of causal

[1] See chapter viii, pp. 209, 210.

Science and Religion

law which science seeks to establish. Some of the movements of our bodies clearly take place independently of our wills. My heart beats, my blood circulates, my digestive processes occur, my hair and nails grow, without the intervention of my will, and, if I am lucky, without the knowledge of my consciousness. In the causation of these bodily movements, then, my will plays no part. Moreover, if my body and a leaded wax effigy of my body of the same shape and weight are tipped over the edge of a precipice, both will fall in the same way and at the same speed, reach the bottom at the same moment and exhibit the same sort of behaviour when they get there, in spite of the fact that my body is animated by a free willing mind and the wax effigy is not.

On the assumption, then, that I have a free will, the movements of my body are divided into two sharply differentiated categories—those which are caused by the immaterial agency of my will and those which take place in accordance with the laws of mechanics and dynamics, laws which are ultimately reducible to the laws of physics, some of these latter movements being to all intents and purposes identical with those which would be performed by any other piece of matter of the same weight, density, shape and size which was placed in the same circumstances.

But the two categories of movements extend far beyond the confines of my body. Consider for a moment those movements of my body which fall into the first category. They are themselves the causes of other movements in the world outside. If, for example, the movements are those of my hand signing a general mobilisation order, or of my finger pressing a button that explodes a mine beneath a battleship, the train of consequences set going by my movements is incalculable. Yet all these consequences and all the movements which the consequences entail, must be assigned to the first category of movements, since, if it had not been for the intervention of my free acts of will to produce the movements of my fingers involved in signing the document or in pressing the button, these movements might

137

not, they probably would not, have occurred. Thus the physical movements that occur in the universe fall into two classes. Some, for example, movements on the other side of the moon, are as far as we can tell, completely subject to mechanical causation—that is to say, the laws of physics adequately account both for them and for the preceding movements in the causal chain which ends in them. Other movements cannot be completely accounted for on these lines. This supposition, involving, as it does, a bifurcation of the material happenings in the universe into what are, from the point of view of causation, two radically distinct classes, is difficult for science to accept.

But further difficulties are involved. An identical action may belong to either of the two categories. Let us suppose, for example, that I cross my legs and will slightly to lift my upper foot; let us suppose further that, as a result, my foot rises two or three inches in the air. Now let us suppose that somebody taps my leg with the side of his hand just below the knee-cap. A nerve is touched and my foot again rises two or three inches in the air, the movement being known as a reflex. The two movements, the willed and the reflex, may be quite indistinguishable. Indeed, so far as their intrinsic characteristics are concerned, they are indistinguishable. Yet one is caused by a material event, the application of a stimulus to a nerve, the other by a mental event, an act of will. Now we are accustomed to hold—indeed in science we must hold—that the same effects are produced by the same causes. Yet in this case two apparently radically different causes produce two identical effects. Moreover, since the two classes of movements—the one caused by a free act of will, the other taking place according to the accepted laws of mechanical causation—are indistinguishable, we are forced to the conclusion that, for all we know to the contrary, *any* movement *may* belong to the first class, since there are no intrinsic marks by reference to which it can be decisively placed in the second. Thus science can never feel certain in respect of any movement on the part of a piece of matter that its causation does not include some incalculable factor. It can never feel

138

Science and Religion

certain, that is to say, that the rule of law which it seeks to establish is in fact completely operative.

A further difficulty is occasioned by the sudden and arbitrary break in the causal chain of physical happenings which the hypothesis of free will entails. Let us consider the movements involved in deliberately withdrawing one's body from the path of a stampeding crowd. The stimuli in virtue of which we become aware of the spectacle of the oncoming crowd are conveyed by purely physical processes to the brain. Light rays strike the retina of the eye, messages in the shape of nervous impulses travel along the optic cord and disturbances are produced in the cells composing the cortex of the brain. So far, the sciences of physics and physiology between them can give an adequate account of all that has taken place. In other words, the mechanical law of cause and effect has so far held good. At this point, however, as a result of the disturbances occurring in the cells of the brain, some effect is produced in consciousness. What does this mean? That when the impulse which travels along the optic cord has reached the brain, it causes an event of an entirely different order, that is to say, an event in the mind which is a conscious event. How this transference from brain to mind takes place we do not know. Presumably, however, it *does* take place and as a result we have the sensation of seeing the crowd, a sensation which is a purely mental event not explicable in bodily terms. Upon the sensation there ensues another mental event, an act of will, which is a decision to take action in respect of that which has been sensed by instructing the nervous system to take steps to remove the body from the course of the oncoming crowd. Thus, once again, the machinery of the body, including the nervous system, comes into action, and, once again, the laws of physics and physiology begin to apply. But they do so after a break in the course of which events of an entirely different order have taken place. The corollary of the admission of free will is then, apparently, that physical science applies to, in the sense of giving a complete account of what happens, up to a point; that at this point there is a break during

139

which it ceases to apply, and that it then begins to apply again exactly as if the break had not occurred.

Such are some of the reasons why science cannot admit the intrusion of a free and spontaneous will in the world which it explores and why, since human beings form part of that world, it is bound to treat them mechanically, regarding their minds, in so far as it regards them at all, *as if* they were parts of their bodies. Yet this supposition will not pass philosophical muster.

That Determinism Stultifies Itself

It is not hard to show why the taken for granted Determinism of scientific method will not pass muster as a philosophy. Such a demonstration would, however, take me beyond the scope of this book. I venture here to treat of one matter only, where many might have been raised, because of its special relevance to the thesis of this chapter.

Suppose for a moment that the denial of free will is conceded. If freedom of willing goes by the board, so does freedom of thinking, since it were hard to suppose that, while that part of the *psyche* which is concerned with what we do is a reflex of bodily conditioning, that part which is concerned with what we think is free from bodily determination. Indeed, it is a common-place of psychology that the two 'parts'—and I put the word in quotation marks to indicate that it implies an inadmissible, spatial metaphor—cannot be separated.

Our thoughts, then, if free will is to be denied, are determined —determined by what? Provided that two reservations are made, we may say that they are determined by the body. (Nobody, at any rate, so far as I am aware, has ever suggested that, subject to these reservations, they are determined by anything but the body.) The first reservation is that the *immediate* cause of a particular mental event may be, and often is, another mental event.

It is because I *want* to eat an apple that my *mind* considers how I may best pluck it; thus, it may be the case that the immediate cause of a particular mental event may be, not a physical event, but another mental event which precedes it. The minimum that must be claimed by those who argue for the determination of mental by bodily events is that at some point the chain of preceding *mental* events is terminated, so that somewhere in the causal ancestry of any particular mental event, a bodily event will be found.

The second reservation is that the bodily event which determines the mental event is itself only the last link in a chain of causally linked physical events that precede *it*. Let us suppose that a man decides to make a run for a train which is just leaving a platform. On determinist assumptions, the *proximate external* physical cause of his decision is the appearance of the successive positions of the train as it slowly leaves the platform, which appearance stimulates the endings of the optic nerves in the retinas of the eyes of the would-be passenger. The *proximate internal* cause of his decision is the electrical disturbances which travel along the optic cord, resulting in corresponding disturbances in the brain. A *complete* account of the cause would, however, include the movements in body and brain, *plus* the whole series of preceding events constituting the would-be traveller's biography culminating in the situation which is referred to as the desire to catch the train, *plus* the whole series of preceding causally linked events which resulted in the train moving just when it did.

Given these two reservations, we should, if we were determinists, be prepared to hold that all mental events are determined by preceding bodily events, and that those mental events which we call acts of thought and will are determined by preceding cerebral events.

Now, some bodily events are immediately caused by events outside the body and in this sense may be said to refer to them. Mental events which are by-products of bodily events will have external reference in the same sense. But can they have it in any other? A thought is usually taken to refer to external events in another sense, this being the sense in which the external event may be said to be the *object* of the thought. In this, which is

Science and Religion

the epistemological sense of reference, it is possible for some of the objects of thought to be future, as when I think that it will rain tomorrow, and others to be what are called abstract, as when I think that it is the tendency of civilisations to develop and decay. The question is how on the determinist assumption can thoughts which have external reference only in the first sense, the sense in which they are the end products of chains of causally linked events, have external reference in this second sense? Rain tomorrow is not *yet* a physical stimulus; the formulation and comprehension of historical generalisations about civilisations not only is not, it can never be, a physical stimulus.

How, then, on determinist lines explain the epistemological relation of thought to its objects? The content of a thought may be, indeed, on the determinist assumption, it *must* be chemically determined in the sense in which the state of a man's blood pressure is chemically determined. But how can it be determined by its object, that is to say, by that which is thought about? If it is wholly determined by the events which are happening in the brain, how can it also be determined by the nature of the 'object' of which it would normally be said to take cognisance? How, in short, can it be influenced by external objects at all, otherwise than as one of the causally linked chain of events of which, if we accept the determinist view, it is the end product? Yet if it is what is commonly called an abstract thought, it is extremely difficult to see how it *could* be determined by such events. For how could an historical generalisation be the result of a physical stimulus?

Now Determinism is itself a system of thought sustained by a closely woven fabric of argument. Why, then, if the conclusions which Determinism asserts are true, should we suppose it to have any epistemological reference to a state of affairs external to the series of thoughts in which the theory of Determinism consists? Determinism certainly *purports* to have epistemological reference. It *purports*, that is to say, to give information about the nature of things; but if it is true in all that it asserts, it can have only causal reference and can, therefore, give information only about the conditions prevailing in the body and the brain of the determinist.

THE CASE OF ERROR

A special difficulty arises at this point in connection with error. We normally regard thoughts as having the property of being true or false. Without embarking upon discussion of the philosophical question of the meaning of truth, we may say that a thought is *prima facie* true, if there is an external fact which it asserts and with which it corresponds; false, if there is no such fact. Thus, if I think that there are twenty people in the room and proceed, by counting, to verify my estimate, I should say that my thought was true. If the counting showed that there were twenty-five, or if I were suffering from an hallucination and there were, in fact, no people there at all, I should say that my thought was false.

The question is, how can a thought which has no epistemological, but only causal reference be either true or false? The only sense in which we could say of such a thought that it was 'true' is the sense in which it did accurately register or reflect the state of the body and brain of the thinker at the moment when he thought it. Now this is obviously an improper meaning of the word 'true'. For it is obvious, I think, that whatever else we may mean by 'true', we do *not* mean being the end-product of a series of events that led up to the thought for which truth is claimed, or being harmoniously related to a general system of events of which the event for which truth is claimed forms part; thus, we might say that a man's blood-pressure was real but not that it was 'true'.

But even if we were to allow this sense of 'true', what meaning could we assign to the word 'false'? How can an event which is in essence a bodily event or which, at least, belongs to the same category as bodily events, *not* fit into the system of events to which it belongs, or how can it *not* be the end-product of the causally linked chain of events which led up to it? In a word, what account can, on determinist premises, be given of error?

148

Science and Religion

The point has been made by Sir Arthur Eddington better than I can hope to make it, and I venture, therefore, to quote the following passage from his writings:

'If, for example, we admit that every thought in the mind is represented in the brain by a characteristic configuration of atoms, then if natural law determines the way in which the configurations of atoms succeed one another it will simultaneously determine the way in which thoughts succeed one another in the mind. Now the thought of "7 times 9" in a boy's mind is not seldom succeeded by the thought of "65". What has gone wrong? In the intervening moments of cogitation everything has proceeded by natural laws which are unbreakable. Nevertheless we insist that something has gone wrong. However closely we may associate thought with the physical machinery of the brain, the connection is dropped as irrelevant as soon as we consider the fundamental property of thought—that it may be correct or incorrect. The machinery cannot be anything but correct. We say that the brain which produces "7 times 9 are 63" is better than the brain which produces "7 times 9 are 65"; but it is not as a servant of natural law that it is better. Our approval of the first brain has no connection with natural law; it is determined by the type of thought which it produces, and that involves recognising a domain of the other type of law—laws which ought to be kept, but may be broken. Dismiss the idea that natural law can swallow up religion; it cannot even tackle the multiplication table single-handed.'

To put this briefly, natural law determines the motions of atoms. But natural law, on determinist premises, also determines the movements of brains and, therefore, of minds. Thoughts are movements of and events in mind. Thoughts, then, are determined by natural law. How, then, can thoughts be false?

The above are illustrations of the contention that science is unable to give a satisfactory account of the relation between body and mind or, I should add, of the operations of the mind. In particular, the categories of true and false which are appropriate to these operations lie outside its scope.

Science and Religion

VALUES

ART

Another sphere in regard to which science has no competence is that of values. Beauty belongs, *prima facie*, to things. It is not emotions which are beautiful but that which arouses them. Beauty, then, would seem to be a quality belonging to the external world which science studies, but since it is a quality which can be neither measured, counted nor weighed, science can give little account of it. Also, while the qualities which are manifestly sensory and are, therefore, accessible to empirical investigation, stimulate each a single sense, as colour stimulates the sense of sight, sound that of hearing, beauty is or can be a common quality of objects which are apprehended by different senses. For if there is *no* element in common in the emotions aroused by a symphony, a cathedral, a picture and a natural scene, why do we refer to them under a common name and assign their investigation and appraisement to a separate branch of philosophy, namely, aesthetics?

Beautiful things, again, are capable of being graded. The music of Beethoven is 'greater', we say, than that of Mendelssohn, the plays of Shakespeare than the ephemeral productions of the contemporary West End stage. What do we mean by the expression 'greater'? The answer to this question is difficult and controversial but it is not an answer that science can supply.

Here, then, is an important area of human experience in which the writ of science does not run. Such accounts as science does purport to provide of man's experience of beauty emanate from the domain of psychology. They are pitifully inadequate. Normally, they take the form of interpreting what we feel for beauty as an inheritance from what our remote ancestors felt for it, which is not to solve the problem but to put back in time the problem to be solved. Or they speak of the sense of harmony, or of the equilibrium of the emotions engendered by contact with works of art, an explanation which leaves unexplained the

K   145

problem of why it is that some works promote the harmony and the equilibrium and not others, and what it is about them that produces these effects. Or they derive our feeling of beauty from considerations of utility—this, they say, is called beautiful because it precisely serves the purpose for which it was made. But if this is all that we mean, why do we go out of our way to invent a special word, 'beauty', to designate what is, on this showing, only useful?—or maintain that we appreciate a natural scene, because it gives us a feeling of security. But why does it and why, assuming that it does, should we say of it that it is beautiful? Why not be content to couch our description exclusively in terms of security?

Art has played a great part in human history; it can be a source of intense pleasure, yet pleasure is only one and not necessarily the most important element in the complex of experiences we derive from it. Art can lift you out of the selfish little pit of vanity and desire which is the self, and incorporate you, if only for a moment, in what is felt to be greater than the self. The peculiar appeal that art makes demands, many have felt, a metaphysical interpretation; art is a pathway to reality or a window through which we view it; it is also, as I suggested above, one of the ways in which God reveals His nature to man.

Now there must, as I have argued above, be *some* quality about a work of art which is capable of producing these effects, effects which have seemed to call for such dramatic interpretation, even if it be a false interpretation. Further, art finds expression in natural *things*; art, in fact, is a 'work', a series of sounds, an arrangement of paints on a canvas, a structure in stone. To this 'work', then, there must belong some quality or set of qualities which produces the aesthetic effect. But this quality or set of qualities cannot be any one of those commonly supposed to be possessed by matter, such as length or breadth or height, softness or hardness, sweetness or the reverse, since of all these science can give an account, analysing them into combinations of molecules whose motions are predictable in

Science and Religion

accordance with natural laws. What, then, are we to say of this quality?

Let me try to illustrate the point at issue. Here are five notes struck at random upon the piano. Hammers hit wires, vibrations are set going in the atmosphere, stimuli are applied to the tympana of the ears, and appropriate resultant effects are conveyed by the inner ear to the brain. Now strike the same five notes in a particular order, so that they form the statement of the theme of a Bach Fugue. In each of these two cases the notes struck are the same; the events in the physical world, the vibrations, the stimulation of the tympana, the disturbances in the brain, are also presumably the same. Only the order and the intervals are different, and of these the intervals need not be. Now, order is not itself a physical thing; it belongs rather to the category of what the Greeks called 'Form'. Of it, and of the difference, therefore, between a meaningless succession of sounds and a theme by which you can be thrilled to ecstasy, science can give no account. I repeat, therefore, that science can give no satisfactory account of art.

ETHICS

Similarly with goodness. It is, of course, possible to explain the facts of moral experience on naturalistic lines. Indeed, since it is so frequently attempted, we may suppose that this interpretation is beset by fewer difficulties than the equivalent interpretation in the case of aesthetic experience. It is hard, however, to conclude that it is any more successful.

Those who seek to analyse what is *prima facie* ethical experience into non-ethical components are faced, as it seems to me, with at least one insuperable difficulty. Let us suppose that ethical judgments have their origins in considerations of individual and/or social expediency, that I say 'This is good' or 'right' now, because 'this' or conduct similar to 'this' was found to be advantageous by my ancestors or contributed to the welfare or security of the social group to which they belonged. What requires to be explained is why, on this assumption, such words as 'good' and 'right' ever came to be invented and used. If ethical expressions do not refer to the specific qualities which they are commonly supposed to designate, how and why were they coined? And, similarly, if there are no such qualities, if what we call 'good' or 'right' is always exhaustively analysable into considerations of utility and expediency, why were the qualities invented? Thus the answer to subjectivism takes the form, not so much of saying that men invented and used these expressions because they recognised certain qualities, 'goodness' for example, or 'rightness' in things with the presumption that the experiences which their recognition involved were evoked by features of the given, as of pointing out that it is not possible to explain how and why they should have gratuitously deceived themselves into thinking that qualities were present in the universe which were not present, and then invented expressions to refer to them. If the qualities did not exist, how could and why should men have deluded themselves into thinking that they did? If they are fakes, what motive could men have had for fabricating the fakes? 'Painful', I say of the toothache, 'rash' of the climb, 'inexpedient' of the investment, but I do not say that these things are 'bad'. If *all* that I mean by such words as 'cowardly' or 'cruel' is 'painful', 'inexpedient', 'misery-promoting', or 'anti-social', why do I go out of my way to use these ethical expressions in relation to the conduct of the poltroon or the sadist, but not in relation to the toothache or the investment? Why, in fact, use ethical terms and make ethical judgments in regard to some cases of inexpediency, but not in regard to others, if there is at bottom no difference between the two classes of case?

Unless the questions I have just asked can receive a satisfactory answer, there is, I suggest, no way of avoiding the conclusion that ethical qualities exist and that ethical judgments refer to them. But—the question must again be pressed—if the qualities do exist, what account can science give of them and of the responses they evoke in us? Given a subjectivist or naturalist interpretation of ethics, given that '"this" is good' means no more than 'I or my remote ancestors or my social group approve of "this"', then the function of the scientist is relevant. Anthropology and sociology can, for example, be invoked to answer the question why my group or my ancestors approve or approved of 'this'. But given that this interpretation does *not* convince us, then we must postulate a sphere of 'what is' into which science does not and cannot enter.

RELIGION

As with art and ethics, so with religion. Religion suggests that man is a member of two worlds or, rather, of two orders of being. By virtue of his body and those parts of his psychological life which have their origin in bodily happenings, he is a member of the natural world. By virtue of the fact that he is a soul or spirit capable of responding to beauty, of making moral judgments and of acknowledging the presence of God, by virtue, also, I should add, of his possession of reason, he is a member of a non-corporeal order of reality. In so far as this is true of him, some of his experiences, at least, will evade interpretation on purely naturalistic lines. Of these experiences science can give no account; nor can it give an account of the mode of their relationship to those other experiences which originate in the natural world, nor determine with any certainty to which category a particular experience belongs.

And this in practice turns out to be the case. Of the movements of our bodies science can give a fairly complete account. Of *some* of them the account is, indeed, quite complete. It can, for example—to revert to the illustration given above—give as complete an account of the behaviour of my body, if this is dropped over a cliff, as it could of the behaviour of a wax effigy of my body. There are, however, some bodily happenings of whose causation, granted the freedom of the mind and will, science is *not* able to give a complete account, and there are other happenings which cannot, as I argued above,[1] be assigned with certainty to either category.

[1] See pp. 137, 138.

Science and Religion

Of those events in my mind which have an ostensible bodily origin, of physical pain, for example, of hunger and thirst and sexual enjoyment, science can again give an account, of varying degrees of completeness. It can, for example, predict with reasonable certainty that, unless I am anaesthetised, I shall feel pain of a certain kind if my finger is pricked with a pin. In regard to those events which are *prima facie* of psychological origin, the writ of science runs a certain distance, though the mode of origination of this category of mental events brings us to the borderland of controversy. Has the feeling of fear, for example, which I experience at the sight of a machine gun spraying a hillside with bullets an origin in the secretions of the adrenal gland? Does the jealousy I feel as I see another man kissing the girl I love originate in a rush of blood to the brain and an increased rapidity of the heart beat, or are the secretions of adrenal fluid, the rush of blood and the rapid heart beats merely the accompaniments or the consequences of the *mental* apprehension of a particular situation? The answer is far from clear. What we can do is to predict with a fair measure of, though not with absolute, certainty that I shall feel fear in the first place and jealousy in the second.

Science can, however, give no account of the activity involved in performing purely mental operations, nor is the certainty which the conclusions of logic and mathematics possess of the same kind as the 'certainty' with which science predicts events in the natural world. It is a certainty more absolute, and it is not subject to time. The difference is the one traditionally expressed in philosophy by the classical distinction between necessary and contingent facts.

The operations of the spirit are still more unpredictable. Of whom can it be said in advance that he will appreciate the music of Bach or become sensible of the existence of God? What, then, has science to say of such experiences? If it is to take cognisance of them at all, it must write them off or explain them away. Thus, religion is, for it, the expression of a sense of guilt, or of need, or of man's feeling of loneliness in the face of the vastness and impersonality of the universe, or of his need for a 'Father figure'. Upon the adequacy of these attempted explanations I have commented elsewhere.[1] Those who do not feel convinced by them will admit the existence of yet another field of experience of which science can give no account. What is more, since the experience must take the form of a response to something in the external world by which it is aroused, the inference would seem, once again, to be that there are spheres of the universe other than the natural sphere which science studies.

SUMMARY

It may be useful briefly to summarise the conclusions of this chapter. I have sought, in the first place, to establish the common-place proposition that there is no conflict between science and religion. Many have supposed that the conclusions reached by scientists in regard to the nature of the physical world and the development of life upon this planet throw doubt upon the religious interpretation of the universe. The argument of the first section of this chapter is that science at least affords no good grounds for this doubt.

I have tried, secondly, to show that the scientific account of the world is a selective account. The selection is dictated by certain specific human interests and determined by certain specific human limitations. It is in no sense a whole account of the whole. There are some grounds for regarding the account as in the nature of an imaginative picture constructed by the mind of a reality which is and must remain unknown to us. Whatever view we take on this controversial issue, this much, at least, is clear: whatever reasons there may be—and many have been alleged—for regarding the religious view of the universe as a construction by or a projection of or an imaginative picture painted by the human mind, apply no less to the scientists' account of it. On this count also science fails to provide grounds for discrediting religion. Thirdly, by way of illustration

[1] See chapter iv, pp. 96–104.

of this thesis, I have cited certain outstanding examples of the failure of the sciences to give an even plausible account of certain areas of human experience.

The upshot of these considerations is to support the view advanced by religion that man is a member of two different orders or realms of being, that it is only of one of these that science takes account, and of that one only in so far as it can be satisfactorily isolated from the other and treated *as if* it were the whole. In other words, science cannot give an account of the impact of the supernatural order, in so far as it makes itself felt, upon the natural, or of the results of that impact. If this is so, there seems to be no necessary reason why we should not accept the conclusion that in the last resort no complete account can be given even of the natural order, which does not make allowance for the intrusion into it of the supernatural. God, in fact, may, for all that science can show to the contrary, be immanent and active in nature. He may at different times in the past, and more particularly in the early days of Christianity, have been more frequently active than He is at the present time. The fact that miracles are contrary to natural law is not, therefore, a reason for rejecting them out of hand. The same may be said of such major intrusions into and interferences with the course of nature as the Resurrection and the Incarnation of Jesus Christ. Once the existence of the supernatural and its total difference in kind from the natural are recognised and admitted, such difficulties as astronomy and geography raise, for example, as to the whereabouts of Heaven and the nature of immortality disappear. For Heaven is not a place but a state, and immortality is not to be conceived as something that goes on for a very long time. To this last matter I shall return in the next chapter.[1]

[1] See chapter vi, pp. 174–6.

CHAPTER VI

Pantheism and Immortality

In this chapter I propose to consider briefly the view that God exists and is wholly immanent in the world. This takes two forms which those who hold it do not always clearly distinguish. Either (i) God is or is identical with the world, or (ii) He is wholly immanent in it in the sense that there is nothing of God outside the world, although not necessarily in the sense that there is nothing in the world which is other than God. According to this second version of 'immanentism', God may be expressed in or contained in or locked up in the world as the soul is commonly thought to be locked up in the body, and just as the soul is wholly contained in the body, yet there is body as well as soul, so, on this second version of the pantheistic view, God is not the world but there is the world as well as God. Most of the objections which I propose to bring against the conception of God as wholly immanent apply to both forms of this view. In what follows, however, I shall be chiefly concerned with the first, which is, I think, the commoner.

WILLIAM JAMES'S MYSTICISM

The straightforward version of the pantheistic view asserts quite simply that God is the world. Everything, then, is God, the desk as well as myself, my toenail as well as my mind and/or soul. A slightly more sophisticated version of this view, while insisting that God is all, represents the individual soul as being separated, at any rate temporarily, from God although still in contact with Him. As an example of this version let us consider the kind of mysticism associated with the name of William James.

Pantheism and Immortality

James calls us back from an arid intellectualism to consider the nature of experience as it is actually lived. Experience as actually lived, he points out, is not made up of clearly defined bits that can be distinguished from one another, nor is it clearly distinguishable from those other bits, which are the so-called 'objects' of the external world affirmed by common sense and explored by science. Experience, he maintained, is a dynamic activity, a flux in which separateness and distinction, the products of the analysing and discriminating intellect, disappear. Thus, there is no separation between one state of experience and another but only an insensible passage through imperceptible gradations.

Again, there is no separation between those clearly defined features or humps of experience which we call consciousness and the dark hinterland of the subconscious from which they spring, and no separation between the subconscious and a 'more' which is, James seems to suggest, the experience of, or the experience which *is*, the universe as a whole. Thus the individual personality lives in sub- or semi-conscious contact with the vast obscure life of the cosmos. It is from this larger life and experience that there comes to most of us, even in our present condition, that strengthening and healing which men call 'grace', and that there *will* come to us in the end liberation from the sense of separation entailed by our individuality, a liberation which Christians refer to as blessedness, peace, salvation, immortality, Heaven and so on. It is in the feeling of continuous contact with this 'more' that, on James's view, the essence of religion in general and mystical religion in particular is to be found, for the 'more' with which we are continuous is none other than that which the religions have known as God.

A somewhat similar conception is to be found in Schopenhauer's account of the universe as a dynamic semi-conscious will, expressing or objectifying itself in innumerable individual expressions which we know as the consciousnesses of apparently separate and distinct 'egos'.

The mysticism of James differs from the traditional Christian

154

Pantheism and Immortality

mysticism both in respect of the fact that the 'more' with which the soul is presumed to be in contact is in a condition of continuous, energetic activity, and in respect of the fact that God so conceived—and James does not hesitate to use the word—is not other than a universe which He transcends, but *is* the universe or is, at any rate, its soul.

Logical Difficulties

This point of view is, as it seems to me, exposed to one outstanding logical difficulty. Either the apparent individuality and separateness of every soul is a fact or it is not. If it is a fact, the universe is not adequately represented as a single, continuous whole of dynamic experience. If it is not, if the universe is in its real nature a continuous whole of unindividuated experience, we must ask how differences arise, or, rather, how apparent differences appear to arise. Granted that the appearance is illusory, how did the illusion, the illusion of which I, for one, am a victim when I believe myself, as I do, to be a separate centre of individual experience, come to be generated, and not merely the illusion of difference as such, but the illusion of just those actual differences between men and men and men and things, which have been developed or, rather, which appear to have been developed? How, in fact, out of a continuous whole of experience do you get the illusion of a multiplicity of individual centres? And if you reply, as James and Bergson did, that the illusion is due to the conceptualising propensity of the intellect, which inserts artificial stops and gaps into what is in fact a continuous flow, whence arises the intellect with its error-creating activity, and why does it insert just those stops and gaps which are worked up, as it were, into the common-sense world of people and things, as we know them, and not others? Do they correspond to features initially given in the flow itself, or do we make our world as we please, carving it, as it were, at will out of the continuous whole which is reality? If the latter, why do we make it as we do? Why, in fact, do we arbitrarily 'carve out' missed trains and broken bootlaces? If, as

Pantheism and Immortality

one cannot help suspecting, the stops and gaps correspond to divisions and distinctions in the 'given' which are actually presented to us, it is difficult to see how it is to be exonerated from being initially characterised by just those differences, or the potentiality for just those differences, which subsequently appear. But in this event, the universe is not adequately represented as a continuous whole of experience.

I do not pursue these difficulties here, since my concern is rather with the theological than with the logical implications of this conception. I want to enquire what sort of provision it makes for religion and the religious consciousness. On the assumption that our consciousnesses, in common with the universe as a whole, are the expressions of a spirit which is wholly immanent in things and which men have not hesitated to call God, what account are we to give of the experiences distinctively associated with religion?

I suggest that this view is, from the point of view of religion in general and of the Christian religion in particular, unacceptable for the following reasons:

I. THAT GOD IS DOOMED

If God is identical with the world or is wholly immanent in the sense of being wholly contained in and bound up with it, He will, it is obvious, share its history and its fate. Now one of the most widely held views as to the future of the physical universe is that it will perish of what has been sometimes called a 'heat death'. The second law of thermo-dynamics requires us to suppose that the energy which is at present contained in and is being diffused from radio-active atoms will ultimately reach a condition of maximum diffusion. Conceive for a moment that the universe in its original condition consisted of a number of carefully done-up parcels which, as time passed, began to unwrap themselves and to distribute their contents higgledy-piggledy in every direction. When a condition of maximum 'higgledy-piggledyness' had been reached, no further distribution would or could take place. Moreover, if such distribution and its consequences constituted the only kind of event known in the universe, no more events of any kind would occur.

Or consider a clock which has been once wound up and has finally run down, or a blob of ink which has been shaken by a fountain pen into a tumbler of water and has gradually diffused itself evenly throughout the water. There will be no further events in the clock and the tumbler. The physical universe is, then, on this view doomed ultimately to reach a condition of eventless stagnation, and if God is wholly immanent in and dependent on it He will, presumably, share the same fate.

Even if we take a different view of the future of the universe and suppose that the physical universe, while expanding indefinitely into space will, owing to the continuous creation of new matter, exhibit what are in effect predominantly the same characteristics throughout an indefinite period of time,[1] God, if wholly contained in the universe, will be subject to sentence of indefinite repetition. For it is hard to see how a Being who is conceived as being wholly immanent in and, therefore, bound up with the *physical* universe, could exist without it, either in the sense of ultimately emancipating Himself from it or of surviving it.

A word may be added with regard to the popular immanentist view put forward in the writings of Bernard Shaw, according to which a force or activity of life enters into matter and forms living organisms in order to further the process of its own development. The philosophy of the Life Force set forth in the preface to the *Back to Methuselah* Pentateuch is not in point of metaphysical principle essentially different from that of the mystical 'more' of William James, of the 'Will' of Schopenhauer, or of the *élan vital* of Bergson. Admittedly, Shaw looks forward to a time when the Life Force will cease to feel the need to objectify itself in matter. 'After passing a million goals,' says Lilith, in the final speech of *Back to Methuselah*, 'they press on

[1] See *The Nature of the Universe* by F. Hoyle, pp. 107–9.

to the goal of redemption from the flesh, to the vortex freed from matter, to the whirlpool in pure intelligence that, when the world began, was a whirlpool in pure force. . . . I will not supersede them until they have forded this last stream that lies between flesh and spirit, and disentangled their life from the matter that has always mocked it.' And again: 'I shall see the slave set free and the enemy reconciled, the whirlpool become all life and no matter.'

No reasons are given for thinking that what is postulated as being immanent in the physical universe can alter its condition and become independent of the universe, but the whole conception of the Life Force, its origin, nature and purpose are shrouded in such obscurity that one does not feel any confidence in making any definite statement in regard to its ultimate status.

My general conclusion is that a God who is so intimately and exhaustively bound up with the universe as is the immanent God of the pantheists, is not the kind of God who fulfils the requirements of religious experience or satisfies the longing of religious need. How could He be, if He is doomed? Emphatically He is not the kind of God whom the great religious mystics have affirmed. For it is difficult to regard Him as a person or, indeed, as anything at all save as the impersonal soul of an impersonal universe. Finally, if He is not a Person we cannot think of Him as sending His Son into the world to save mankind.

II. THAT THE WHOLE IS NOT NECESSARILY MERITORIOUS

Religion cannot, I think, divorce itself either from value or morality. Let me take the point first in regard to value.

(*A*) If God is wholly immanent in the universe, then either there is nothing in the universe deserving of worship or the whole is, since, even if there were some element in the universe other than God it would, on this view, be impossible to separate that element from God in such a way as to enable us to recognise the latter as God and to recognise also that, being God, It or He

158

was worshipful, while at the same time discerning in regard to the former that it was not God and was not worshipful. Now it seems to me self-evident that religion demands that there should be something in the universe which is worthy of worship, something which can serve at once as an explanation and source of, and also as a focus for, our emotions of reverence and awe. I conclude, therefore, that on this view we have no alternative but to regard the whole as being valuable and worshipful and this conclusion is one which most pantheists have been willing to accept.

The question then arises, is it in fact true that the whole is deserving of worship? It cannot, I think, be so deserving unless it has merit. What meaning, then, in this connection can the concept of merit bear?

In answer to this question I venture to make three points.

(i) It seems to me that, if everything is meritorious, then nothing can be, since to claim merit for everything is to deprive the concept of merit of meaning by depriving it of contrast. The concept of merit, in short, has meaning only in relation to something that is without it, or that has less of it. Unless merit characterises some things and not others, it loses distinctiveness as a characteriser, since there is nothing from which to distinguish it.

(ii) If the whole has merit, the parts cannot be wholly without it. Am I, then, to rejoice because in sharing the universe with tapeworms and excrement, I share with them its merit? And is it really true that a toenail has merit in the same sense as that in which a good moral action has?

(iii) The conception of merit seems to me to entail the concept of a person, since only a person can be morally meritorious. Now, I do not find it easy to conceive that the tapeworm, the excrement and the toenail form part of a person or that the whole is a person. As for aesthetic merit, much of the universe is clearly ugly, just as much of it is clearly evil.

(*B*) This last consideration brings up the question of morality. Does the kind of mysticism which W. James sponsored make any adequate provision for the fact of evil? I cannot see that it does.

Pantheism and Immortality

If God is everything and everything is God, how can there be evil in the world, unless God is Himself evil? Christianity seeks to provide for the fact of evil by taking man's individuality and freedom seriously and asserting—what is only too obvious—that individual men have used their freedom to choose wrongly.

But this form of explanation is denied to a view which either holds (i) that I and my acts of will are divine, since God is all or in all, or (ii) postulates my subconscious continuity with a 'more' from which or whom intimations are conveyed to me of the direction in which 'the more' desires or intends—if desire or intention can properly be attributed to it—my character to develop and my moral choices to be made. For if God is all, what is to prevent these intimations being carried out? What barrier can or could exist between me and God, to cut me off from God's grace and so to prevent me from choosing and acting as God would have me choose and act?

THE DIFFICULTY IN REGARD TO FREEDOM

This difficulty comes out again clearly in connection with that form of the immanentist view which Shaw popularised under the name of the Life Force. The difficulty is in the first place a difficulty in regard to freedom. It is never clear to what extent, for Shaw, the individual is free. Is he merely a vehicle for the canalisation and subsequent development of the Life Force, or can he win some measure of freedom from life's promptings? In the first event, he is a mere fountain-pen for canalising the stream of life, no more responsible for what he does than is the pen for what it writes. It is fairly clear that Shaw does not mean this. For if the individual were not in some sense free, the admonitions and exhortations and injunctions of which Shaw's practical philosophy consists would be beside the point. To be told, for example, that your success (or duty) in life consists in being used in pursuit of its purposes by the power that made you, clearly implies that it is open to you to resist being used in this way, open to you to follow your own purposes, open to you, in fact, to fail.

Pantheism and Immortality

This, I have no doubt, *is* Shaw's view. We are, at best, imperfect instruments of life's purpose. In particular, we busy ourselves with our own concerns instead of using ourselves up in life's service, and although life does its best to point out to us, through the instrumentality of Shaw and other wise men whom it sends into the world 'to give conscious expression to its instinctive purpose', the way it would have us go, and encourages us to follow that way by contriving that the life of direct pleasure-seeking will be unrewarding even in terms of pleasure, nevertheless, we do, in fact, all too frequently go astray.

Assuming, then, that we do have freedom, three difficulties present themselves. (*a*) First, is our freedom only a freedom to go wrong? Are we, when we go right, when, that is to say, we go about life's business, mere automata, responding to the promptings and impulses that reach us from the force of which we are expressions, whereas when we assert our wills and go our own ways, when, in fact, we thwart life's purposes, we are acting as self-determining individuals? This is a depressing view to take of human free will. (*b*) If we are free, whence do we derive the energy which enables us to pursue a course divergent from life's purpose in regard to us? Granted that we are instruments of life, how can the instrument turn against the hand that wields it? If God is not all that there is but is, nevertheless, wholly immanent in what is, if, that is to say, matter be admitted in the universe as well as God, and God is wholly immanent in matter, then the difficulty might conceivably be overcome by assuming that matter may intervene, as it were, between the main stream of life and its individual expressions, and by intervening act as a temporary insulator, conferring a degree of freedom upon the individual expressions of the Life Force, much as a line of rocks lying athwart a river will diversify and deflect it into a number of different streamlets, each of which follows its own direction, though *the energy* with which it follows is that of the parent river. This suggestion is not unplausible; but besides making use of a metaphor which may well be inadmissible, it derives the fact of freedom from the inter-position of matter which limits the power of life over its individual expressions. Shaw himself never, so far as I know, tackles this difficulty.

In general this suggestion, which entails the existence of matter in the universe as well as that of God, of matter, more-over, which intervenes to thwart God's intentions in regard to creatures He has made, is more akin to a dualistic than to an immanentist view.

THE DIFFICULTY IN REGARD TO MORAL EVIL

(c) But how, in the third place, *can* the individual expressions of a divine Principle act wrongly and what could it mean in a pantheistic universe to say of them that they do act wrongly?

I venture the opinion that, as I hinted in an earlier chapter,[1] neither Shaw nor any of the other immanentists have taken the fact of evil seriously. Read Bergson, Alexander or Shaw, all of whom are in their different ways expositors of the doctrine of creative evolution, and it is difficult not to reflect upon the appositeness of their philosophies to the circumstances which prevailed in the western world during the era of triumphant progress which came to an end in 1914.

According to these philosophies, there is nothing existing in the universe higher than the spirit that is man or that is in man; hence, there is no impediment to bar man's path and there are no absolutes existing independently of his will to check human ambition or to limit its achievement. Nor is there anything in the world that can ultimately withstand his will. Having raised himself by dint of his own efforts from the level of the animals, he will probably continue to evolve into something greater than himself. (Nietzsche, it will be remembered, was still prating of the Superman.) Man, in fact, is the highest expression of the spirit of the universe, a spirit which will one day, if it has not done so yet, raise itself in and through his agency to the level of the divine. God, in fact, as Alexander suggested, is

[1] See chapter iii, pp. 81, 82.

waiting to be evolved by man's efforts. When He arrives, He will be man's handiwork and man's descendant.

This is the very crest of the wave of human optimism. Nowhere in these philosophies is there any suggestion that there may be something fundamentally wrong with man, that evil may be endemic and ineradicable in human nature and, therefore, in the order of reality to which human nature belongs.

And so we come to the view of evil which I discussed and criticised in an earlier chapter,[1] which represents evil as a by-product of circumstance, or a characteristic incidental to our condition of imperfect evolution, with the corollary that to remove the circumstance is to abolish, to evolve more fully, to supersede, evil.

To hold such a view in regard to evil is, I have urged, tantamount to a refusal to take evil seriously. I now add that the pantheistic view of the universe in any of the forms in which I have been considering it is precluded from 'taking evil seriously', in the sense of holding that evil is endemic and ineradicable in the universe, as we know it, and that in us sin is 'original'. It is difficult enough in all conscience to provide a tolerable account of evil which is consistent with the assumption that God is transcendent (as well as immanent) and that He created the world. But to regard Him as *wholly* immanent means that we must regard Him as infected with the evil with which the universe is so palpably shot through, as an alternative to writing off evil as a temporary incident or by-product of circumstance. Now this, if there is any substance in the considerations advanced in chapter iii, is gravely to misread the significance of our experience.

[1] See chapter iii, pp. 56–63.

Pantheism and Immortality

III. THAT PANTHEISM DESTROYS THE SIGNIFICANCE OF INDIVIDUALITY

(i) THE PERSONALITY OF CHRIST

It destroys it, first of all, in respect of its bearing upon the nature of Christ. If pantheism is correct, there is only one level or order of reality, the level of the cosmos in which God is wholly immanent or, if God *is* the cosmos, the level of God. Thus the distinction between a natural and a supernatural order, from which the natural order takes its rise and in terms of which it receives its explanation, falls to the ground. There is, then, no such thing as a supernatural order or a supernatural being. It follows that Christ was not a supernatural being. What, then, was He? Answer, on this view, a man like the rest of us—a very good one, admittedly—but still a man who was born like any other man at a certain point in history and gave utterance to a certain number of rather unpractical ethical precepts.

I have no qualifications for seeking to assess the significance of Christ, or to determine the nature of His personality. I confine myself to making two points which seem to me to be clear. (*a*) First, if Christ is no more than a teacher of ethics, He is not a very impressive one. Many of His ethical precepts appear in the teachings of the other higher religions; others form part of the stock-in-trade of the Greek philosophers. Again, Christ's teaching as it has come down to us is fragmentary and unsystematic. On a great many important matters of conduct He has little or nothing to say. His teaching in regard to the rôle of man, the citizen, touching his relation to the State is very inadequate. He attributes little value to the intellect. Nevertheless, much of what He has to say is exasperatingly obscure and He chides people because they do not understand Him. He is often angry and strikes one as being sometimes unreasonable. What, for example, could be more reasonable than the request of the Scribes and the Pharisees for some *evidence* that He was the supernatural person that He claimed to be? Yet how frequently and how bitterly He breaks out at them for asking for 'a sign'.

Considered *merely* as an ethical teacher, Christ is inferior both to Buddha and to Socrates.

(*b*) I conclude that it is not possible to explain the hold of Christ over the minds of men on the assumption that to say of Him that He was an ethical reformer or an original, ethical thinker or that He was a very good man, is to say all that can be significantly said; still less is it possible to explain the subsequent history of Christianity. The miraculous element in Christianity, the Incarnation, the miracles themselves, above all the Resurrection, would seem, therefore, to me, to be essential parts of Christianity, if only because without them I do not see how it is possible to explain the tremendous impact which Christ has made upon men's minds. It is impossible, also, to explain the subsequent history and influence of the church. Christ, then, I conclude, if we are to make sense of the history of Christianity, must have been in part a supernatural as well as in part a natural person. Now if the view under consideration in this chapter is true, He could not have been supernatural.

(ii) THE SIGNIFICANCE OF HUMAN INDIVIDUALITY

In the second place, the pantheistic view destroys the uniqueness of the concept of individuality in its application to man. The age in which I grew up tended to look coldly upon individuality, representing it as a temporary stage in a biological process which would transcend it or, if it took the concept of spirit seriously, as a temporary phase in a *spiritual* journey which looked forward to the transcendence of individuality as its goal. As an example of the former tendency I cite the attitude to individuality adopted in *The Science of Life* by H. G. Wells, G. P. Wells and Julian Huxley. After describing the nature and habits of a number of marine and fresh-water creatures such as feeding-polyps and blastostyles, which can apparently be regarded at will either as individuals specialised to form a colony or as cells in a single individual which *is* a colony, the authors

165

proceed to observe that individuality is not a precise but is an elastic concept. As such, it is a matter of degree and of emphasis. We are then warned against supposing that the existence of discrete individuals is the only form of existence which life can assume. Thus, 'in Obelia the reality is not a number of separate individuals but the plastic living tissue growing and budding and branching, throwing out now a feeding-polyp, now a blastostyle . . .; not definitely committed to any one of these kinds of body, but sprouting and reorganising itself as circumstances determine. It is a living continuum; a mob of cells which may be turned to this or that'.[1]

Even in the case of ourselves there is an underlying reality, namely, the race which is other than we are and other apparently than our sum; we are but the race's incidental offshoots. From the biological point of view, the thing which continues is not the human being but human protoplasm: 'Human protoplasm lives on and may live for ever; human individuals are the temporary shapes that it assumes—excrescences, so to speak, that the race throws out as the Obelia stuff throws out polyps.'[1] And so to the conclusion that the 'living material race', rather than the highly complicated cell-communities that we call individuals, is the 'enduring reality'. Individuals come and go, and, far from being necessary forms of life, will probably be superseded. Inevitably, the biological view discards such conceptions as that of the soul and takes an epiphenomenal view of mind.

Intermediate between this and what may be called a fully spiritual attitude to the mind and soul as constituting the essence of individuality are a multitude of contemporary speculations which also tend to regard individuality as temporary. Thus in Olaf Stapledon's exciting work, *Last and First Men*, which envisages the future of our species first upon this planet and in the more remote future upon the planets of other stars in the Milky Way, individuality is to a large extent superseded. Individuality does, indeed, still persist for the performance

[1] H. G. Wells, G. P. Wells and Julian Huxley, *The Science of Life*, p. 150.

Pantheism and Immortality

of special functions, but the greater part of human experience —one is precluded from writing 'individual experience'—is now that of the group consciousness of the species, in which individual consciousnesses are merged, much as its partial expressions and apparent differences are ultimately—though the ultimate here is one of logic rather than of time—merged and reconciled in Hegel's Absolute. Each element in the group consciousness enjoys the pleasures and suffers the pains of all. Or—as an alternative mode of expression—Stapleton speaks of a group mind or consciousness which is engendered by the coming together and merging of a colony of individual minds, the experience of which is more than and richer than the sum total of the individual experiences of each of the individual minds which participate in and are merged in it. We are invited to think of this merging of purely individual experience in that of a whole which transcends it as constituting an advance.

ALDOUS HUXLEY ON THE NATURE OF THE UNIVERSE

The most persuasive form of the belief that individuality is not a permanent but is a transitory category, in its application both to the human soul and to the soul or spirit that pervades the universe, is to be found in the later works of Aldous Huxley. Huxley in his more recent writings has laid great stress upon the significance of the deliverances of the mystical consciousness. They point, he thinks, strongly in the direction of the Buddhist doctrine that 'God' is infinite and non-personal and that in this infinity the individual soul will ultimately be merged. For 'the individual is an abstraction from reality. Separate individual existents are illusions of common sense'.

As the doctrines of Eastern mysticism have recently achieved some vogue in intellectual circles in the West, a vogue for which Huxley's writings are in part responsible, I propose to devote a little space to a summary of his view. This will be found most clearly set forth in the chapter entitled "Beliefs" (chapter xiv) of his book, *Ends and Means*.

167

Pantheism and Immortality

For many years, Huxley tells us, the question of the meaning and purpose of the universe had, for him, no meaning, since, for him, the question 'Does the world as a whole possess the value and meaning that we constantly attribute to certain parts of it . . . and if so what is the nature of that value and meaning? . . . is a question which, a few years ago, I should not even have posed. For, like so many of my contemporaries, I took it for granted that there was no meaning'.

For various reasons, partly of theory, partly of practice, which he cites in detail, he has revised this view and now takes a more constructive one. This may be summarised as follows:

(i) The Buddhist doctrine that desire is the source of illusion is correct. In the degree in which it has subdued desire the mind wins free from illusion and sees clearly. Hence in practice we must cultivate 'non-attachment'.

(ii) In so far as we are successful in this, we enter into certain states of consciousness in which the individual consciousness 'obtains direct experience of a spiritual unity underlying the apparent diversity of independent consciousnesses'.

(iii) In obtaining and enjoying this experience we realise that personality is not an ultimate fact and that it is 'possible for individuals to transcend the limitations of personality and to merge their private consciousness into a greater impersonal consciousness underlying the personal mind'.

(iv) The true nature of the universe which is discovered 'beyond the frontiers of the average sensual man's universe' is then revealed as 'a spiritual reality underlying and unifying all apparently separate existence—a reality with which [the mystic] can merge himself and from which he can draw moral and even physical powers which by ordinary standards can only be described as super-normal'.

We are further told that in the experience of this universal consciousness 'it is possible for individuals to pass to another level of being' in which their experience 'is not their own emotion, their own volition, their own knowledge, but an unnamed and perhaps indescribable consciousness of a different kind, a

Pantheism and Immortality

consciousness in which the subject-object relation no longer exists and which no longer belongs to the experiencing self'.

(v) Since the underlying reality is not a person, it is without ethical qualities. Huxley quotes with approval Eckhart's 'God is not good'.

(vi) What, then, is goodness? Answer, 'the means by which men and women can overcome the illusion of being completely independent existents and can raise themselves to a level of being upon which it becomes possible to . . . realise the fact of their oneness with ultimate reality . . . and in some measure actually associate themselves with it'.

(vii) Nevertheless, while embodied we can never wholly transcend our 'animal nature' and the needs which it engenders and we can never, therefore, wholly transcend our separatism.

(viii) Finally, the extent to which we realise our essential oneness, or, alternatively, the extent to which we emphasise our (apparently) no less essential, albeit partial, separateness, depends upon ourselves. 'Goodness is the method by which we divert our attention from the singularly wearisome topic of our animality and our individual separateness.' 'Virtue', in fact, 'is the essential preliminary to the mystical experience.'

The conclusions of the view that I have so briefly summarised are these:

(1) That God is not a Person but is a universal spirit.

(2) That we ourselves are expressions of this spirit.

(3) That our individuality is temporary and not ultimate and that our destiny is to be ultimately merged in the spirit.

(4) That we can make some progress in this direction while our souls are still incarnate in bodies. This we do by cutting off desire at the root and cultivating non-attachment.

Conduct, then, which, so far as its ethical characteristics are concerned, cannot be understood apart from metaphysics should be directed to overcoming individuality. We are good in so far as we cease to be individual.

There are three main reasons why I find this view unacceptable of which one is logical, another ethical and the third personal.

Pantheism and Immortality

(1) LOGICAL

If reality is a single universal consciousness, how does it come to be split up into, or get expressed as, a number of individual consciousnesses?

(i) In the first place, why should it do so? What conceivable point could there be in such a proceeding? All action, nay, more, all self-expression implies purpose. It is undertaken for an end. Now, the notion of purpose entails desire or need, the need to realise the purpose, the desire to achieve the end. It is difficult to see how or why a universal consciousness which is identified with the whole could entertain a desire or feel a need to achieve any purpose or to realise any end; difficult, indeed, to understand how it could need or desire anything at all. But if it has no desire, no need, it could have no motive for self-expression, if self-expression be the appropriate word. For desire presupposes lack; we do not desire that which we already are or that which is already ours. Now, a universal consciousness identified with the whole of reality could not, presumably, lack anything, for already it is all that there is.

Again, the concepts of need and purpose imply impediments, obstacles, frustration. We do not aim at what we possess or purpose to achieve what is already accomplished. If, then, there is to be desire, if motive, if need, if aim, if end, there must be something which stands between us and possession, something which impedes realisation and denies accomplishment. But a universal consciousness, if it is truly universal, is all-embracing and all-inclusive. What, then, could it lack, or what could there be other than itself to impede its achievement of aim or to frustrate its accomplishment of purpose?

(ii) How, in the second place, *could* it do so?

(*a*) If we take the Buddhist and neo-Buddhist doctrines as outlined by Huxley, seriously, we must suppose that the universal consciousness *is* reality, while individuals are only potentially real, since individuality belongs to the world of appearance and not to that of reality. Hence the differences between things and people are unreal in some sense in which their wholeness and oneness are real. Hence the universal consciousness, in expressing itself in individual consciousnesses, or in generating or producing them—it is difficult to know under what term the implied relationship can be most appropriately envisaged—is expressing itself in something less real than itself. But how could reality become, how could it even cause, that which is less than real, even if it could be supposed to have a motive for becoming or doing so?

(*b*) Either the difference and separation which individuality entails are real or they are not. If they are not real, the belief that they are is illusory. How, then, could a universal consciousness which is reality and which is the whole of reality generate or give rise to error? Nor can those who uphold this view have recourse to the explanation that error is illusory. For it is certain that I *think* that my individuality is real and that I am different from my neighbour. Let us suppose that I am mistaken in thinking this, that I am in reality one with him, as the monists assert. Then either my mistake is real or it is not real. If it is not real, then it is not *really* a mistake to think that I am different and I *am* different and difference is real. But if the mistake is real, then, presumably, it is real in some sense in which the separateness and the difference are less than real. The universe is thus saddled with the attribute of *real* and not merely *apparent* error. Hence, if the universe is a single consciousness and differences are illusory, then granted that error is real, this consciousness must itself be infected through and through with error. This is not, so far as I am aware, a view which any thinker has held.

If, on the other hand, difference and separateness are real, the question must be pressed, how are we to conceive them as being generated in and evolved from the bosom of a single, universal whole of consciousness? If the consciousness is, indeed, a perfect and complete whole or unity—and would not determination of any kind infringe its flawless universality, in the sense in which an individual personality, for example, is distinguished from pure universality by reason of the determinations by which the personality is characterised?—how does the possibility of finite development from, or even of finite experience within it arise? How, to put the point differently, does the principle of difference appear in and develop from perfect oneness? Complete unity can no more serve as a ground for the reality of difference and separateness, than it can for the illusory appearance of difference and separateness?

To sum up this objection, the universal ground of things is not the same as the sum of all possible developments from that ground —why, indeed, if it is or could be, was the process of development ever initiated? Once the difference be granted, we must ask how the universal ground can be conceived responsible for originating that element, whether it be regarded as negativeness, partiality, limitation or finiteness which produces *apparent* error, *apparent* multiplicity and *apparent* separation between knowing mind and known object? We are told that these 'manys' are 'ultimately' one. The distinction between 'ultimately one' and 'one' is not clear. But if the word 'ultimately' means anything, 'ultimately one' implies a contrast with something other than oneness now. How that something other could have been generated from the unity of the universal consciousness or could become merged into it without carrying back with it into the 'one' the principle of difference—a principle which entails as a minimum that there does *appear* to be a difference between the world as it appears and the world as, on this view, it really is— is the insuperable difficulty which seems to be implicit in the whole conception of a universal consciousness which is identified with the whole of reality.

(2) ETHICAL

(i) I do not see what even remotely plausible explanation can, on this view, be given of the problem of evil. The problem of evil has been considered in an earlier chapter[1] and I do not propose

---

[1] See chapter iii.

again to dilate upon the difficulties which attend any view which refuses to take the fact of evil seriously. As I have indicated above,[1] a view which regards reality as consisting of a single universal whole or unity, whether or no it identifies that whole or unity with the totality of the universe, is faced with the difficulty in a particularly obnoxious form. Either it must write off evil as being in some sense illusory, as not wholly real, or it must regard the whole or unity as being itself infected with evil. The conception of the reality of the universe as a universal consciousness is not immune from this difficulty.

(ii) The view seems to deprive individual striving and aspiration both of point and of motive. Of point, because it is never made clear *why* an individual soul should seek to transcend its individuality by achieving absorption in a universal consciousness. What adequate reason is given for our wishing to do so? Why should individuality seek to abolish itself? And what of the universal consciousness ? What purpose could conceivably be served on the part of the universal consciousness with which reality is identified—if, indeed, to revert to our logical difficulty a universal consciousness can be said to have a purpose—by diversifying and expressing itself in a finite number of individual consciousnesses with a view apparently—if all goes well and each individual consciousness attains such degree of perfection as is possible to it—to their again being merged in the universal consciousness? For the end of the whole process is, so far as can be gathered, the return of all individual consciousnesses to, their merging in the universal consciousness from which, presumably, they took their rise. The end of the process is, then, a single universal consciousness. But so also was the beginning. What, then, can be the point of a process, if indeed it can be rightly termed a process, which is such that while involving pain, evil, illusion and finiteness by the way, its end is not other than its beginning?

It deprives individual striving and aspiration of motive by robbing the individual's struggle to improve himself of incentive.

---

[1] See pp. 162, 163.

Pantheism and Immortality

If I *desire* loss of individuality by absorption in a universal consciousness, and can feel a reasonable assurance that, in so far as I transcend my own individuality I shall achieve such absorption, well and good—I shall struggle to overcome desire, to cultivate detachment and to transcend the limitations of my individual personality. But if I do not, what motive can I have for so striving? Now, moral endeavour constitutes in some form, however modest, an element in every life: moreover, it is the essence of the moral life. The effect of this view is to deprive it of its significance.

(3) PERSONAL

The point that I have just sought to make in general terms I venture to illustrate by personal reference. Speaking for myself, I cannot detect any impulse, still less any sense of obligation to strive to deserve immortality by the effort and endeavour to become a morally better person, if that immortality is not to be *mine*. For a condition in which I shall cease to think, to feel as an individual or, indeed, to *be* an individual, is a condition in which *I* shall cease to be at all. Now why should I hope or seek to realise such a condition, unless I take my individual personality to be of no account? But if it *is* of no account, why am I to take trouble with it? It is only the conviction that my individuality possesses not merely the value of occasional contingent, personal happiness, but a value which belongs to it of necessity because my individuality is of interest to God who created it, that makes it worth troubling about one way or the other. In other words, it is only because I believe myself to matter, not merely for and to myself but in the eyes of God, that I shall try to win His approval by becoming a better man. Now in this endeavour I am convinced that God can assist me and will indeed do so—since He approves of it—if I pray for His assistance and seek to deserve it. Christianity, moreover, tells me that He will not only assist me personally by the bestowal of grace, but that He has assisted mankind as a whole by sending His Son into the world to win for men by His suffering and

174

Pantheism and Immortality

death the chance of eternal life and to provide them with an example of right living, by following which they may come to deserve it.

Now these beliefs of mine, beliefs which have become, for me, the presuppositions of moral effort and aspiration, themselves presuppose (i) that God is a Person with a mind and will not wholly unlike my own and (ii) that I myself am an individual human being whose moral welfare is of interest to Him. If my individuality were temporary and contingent, I should be unable to account for my conviction of His interest and concern. For why should a God, Who is eternal, concern Himself with the moral welfare and destiny of a creature who is accidental and ephemeral to the point of sending His Son into the world to suffer and to die on that creature's behalf?

It may be objected that I have spoken so far only of myself and of my conviction; I hasten, therefore, to add that my questions have no special personal preference. Hence, it is not merely a question of asking why I should strive for the improvement of a creature who is to be superseded and merged, for an immortality, therefore, which is in no sense mine; the question is why I should so strive for the achievement of an immortality which is not, in fact, *anybody's.* What is the universal consciousness to me or to anybody else, that we should so sweat and struggle that we may be lost in it? Nor do these questions, any more than the conviction which underlies them, presuppose that I have any clear-cut conception of what individual immortality entails; for I do not, of course, know even in outline.

THE CONCEPT OF INDIVIDUAL IMMORTALITY

Three things, however, I would venture to affirm, and these not of my own discovering but as conveyed by the insight of those who are both wiser and more experienced than I, an insight which has found a response in my own consciousness.

(i) It seems to me, then, in the first place, that I must believe two things. (*a*) That immortality cannot be adequately regarded in the light of an infinite prolongation of an existence like the present with all that shames it omitted. It is not the continued existence for a very long time of my personality, as I now know it, but without pain and without sin, and with God hovering somewhere in the background, but considerably nearer and clearer than He is now. (*b*) That, nevertheless, the creature who experiences immortality must still in some sense be recognisably myself.

(ii) It seems to me, secondly, that immortality is not a primitive but a derivative concept; it derives from God. God is the central fact, God whom one aspires, or whom in one's best moments one aspires to know and to love. The central thought about life after death is that provided that certain conditions touching one's life here upon earth are satisfied, it will be a life of intercourse with God. Given intercourse with God, immortality seems to be entailed by the notion of it, for it is repugnant to our reason to suppose that such intercourse, once we have been deemed worthy to achieve it, can be interrupted or discontinued. Or can we suppose that once admitted to intercourse with God, we can deteriorate and become again unworthy of that intercourse? Hence the achievement of intercourse with God entails the notion of its indefinite continuance, entails, therefore, the notion of immortality.

(iii) It seems to me, thirdly, that this intercourse with God in which, as I conceive it, immortality consists, cannot be something totally disparate from any experience that we have on earth—if it were, how could we conceive it?—but will be a prolongation, intensification and assurance of the continuance of the highest and best experiences that we enjoy in our present earthly condition.

While these experiences are characteristically human, they are nevertheless experiences of that which is not human at all, of, in fact, Value.

Pantheism and Immortality

The Three Values

In regard to the nature of Value, the traditional view affirmed in the *Philosophia Perennis* seems to me to be correct. The Values, on this view, reduce themselves to three, Goodness, Truth and Beauty. As I have suggested elsewhere,[1] they are both objective in the sense that they are found by the human mind—found as given in things—and not projected into things or contributed to them by our own minds, and ultimate, in the sense that whatever we value can be shown to be valued because of the relation of the thing valued to some one or other of the three Values. Thus while other things are valued as means to one or other of these three, *they* are valued as ends in themselves.

Moreover, these Values are not just arbitrary, pieces of cosmic furniture lying about, as it were, in the universe without explanation, coherence or connection, but are revelations of a unity that underlies them, are, in fact, the ways in which God reveals Himself to man. Hence those human activities which consist in or which arise out of the pursuit of Truth, the cultivation of moral Goodness or the creation and enjoyment of Beauty, are such that we cannot help but value and revere them.

But at this point I would make a distinction which I find it difficult to express. It seems to me that there is an everyday natural experience of the Values which should be distinguished from occasional outstanding experiences which demand supernatural interpretation.

Examples of our everyday natural experience of Goodness, are of a man's honesty, that of a tradesman, for example, in his small daily dealings; of Truth, the appreciation of formal intellectual relations in, for example, algebraic equations or in the laws of logic; of Beauty, the seeing of a pretty face in the street or a patch of spring flowers in a wood. These things we must value since they are good of their kind, but they seem to

---

[1] See chapter v, pp. 145-9 and my book *Decadence* in which the position is argued at length.

me to carry no metaphysical significance. They are accidental and contingent, that is to say, they throw no light upon the fundamental nature of the universe and demand no explanation in terms of a metaphysical theory which reaches beyond themselves.

There are, however, other experiences with which from time to time our lives are graced in all three spheres. These I cannot attempt to describe for, indeed, they are ineffable. Nevertheless, all who have enjoyed any tincture, however faint, of these experiences will recognise them for what they are. They include the experience of a sunset or of a great view from a mountain top; they include, also, some great act of heroism or self-sacrifice and they are illustrated by a life which is devoted to the disinterested pursuit of Truth.

Of these experiences, four characteristics may be predicated. First, they are not merely contingent but convey a sense of their necessity; we realise, in fact, that they could not be other than they are, the universe being what it is.

Secondly, they are not arbitrary but are felt to be significant, significant of something beyond themselves. We feel that the reason *why* they could not be other than they are is that they reveal something of the nature of the universe. The universe being as it is, it is inevitable, we feel, that there should be occurrences in it and areas of it that exhibit these features and that we should experience them—or, rather, for most of us do not, after all, experience anything of the kind—that we should experience them *provided that our minds and spirits are rightly attuned.* Now these experiences, when we have them, are strangely moving.

NATURE OF AESTHETIC EXPERIENCE

Thirdly, they bring with them a sense of release, release from the needs and desires, the wants and cravings, the driving impulse of daily life.

Our normal day-to-day experience is that of a surge of impulses, a battlefield of desires over which we can only at

Pantheism and Immortality

length and after a lifetime of setback and of struggle, attain a degree of mastery through the achievement of a self-discipline which is itself the outcome of desire made rational. Wishing, fearing, craving, hoping and willing, we may never, except in the rare moments of aesthetic enjoyment or the secure possession of truth, be at rest. We must be for ever doing and stirring, meddling, changing and improving. But in the appreciation of pictures, of great music or of nature—I have put this in aesthetic terms, for it is in that direction that my own experience has chiefly lain—we get a momentary and fleeting glimpse of the nature of that, the full knowledge of which may be conceived as constituting at least in part our true end. For that moment, and for so long as the glimpse persists, we realise in anticipation and almost, as it were, illicitly, the nature of the end. We are, if I may so put it, for the moment *there*, just as a traveller may obtain a fleeting glimpse of a distant country from a height passed on the way, and cease for a space from his journey to enjoy the view. And since we are for the moment *there*, we experience, while the moment lasts, that sense of liberation from the drive of life which has been noted as one of the special characteristics of aesthetic experience. We who are part and parcel of the evolutionary stream stand for the time outside and above the stream, and are permitted for a moment to to be withdrawn from the thrust and play of impulse and desire. We feel neither need nor want and, losing ourselves in the contemplation of a reality which is other than ourselves, become for the moment selfless. When we experience those significant combinations of forms or sounds to which we give the name of beautiful in art, our contemplation is, in a word, *will-less* in its character.

But, fourthly, if in the aesthetic experience we are like travellers resting on our journey and refreshing ourselves with a view of the goal to which our steps are directed, we may not rest for long. That it should be at once unexpected and intermittent is characteristic of our pleasure in the beautiful in whatever form it is presented. Beauty often takes us, as it were,

Pantheism and Immortality

by surprise, whether it comes to us as a sudden view of a landscape, as a harmony of shape and line, or, it may be, as music
accidentally heard from an open window in the street. Nor is
the reason far to seek. Aesthetic appreciation is unconditioned
by considerations of space and time and, while it lasts, lifts us
out of the arena of moral struggle and conflict in which our daily
lives are passed. For this reason we are not allowed to indulge
it overmuch. And so, before we are even fully assured that the
vision of beauty is ours, we are caught up and thrust back into
the whirlpool of want and need, of striving, loving, and fearing
which is our day-to-day experience as individuals. This no
doubt is the reason for the fleeting and ephemeral nature of
even the most lasting aesthetic experience; to this it owes its
unsatisfactory and tantalising character. There is no sky in
June so blue that it does not point forward to a bluer; no
sunset so beautiful that it does not awaken the thought of a
greater beauty. The soul is at once gladdened and disappointed.
The veil is lifted so quickly that we have scarcely time to know
that it has gone before it has fallen again. But during the moment
of lifting we get a vision of a something behind and beyond which
passes, before it is clearly seen, and which in passing leaves behind
a feeling of indefinable longing and regret. Only the mystic
achieves a vision which is in any degree lasting, and to achieve
it he must surrender most of what men call the goods of life.

And strangely, the longing and regret are for what is somehow
familiar. There is an element of nostalgia in aesthetic experience
which finds expression in philosophies of pre-existence from
Plato's theory of Reminiscence onwards. The vision which is so
tantalisingly vouchsafed to us is of a place to which we have
already been and from which we should never have been parted.
So strong is this feeling that, not only while it persists but even
after it has passed, it brings to some the conviction that what
they have so briefly glimpsed is in some sense their real home,
to which they have come back after a long absence; and, as the
vision passes, they are filled with sadness at returning again to
the world of their exile.

180

Pantheism and Immortality

These characteristics of our highest experiences, characteristics which I have tried to convey in terms of aesthetic experience, though they are by no means confined to this, are, I believe, most plausibly to be explained on the assumption that in them we obtain a fleeting glimpse, a foretaste, as it were, of the nature of that reality which is God. In so far as I can conceive the notion of immortality at all, it is under the guise of a mode of existence in which what in these experiences is precarious is made secure, what is obscure is made clear and what is fleeting becomes eternal.

CHAPTER VII

Transcendence and Immanence

THE TWO ORDERS OF REALITY

Having considered and rejected a number of views as to the nature and interpretation of the cosmos, I shall try in this chapter and the next to state the one which seems to me to be open to the fewest objections. It is, briefly, what I take to be the traditional Christian view, namely, that the universe is to be conceived as two orders of reality, the natural order, consisting of people and things moving about in space and enduring in time, and a supernatural order neither in space nor in time, which consists of a Creative Person or Trinity of Persons from which the natural order derives its meaning and in terms of which it receives its explanation. This supernatural order is fully real in some sense in which the natural order is less than real; it is also perfect in a sense in which the natural order is morally imperfect. The eternal reality which is the supernatural order is related to the natural order. The nature of the relationship depends at least in part upon the living human souls which are denizens of the natural order. It is of great importance—at least to them—to ensure that the relation is a right one.

The supernatural order is not susceptible of investigation by the same methods as are effective in the natural sphere. Man's knowledge of it must either be vouchsafed by divine revelation or sought by submission to special discipline or achieved by obedience to a revealed law. The supernatural order may from time to time manifest itself in natural phenomena, but these manifestations are not predictable and controllable in the way that natural phenomena are. Divine

Transcendence and Immanence

revelation, that is, such information as is vouchsafed to us in regard to the supernatural order, is consistent with reason and may, indeed, find support from the use of reason, but the knowledge which it conveys cannot be attained by the operations of reason alone.

Thus, the believer in Christianity holds that he is possessed or can become possessed of a source of knowledge other than and distinct from that obtainable by scientific investigation. He maintains, therefore, that there are limits beyond which scientific knowledge can never hope to pass. Some of these limits were indicated in chapter v.[1] Thus, science and religion need not (and cannot, when rightly conceived) be antagonistic. Science can at best only support religious conviction; it cannot be its ground or source.

Of the various explanations of the universe that have been proffered, this, though far from exhaustive, and resting to a large extent on speculative hypotheses which those who hold it receive on 'faith', covers, in my view, a wider area of the facts given than any other.

Of the many difficulties of this explanation, that which touches the nature of the relation between the two orders has historically provoked the most damaging criticism. It is to a consideration of this question that this chapter and the next will be devoted. Briefly, the relation seems to me to be one both of transcendence and immanence. The supernatural order, that is to say, is both other than and independent of the natural order, and it is also present in the natural order; it expresses itself in it, and makes it to a considerable extent what it is.

SOME ILLUSTRATIONS

I will begin by trying to illustrate this undoubtedly difficult conception. Consider the movement of a sonata. It is a collection of musical sounds, notes and phrases which science analyses into vibrations in the atmosphere. Such analysis does not, however, give a complete account of it; for it is also a series of notes and

[1] See chapter v, pp. 135–151.

phrases arranged in a particular pattern. This pattern prescribes the order in which the notes are arranged and the intervals between them. The pattern is imposed by the mind of the composer. The sounds as arranged in the pattern are at once the expression and the embodiment of the musical idea which the composer conceives. Many would say that the sounds as arranged in the pattern constitute a unity or whole. In using such an expression they would, I think, wish to imply, first, that the whole is more than the arithmetical sum total of the different sounds; secondly, that the sounds, when heard in the context of the whole are, precisely because of their relation to the whole and to one another, different from what they would have been, if they were taken out of their context and heard in isolation. It is because of the immanence of the musical idea that the sounds are arranged as they are and sound as they do. If it were not immanent, the arrangement would not occur and the sounds would sound differently. Nevertheless, most people would agree, the immanent idea is not exhausted or used up by any one embodiment of it in a particular set of sounds. For a musical idea is more than any particular rendering of it, more, indeed, than any number of renderings of it. It would still exist in the composer's mind even if the music which embodied it were never written down. This could be put by saying that it transcends the renderings of it.

A nation, most people would say, especially if it has a long tradition behind it, is more than the sum total of the individuals who at any given moment may happen to be living and constituting the nation. The conception of the nation includes such subsidiary ideas as a continuing tradition, a way of life and belief, a scale of values, all of which, when taken together, constitute a mould or formula within which each successive generation of individuals grows and develops. The members of a nation have become what they are because of the influence of the mould upon them; it stamps them with its impress. The national ethos and culture, as we say, make them what they are. In this sense, the ethos and culture of the nation are immanent

184

Transcendence and Immanence

in the citizens. Because of this immanence, the members of a national community constitute a whole, and because of their relation to the whole and to one another they are different from what they would have been as isolated individuals. Nevertheless, the tradition, the way of life, the scale of values, are not *exhausted* by any particular generation that happens to exemplify and live in accordance with them. They persist, most people would say, from generation to generation. The nation, then, in this sense, transcends its members. Whether, as in the case of a musical idea, it would exist apart from the particular individuals who happen to embody it, is a controversial question. I should say that it would not. For this reason, though it illustrates the transcendence-immanence relation, it differs from the musical illustration just given.

Consider now a personality. It is interesting, first, to consider the account which the sciences might give of a personality. Of its different ingredients the sciences have, indeed, much to tell us. Each separate aspect of a human being is assigned to a special science, and of this aspect the relevant science purports to give a reasonably full account. We will suppose that these various accounts are drawn up and collated. We will imagine ourselves to begin with the physiological account in terms of tubes and pipes, nerves and bones and blood vessels. These, presumably, can be analysed into their chemical compounds, and there will be, therefore, a chemical account in terms of molecules and elements. These, again, can be analysed in terms of their atomic constituents and to the chemist's, therefore, we must add the physicist's account. There is also the psychologist's accounts of a man's consciousness in terms of mental events, images, sensations and so forth, with special departmental accounts such as the behaviourist's in terms of language habits and conditioned reflexes, and the psychoanalyst's in terms of unconscious desire and promptings of the libido. From other points of view there is the "economic man" and there is the "median man" of the statistician; there is man from the standpoint of the biologist and man as he appears to the anthropologist. Each of these accounts

Transcendence and Immanence

could in theory be made accurate and complete—complete, that is to say, so far as it goes; yet each would be couched in different terms. To say that no one of these accounts conveys the whole truth about a man, but describes only some particular aspect of him which has been selected for special attention, would be to state a commonplace.

But we can go further. Let us suppose that all the different accounts, the physiological, the chemical, the physical, the psychological, the behaviouristic, the psychoanalytic, the economic, the statistical, the biological, and the anthropological were collated, supplemented with other accurate but partial accounts and worked up into a comprehensive survey, they would still fail to constitute *the* truth about a man. And they would fail to do this, not because some particular piece of information had been left out, or some particular point of view forgotten—for no matter how complete the collection of scientific accounts might be, the truth would still elude them—but because they would remain only a set of separate accounts of different parts or aspects, and a man is more than the different parts of aspects which are ingredients of him. True knowledge of a man is not, in other words, the sum-total of the complete and accurate accounts of all his different aspects, even if these accounts could be made exhaustive. True knowledge is, or at least includes, knowledge of the man as a whole. To know a man as a whole is to know him as a personality, for a personality is the whole which, while it integrates all the parts and so includes them within itself, is, nevertheless, something over and above their sum. Now to know a man as a personality is to know him in a manner of which science takes no cognisance. It is to know him as a friend.

The whole personality is, then, more than the sum of the parts upon whose combination, according to the account given by the sciences, it supervenes. But suppose that to think of the personality as resulting from the concurrence of a number of parts was misleading from the first. Suppose that the personality is logically prior and that the parts derive from it, in the sense that

Transcendence and Immanence

it is in the parts that it expresses itself and finds its embodiment. And first, in the bodily part: a man's mouth, we would say, tells the discerning observer much about the man; if he is happy, good-tempered, cheerful, the corners of his mouth tend to turn up; if gloomy, irritable, depressed, down. A man's nature, again, is thought to be expressed in his smile. It is charming, friendly, sweet or hypocritical. Or, a man's nature is expressed in and is deducible from a grooved forehead and lines about the eyes; the eyes, we say, are the windows of the soul. There are refinements in these matters. Thus Shaw talks of the wide spreading nostrils of the dramatic orator and the long upper lip of the professional comedian. Even a man's gait, confident and jaunty, or drooping and dragging, tells us something about his nature.

It is expressed, secondly, in his psychological life. His moods, tempers, hopes and fears, are all, psychology teaches, expressions of a certain type of nature. They do not constitute the nature, they are the ways in which it shows itself. All these are ways of expressing the truth that the personality is immanent in the 'parts', immanent in the bodily behaviour, immanent in the psychological moods. The 'parts', as in the case of the other illustrations, are what they are because of their relation to one another and to the immanent whole which expresses itself in them. In the case of this illustration, it is hard to think of the 'parts' as existing separately from the informing personality; in so far as they can be conceived of as doing so, they would, it is obvious, be different in isolation from what they are in the context of the personality.

Christianity regards the whole which I have been calling the personality as an immortal soul which will survive the break-up of the body, even if it did not precede its formation. If this is true, there is a sense in which the personality is more than its expressions both in the body and in the psyche, so that besides being immanent, it is also transcendent.

I have tried by means of these three examples to illustrate— I have not, it is obvious, explained—the transcendence-immanence relation.

187

Transcendence and Immanence

In my view, the relation of the two orders of reality referred to above is a relation of this kind. I propose to develop this view as it bears upon certain well-known philosophical issues, namely, the relation of body and mind, the relation of universal and particular, the relation of value and fact, and the relation of God and the world. First, however, I propose to give one or two examples of what seems to me to be the inadequate, the palpably inadequate, treatment of these issues by science. Interpretations in terms of the transcendence-immanence relation will be suggested in the next chapter.

TREATMENT OF MIND BY SCIENTISTS. ITS INADEQUACY

I will begin with the vexed question of mind and of its relation to the brain. It seems to me that no science has as yet succeeded in giving an even plausible account of mind or of its relation to the body and brain. I referred in the second chapter to the inadequacy of Mr. Hoyle's account, an account which, it will be remembered, postulated that the mind must possess 'detectable physical connections'. Mr. Hoyle also declared his inability to think of immortality save as an experience on the part of a mind that animated some sort of body. I propose to dwell for a moment on this account, as it illustrates very well the attitude, whether explicit or implicit only, which so many scientists adopt towards the mind.

Mr. Hoyle pictures man as finding himself pitchforked, without so much as a 'by your leave' into 'this wholly fantastic Universe with scarcely a clue as to whether our existence has any real significance'. Now it is, I should have thought, obvious in the first place, that our existence *can* have no significance if mind is not an independent principle, but is derivative from matter being attached to matter by 'detectable physical connections'. Yet if the mind has no 'physical connections', I do not see how a scientist, *in so far as he follows the classical methods of science*, can hope to give an account of it. I shall return to this point in a moment.

Mr. Hoyle goes on to express surprise that the Hebrews should be credited with an understanding of human beings.

Transcendence and Immanence

It would, indeed, be surprising if the only kind of human experience is that which entails the existence of our bodies and sense organs, is, in fact, sensory experience, and if the only kind of knowledge is the knowledge that science derives from sensory experience. Yet these precisely are the assumptions which underlie the concepts of mind and immortality quoted in an earlier chapter,[1] according to which not only must a mind have 'physical connections', but 'survival after death would be meaningless and unthinkable without some interaction with the physical world', and immortality, since it goes on for a very long time, must be very boring. In general it may be said that there is no hint of a suggestion in Mr. Hoyle's writings that there may be such a thing as spiritual experience which is of a different order from bodily experience, that the mind may be genuinely different from the body and may on occasion enjoy experiences which are independent of its relation to the body and which own a source other than that of the body, that there can be a mode of existence which is timeless, and that there can be truths which are not stateable in terms of the concepts and not demonstrable by the methods employed by science. In other words, Mr. Hoyle's treatment of the cosmos in general and of mind in particular is vitiated by reason of his failure to contemplate the possibility that science and the information that it provides may not be exhaustive, that there may be other methods of approach to the cosmos and that religion may be one of them.

It is precisely this kind of inadequacy which makes itself felt in connection with so many scientists' accounts of mind. The inadequacy springs in each case from this same failure on the part of scientists to emancipate themselves in fact from the domination of the materialist concepts of which, as scientists, they habitually make use, however strongly they may repudiate them in theory. As a consequence they think of mind after a material model, and more particularly do they think of it as an entity or activity which occupies space. This parochial concept of mind is, in its turn, due to a parochial identification of reality

---

[1] See chapter ii, pp. 42–4.

189

Transcendence and Immanence

with that which can be seen and touched or which is at least of the same nature as that which can be seen and touched. This limited concept of mind, this parochial treatment of the real, is so pervasive both in the thought of scientists and in the attitude of common sense which is derived from science, that I propose to illustrate it by a further example from an eminent, contemporary scientist, Professor Julian Huxley.

THE TREATMENT OF DEVELOPMENT AND PURPOSE BY JULIAN HUXLEY. ITS INADEQUACY

Starting from purely materialist preconceptions, Huxley, more reasonable but less consistent than Hoyle, does his best to make provision for the existence and activity of a mind which has cut loose from its moorings in matter, and to smuggle into his universe an element of value after which this mind aspires. In a recently published survey of biological thought,[1] in the course of which contemporary conclusions in regard to evolution are summarised for the benefit of the biological layman, Huxley makes the following points:

(*a*) There is every reason to believe that 'living matter developed automatically out of non-living matter', hence

(*b*) No 'vital force' or 'other special form of energy' is required to account for the phenomenon of life or to constitute it.

The world, then, consists of matter in space and of nothing but matter since life, which is identified with 'living matter', is not different *in its essential nature* from the matter from which it originated. For the effect must be of the same nature as the cause unless, of course, we are prepared to endow matter with the capacity for creation; but I doubt whether Huxley, who finds it difficult to accept the notion of a creative *mind*, would entertain the notion of creative *matter*, that is, of matter endowed with the capacity to bring forth from itself by the laws appropriate to itself something which is not only other than itself but totally different in its nature from itself. In spite of its

[1] Published in the *News Chronicle* in October 1950.

Transcendence and Immanence

origin and nature, life, that is to say 'living matter', as expressed in human minds—if, as to which I am doubtful, 'expressed' be the correct word to describe the relationship—can become (i) 'conscious and aware of itself' and (ii) conscious and aware of value. 'New factors,' says Huxley, 'such as conscious values begin to count in evolution.' (I take it that this loose phrase does not mean, as I think it ought to do, that the values are themselves conscious—I doubt, that is to say, whether Huxley means that Truth, for example, the truth that $a^2 - b^2 = (a+b)(a-b)$ achieves consciousness, or that Beauty, for example, the beauty of the second movement of Bach's Double Violin Concerto is conscious. I take him to mean merely that minds become aware of and respond to the truth of the conclusion and the beauty of the music.) (iii) Mind can further transmit its own characteristics otherwise apparently than through 'the physical mechanism of heredity'. Huxley seems to mean by this that mind can *directly* transmit what he calls the 'accumulation and variation of experience and tradition', so that the individual's initial inheritance is no longer restricted to the chemical factors, the genes, which constitute 'the physical mechanism of heredity'. Mind, moreover, can in certain respects win free from matter and consciously direct the evolutionary process, as the result of which 'change can now be hundreds of times more rapid'. Change, indeed, can now be more than change; it can be 'a broad tendency towards improvement'.

As regards point (i), I would ask, is the notion of conscious matter really thinkable? I have tried hard to envisage it but without success. Is this, perhaps, evidence of my imaginative poverty or is it, as I believe, that the conception of bits of matter, that is to say, charges of positive and negative electricity being conscious of themselves and of other things and striving after improvement, is strictly unthinkable, *unless, of course, they are directed or animated by a mind*, in which event it is the *mind* that is conscious, and not the bits of matter?

As regards (ii), how can 'living matter' be aware of value unless value exists independently for it to be aware of, or unless living

191

matter itself produces the values of which it is aware? In the former event, the universe does not consist exclusively of matter and of 'living matter', but contains 'values', whatever these may be, which are presumably not analysable into the movements of charges of positive and negative electricity. (If they were so analysable they would be only matter in another guise and not values at all.) In the latter event, matter produces out of its own bosom, as it were, not only mind but Truth, Beauty and Goodness, assuming for a moment that these are examples of what Huxley means by values. But if this is so, the difficulties raised in (i) occur in a new form. Can protons and electrons really be, or, alternatively, can they *produce* Truth? Or can their movements in space be or produce Truth? The notion that they are or can seems to me to involve a hopeless confusion of categories like the notion of 'purple quadratic equations' or of a 'square cricket eleven'.

On point (iii), I have two comments. (*a*) The notion of 'improvement' clearly entails not only change but change in a certain direction, in the direction, presumably, of more of that which is good. But the notions of 'good' and of 'increasing good' involve standards of measurement by reference to which worth and the degree of its increase can be assessed. These standards themselves imply values, the value in the case in question known as Goodness or Good. But a standard of measurement must be other than the process, or thing which it is invoked to measure, as the statement 'Tom is eight inches taller than Dick' entails the notion of height which is other than both Tom and Dick. Hence the standard of measurement which Huxley's concept of 'improvement' entails cannot perform the function which is required of it, if it is *not* other than, but is merely developed by or is an emanation *from* the process which it is invoked to measure. (In the analogy, Tom and Dick cannot develop out of themselves the standard of measurement by which their respective heights are assessed.)

(*b*) Mind cannot consciously direct the 'evolutionary process' or directly transmit its own characteristics, unless it achieves a degree of emancipation from determination by matter, unless, in fact, it is free.

Now nothing, so far as I am aware, has been advanced by either physicists or biologists to suggest that the movements of matter (with the possible exception of the movements of microscopic particles)[1] do *not* obey the laws of physics and chemistry and are not, therefore, determined. Hence of two things, one; either the movements of 'living matter' are also so determined, in which event it is difficult to see how matter can achieve consciousness of itself or direct the process of evolutionary change towards 'conscious values'; or 'living matter', in respect at least of some of the things it does, does *not* obey the laws of physics and chemistry, and either obeys some other laws or is free from *complete* determination by any laws. If the former, what are these 'other laws'? If the latter, then Huxley is endowing 'living matter' with most of the characteristics which Christians would wish to claim for life, for mind and for spirit.

SUMMARY

.As I do not profess to understand Huxley's treatment of what he calls 'life' I cannot hope to make it plain to readers. I cite it because it illustrates and embodies the fundamental confusion arising from the attempt to intrude the concepts and methods of science into spheres in which they are inapplicable. Like Hoyle's treatment of mind, Huxley's treatment of life illustrates the limitations of the scientific method when applied to what are essentially philosophical problems. Like Hoyle, Huxley assumes that matter is both fundamental and universal. In theory he admits life in the form of 'living matter', but 'living matter' is either matter in disguise, or else it is life which has emancipated itself from and achieved independence of its material origin. But such independence can, on the materialist premises from which Huxley starts, only be achieved at the price of gross inconsistency. The problems involved are not so much solved as ignored.

[1] Heisenberg's *Principle of Indeterminacy* affords perhaps a possible example.

Transcendence and Immanence

I draw three conclusions, first, that life, mind, spirit and value cannot be adequately conceived in material terms as off-shoots of or emanations from matter; secondly, that they are non-spatial; thirdly, that on both counts, science is disabled from giving an adequate account of them.

Starting from these conclusions as premises, I propose to try to give some account of the relations between the two orders or levels of reality to which, in my view, spirit and mind on the one hand and matter on the other respectively belong.

The Mystery

Yet such a statement of intention is, I am afraid, disingenuous, since, for me, it is of the essence of the matter that no intelligible account of this relationship can be given. God, we are told in the Book of Genesis, 'Formed man of the dust of the ground, and breathed into his nostrils the breath of life; and man became a living soul.' If this is, as I believe, a symbolic description of what is indeed the case, then, I would suggest, we cannot expect to understand the nature of a relationship whereby the breath or spirit of God is materialised or embodied or incorporated in something that is not, or is not at any rate directly, God. And we cannot for two reasons, first, because God's mode of working is only too likely to be beyond our understanding; secondly, because since one of the terms in the X—Y relationship, namely, X which, if I am right, both transcends and is immanent in Y, belongs by hypothesis to a different and supernatural order of reality, its relation to Y, which belongs to the familiar, natural order, must also partake of, or at least be infected by, the supernatural. If the relation were *wholly* natural, then both the related terms would require to be natural, but a natural relation between two terms both of which are natural is not the kind of relation that I have in mind when I say that the relation of God to the world, of spirit to matter, and of mind to brain, is the transcendence-immanence relation which I began by trying to describe. The task that I propose demands a chapter to itself.

194

CHAPTER VIII

The Relation between the Natural and the Supernatural

I. THE BODY-MIND RELATION

I will begin with the relation between mind and brain. This, as I said in the last chapter, I believe to be indescribable because it is, by us, incomprehensible. The mind is, it is clear, constantly interacting with the body and brain, yet all attempts to envisage the mode of this interaction have been lamentable failures. It is because of this failure that Cartesian Dualism is an almost universally condemned concept—it is enough to assert of a theory that it savours of Cartesian Dualism to condemn it out of hand—and scientists have been driven to adopt the desperate expedient of suggesting that mind is only an offshoot of or development from the body and brain, and is not, therefore, fundamentally different in its nature from the brain which produced it. Again, because of this failure, Professor Ryle has been led in a recent, justly celebrated book to disavow the whole concept of mind as a 'ghost in the machine', without succeeding in indicating, at any rate to one reader, what he would put in its place. In a word, everybody is dissatisfied with Cartesian Dualism.

Yet the ground for dissatisfaction lies, surely, in the presumption that the relation between mind and brain is, or at any rate should be, intelligible by us, and that it should, therefore, be possible to give an intelligible account of it. But suppose that it is not intelligible. Suppose that, like all the manifestations of the

Relation between Natural and Supernatural

supernatural in the natural order, it is a mystery. Suppose that we not only do not, but cannot understand how an immaterial activity can inform a material medium in which it is manifested. By committing this initial act of agnosticism we reap certain very great advantages.

RELEVANCE OF PARA-NORMAL PHENOMENA

We are, for example, no longer completely at a loss to find an explanation for para-normal phenomena such as, for example, telepathy and telekinesis. On the contrary, extra-sensory perception which, in all the forms of its manifestation, is so baffling to orthodox science and psychology, ceases on this hypothesis to be unintelligible or, rather, it becomes no more unintelligible than normal perception. Let us suppose that the cumulative evidence for the occurrence of para-normal phenomena is now so strong as to compel their acceptance by unprejudiced minds. Let us further grant that no explanation of their occurrence has been put forward which is even remotely plausible. These phenomena, then, constitute something of a scandal in the scheme of the cosmos drawn up by science, a scheme into which they so resolutely refuse to be made 'at home'. Hence science either ignores them or seeks to explain them away. But the scandal is scandalous only if we assume that normal sensory perception is something that we can understand and of which we can give an account. Suppose that normal sensory experience involves, as it certainly appears to involve, some kind of interaction between brain and mind. Then, if I am right, the occurrence of normal sensory experience is also incomprehensible and inexplicable and it is only familiarity that leads us to take it, as it were, for granted. On these assumptions, the facts that we cannot explain how a mind can know what is happening in another mind (telepathy) or be aware of what is going to happen before it does happen (precognition) or be conscious of occurrences not present to the sense organs of the body which the mind animates (clairvoyance)—these and similar facts lose their special quality of outrage. I do not mean

196

Relation between Natural and Supernatural

by this that these happenings are not mysterious and unaccountable. They are both. But they are not mysterious and unaccountable otherwise than as normal experience of the external world, or as normal 'experiences' of other people's minds by inference based on the observation of bodily behaviour are mysterious and unaccountable. On the contrary, they can now be fitted into a frame which is, as it were, already prepared to receive them.

And there is another point. If we accept the tacit presupposition of the sciences that the mind is in some sense a thing in space and is, that is to say, in its real nature material, then it is by no means impossible to understand how it could interact with a particular brain, that brain, namely, with which it is spatially connected. But how, on this basis, explain its apparent interaction with another?

Now one of the most striking features of para-normal psychological phenomena is the power apparently possessed by mind to act upon matter *other than* that of the brain belonging to the body which the mind would normally be said to animate. This apparently extra-cerebral activity of mind is expressed broadly in four ways. (i) (*Telepathy*) A mind may directly influence and be influenced by another mind in circumstances in which the normally accepted explanation of our knowledge of other minds, that is, by inference from the observation of the bodies which these other minds animate, is ruled out by reason of the fact that the movements of the bodies in question are not perceptible to our senses. (ii) (*Clairvoyance*) A mind can on occasion be aware of what is happening at places whose spatial location is such that the mind could have no knowledge of them through the normal channel of stimulation of the sense organs. (iii) (*Telekinesis*) A mind can apparently directly influence the movement of pieces of matter otherwise than through the agency of the body which the mind animates. Hence the phenomena to which Dr. Rhine has given the names of 'telekinesis' or 'psycho-kinesis', defined by Professor H. H. Price as 'the influence of thought upon matter independently of the muscular mechanism of the body'. (iv) (*Post- and Pre-Cognition*) A mind can be directly aware of events which occur at some point in time other than that at which the awareness by the mind would itself normally be said to occur, either in the case of what appears to be direct knowledge of the past, or in the case of apparent knowledge of what is about to happen in another mind before it does, in fact, happen (pre-cognitive telepathy).

Now all these apparent capacities of mind are difficult, if not impossible, to explain on the assumption that a mind is a thing in space and in time, and is tied by a necessary and unique bond—Mr. Hoyle's 'detectable physical connections'—to a particular brain.

But suppose that it is not in space, then the fact of apparently direct communication with other minds (telepathy (i)), though it still presents difficulties, does not present the particular kind of difficulty which I find overwhelming on the common assumption that it is in some sense spatially connected with one particular brain, which brain it alone among minds causally affects, and by which it alone among minds is causally affected. For there is no *necessary* reason why a mind which cannot be correctly described as being any*where* should causally affect and be affected by a brain located in one particular region of space rather than by a brain occupying another region. Hence, if a mind is not in space, it could make contact with another mind either by causally affecting and being affected by the body and brain which that other mind would normally be said to animate or, directly, without the intermediation of any brain.

So with clairvoyance, (ii). If a mind owns a unique and necessary relation to one, and only one, material thing which is a particular brain—as it would do if, for example, it were an emanation from, or a function of, or an extension of that brain —it is hard to see how it could be directly aware of scenes and events other than those scenes and events which are causally connected with events in that brain via the normal channel of stimulation of sense organs and transmission to the brain of neural disturbances in consequence of the stimulus. It is still harder to see how it could affect and even interfere with the movements of pieces of matter *otherwise than through the brain and muscular action of the body* which it would be commonly said to animate. But if it is loose from the brain, loose in the double sense of not being dependent upon the brain for its existence and of not being confined in respect of its activity to the area of space which the brain occupies, then its apparent ability to affect and be affected by occurrences in matter situated at a distance from the brain and body which it would be normally said to animate is no longer incomprehensible—at any rate it is no more incomprehensible than its power of affecting and being affected by that brain and body.

Hence telekinesis (iii), the mind's apparent power of direct interference with the movements of matter—in the case of Dr. Rhine's experiments, the movements of dice ejected by a mechanism down an inclined plane were apparently affected by acts of willing on the part of observers—is neither more nor less mysterious than the mind's apparent power of interfering with the movements of the brain and the body in the case of any *prima facie* freely willed action as, for example, when I will to raise my arm in the air.

I hesitate to embark upon a discussion of the questions raised by the apparent facts of pre-cognition and direct knowledge of the past, (iv), owing to the difficulties of the problem. I venture, however, to make two points. First, the notion of a piece of matter, or of a mind which is epiphenomenal upon matter, being aware of an occurrence at some time in the future, an occurrence, therefore, which is not yet, seems to me untenable; for I do not see how matter can be affected by non-existent events. Yet minds do seem to be in some sense aware of the future, as, for example, in the perfectly normal and accepted cases of foresight and expectation.

It is, of course, the case that the apparently direct cognition by a mind of events in another mind which have not yet occurred (pre-cognitive telepathy) certainly *seems* to involve a knowledge of the future at once more direct and immediate than is involved in foresight and expectation. I confine myself to making the very limited point that pre-cognitive telepathy which would, I think, have to be ruled out *a priori* on the assumption of a material or purely epiphenomenal mind, is not necessarily inconceivable in the case of a mind which is not in space and which may in respect of a certain part of itself be not in time.

For, secondly, there is, as I shall urge in a moment,[1] an element or factor in the mind—or, as I should in this connection prefer to call it, the soul—which is timeless. Granted that this soul is immortal, as Christianity teaches, receiving immortality at its creation as a gift of God, the existence of this timeless element or factor is, I think, necessitated. Moreover, the phenomena of mystical experience certainly seem *prima facie*, to demand some timeless element in our total psychological make-up, since all the reports of this type of experience agree upon the attribute of timelessness by which it is characterised. Now, I do not wish to suggest that it is easy to see how a timeless mind (or soul) can be aware of events which have not yet occurred; I content myself with pointing out that such a possibility is no harder to envisage than its awareness of and apparent participation in events which are occurring in what is called the present.

In short, as with space, so with time. How a spaceless mind can interact with a spatial brain we do not know; I am content to point out that this is neither harder nor easier to envisage than that it should interact with some other spatial brain or with a piece of non-cerebral matter. Similarly, how a partially timeless mind can have a cognitive relation with events occurring in present time we do not know; I am content to point out that it is neither harder nor easier to envisage than that it should have a direct cognitive relation with some other region of time as, for example, future time.

[1] See the suggestion on pp. 201–3.

Relation between Natural and Supernatural

MAN AS THREEFOLD

I venture to develop in an admittedly purely speculative direction the hypothesis that there is included in the make-up of the human personality a timeless element. My excuse is that, where so much is in any event speculative, the fact that we should be in a position to urge on behalf of a particular speculative hypothesis that, if it were true, it would cover a number of facts which seem to be inexplicable on any other, is not to be lightly dismissed. The hypothesis in question is as follows.

The traditional division of the human being is not twofold into mind and body, but threefold into mind, body and soul or spirit. I suggest that this traditional division may approximate more closely to the truth than any other.

THE SOUL

The spirit is the seat of personality, is, in fact, the essential self and is timeless. It's true home is not in this but in another order of reality. In fulfilment of a purpose it is incarnated in a body or, perhaps, in a number of successive bodies, and so intruded in the time order for a definable period or periods of time. The spirit so conceived is analogous to what the Hindus call the Atman, with the exception that, as Christianity has always insisted against Hinduism, it is inalienably individual. Its individuality, that is to say, is not merged after death in a sea of universal consciousness, but sustains immortality without losing its individuality. The soul is normally inaccessible to us but I conceive that in certain psychological conditions the soul rises, as it were, into consciousness or, more precisely, our normal everyday consciousness penetrates on occasion through to the soul. I should suppose, though I speak without experience, that it is the soul which is the recipient of mystical experience; also, I imagine, of certain kinds of aesthetic experience. One does not, for example, have to be a mystic to respond to Charles Kingsley's rhetorical question, 'Have you not felt that your real soul was imperceptible to your immediate vision except in a

Relation between Natural and Supernatural

few hallowed moments?' Kingsley has just been describing the nearest thing to mystical experience of which most of us are capable or with which most of us, at any rate, are acquainted, namely, certain moments of transport or tranquillity that we enjoy in our intercourse with nature. His account so closely corresponds to my own experience that I venture to quote it: 'When I walk in the fields, I am oppressed now and then with an innate feeling that everything I see has a meaning, if I could but understand it. And this feeling of being surrounded with truths that I cannot grasp amounts to indescribable awe sometimes.'

The concept of the soul, as I am seeking to describe it, obviously answers in certain respects to some psychologists' descriptions of the unconscious. In certain respects, but not in all.

The soul, as here conceived, has not, for example any affinity with the sexually pervaded unconscious whose denizens, the 'libido', the 'id' and so on dominate the thinking of the Freudian psycho-analysts. There are, however, two respects in which what psychology, and notably Jungian psychology, has to tell us about the soul, tallies with what I am attempting here to convey. First, the soul is the source of genius and the medium of inspiration. I have often been struck by the fact which has never, so far as I know, received adequate comment, that the spheres in which the infant prodigy appears are three and three only, namely music, chess and mathematics. It is significant that none of these spheres derives its material from life. What I would suggest is that children of outstanding capacity in these spheres bring something with them into this world, that this something has its origin and abiding place in what I am calling the soul and that, as experience of life at the ordinary level of consciousness accumulates, the soul and its precious inheritance is increasingly overlaid so that the gifts of the prodigy fade as adolescence approaches.

Secondly, it may be that the sub-conscious essence or foundation of our personality which I am identifying with the soul, is in touch with a something 'more'. If there are higher spiritual agencies at work in the world, agencies which touch and quicken us, enriching us with what we call our gifts in inspiration and responding to our solicitations in prayer, their point of contact and communication with us, the point at which, as it were, they touch us, is the soul. My view that this region is normally inaccessible to consciousness is consistent with the well known fact that we are often unaware of the sources of our inspiration and ignorant how the healing and strengthening influences that bear upon us when, as we say, our prayers are answered, do their work. I am suggesting that the soul, which is a normally inaccessible region of our personality, is not only the medium, but the necessary medium through which this work is done. God, to use the language of religion, influences man through his soul. The soul, then, is the vehicle of God's immanence. It is that in respect of which we are, if not divine, at least in contact with the divine. Thus, it is only when the hubbub of ordinary life and consciousness dies down that, as the Bible has it, the still small voice of God can make itself heard, heard that is to say, by the soul of which at the moment of being influenced, but only *at that* moment, we are conscious. The phenomena of spiritual healing and spiritual regeneration are also most plausibly to be explained on the assumption that God, in response to prayer, acts upon us through the soul to heal the body and strengthen the mind.

THE MIND

Mind is brought into being in consequence of the contact of the soul with the natural, temporal order, which results from its incorporation in a physical body. It is brought initially into being in the form of ideas. More precisely, ideas emerge on the combination of soul with body much as water emerges on the combination of oxygen and hydrogen, and it is the cluster of these emerging ideas which constitute a mind.

Since a mind comes into existence as a by-product of the soul's incarnation in matter, its existence is temporary only. Moreover, it is not in the mind that the unity of the person resides, so that the arguments advanced by Hume and later by

Relation between Natural and Supernatural

William James against the conception of the substantial or unified self, arguments which at the level of psychology it is extremely difficult to rebut, are beside the point, seeing that the unity of the self resides elsewhere, resides, in fact, in a region which is normally inaccessible to consciousness.

To put the point in another way, soul or spirit, when brought into contact with matter by incarnation in a body, expresses itself initially in a succession of ideas. A mind is simply the bundle of the ideas which constitute it at any given moment. Hence ideas are primitive and mind derivative.

Some of the advantages of the 'bundle' theory of the mind are: (a) It allows for the fact that the unity of a mind may be and, indeed, obviously is a matter of degree. Some minds are much more integrated, are, that is to say, much more closely knit bundles of ideas than others. This fact is extremely difficult to explain on the assumption that the mind is by nature a unity. (b) It allows for and, indeed, fits very well the cases of dissociated and multiple personality. For the ideas in which a soul which is incarnate in matter expresses itself may cluster not in one system, but in two. These two systems or clusters may take control of the body at different times. But while covering the undoubted fact of multiple personality, which is no more than an extreme case of those temporary clusterings of psychic elements which make up the stream of moods, desires, aspirations, modes of feeling and behaving, whose kaleidoscopic succession constitutes our everyday consciousness, the hypothesis nevertheless makes provision for the continuance of the real unity of the person, a unity which, on this view, is eternal, by locating it, not in the mind but in the soul.

(c) It allows for the fact that ideas may (i) sometimes wander, as it were, from the bundle to which they normally belong and temporarily form part of another bundle (telepathy), and (ii) directly influence a piece of matter other than the brain which is their normal medium of contact with the physical world. This hypothesis brings telepathy and telekinesis under the aegis of a single principle of explanation.

Relation between Natural and Supernatural

(*d*) Possibility of Survival. It allows for the facts that ideas may (i) get loose from the 'mind' which they normally constitute; (ii) survive for a time the break-up of that mind and of the body which it animates; (iii) form part of the idea bundle which would normally be regarded as another mind; and (iv) form a temporary 'mindlet' on their own which can animate some other body, for example that of a medium in a trance, and which may persist for just so long as the trance continues. The suggestion may be further ventured that it is this 'mind' or 'mindlet' which is responsible for originating the so-called spirit communications which it is equally difficult to dismiss, or, on any normal theory of the mind, to account for—on any normal theory of the mind or, I would add, on any acceptable theory of survival. That I should survive as an immortal soul in the sense which religion affirms is a glorious, that I should be totally extinguished at the break-up of my body, a tolerable destiny. But that I should survive as a kind of Homeric ghost, a wraith, not more but less than a man, whose melancholy and wistful existence is devoted to establishing contact with the things and people that I have known upon the earth, the vehicle of my communications, the séance room through whose dimly lit purlieus the quack so assiduously and so successfully hunts the dupe, their content, the twaddling ethico-religious uplift of 'messages' whose maudlin sentimentality, no less than their intellectual imbecility, suggests the regrettable conclusion that, even if ghosts have or are souls, they have no brains—*that* seems to me a prospect of such horror as only a malicious demon, imbued by an incorrigible hatred of humanity, could have devised.

Indeed, the survival of the self, if considered apart from religion, is something that will not bear thinking about, for what, apart from the hopes derived from religion, could it mean but the indefinite and perhaps eternal continuation of a person as bored and boring as I know myself to be, with all my faults and imperfections heavy upon me? That is the kind of survival whose burden Adam has immortalised in the famous speech of the first play of Shaw's *Back to Methuselah* Pentateuch:—'If only

Relation between Natural and Supernatural

I can be relieved of the horror of having to endure myself for ever! . . . If only the rest and sleep that enable me to bear it from day to day could grow after many days into an eternal rest, an eternal sleep, then I could face my days, however long they may last. Only, there must be some end. . . . I am not strong enough to bear eternity'—the kind of survival whose prospect Mr. Hoyle rightly deplores.[1]

(e) *Spirit Communications.* Yet if we reject the religious approach which fits survival into its place within the framework of a system ready fitted to receive it, it is difficult to see what other kind of survival can be looked for. Granted, however, that what survives is not a mind after the model on which a mind is normally conceived, but is a particular bundle of ideas and of what psychologists call 'traces', which achieves the status of a 'mind' in association with the body of the medium which it temporarily animates, then the low intellectual content of 'spirit communications', becomes intelligible. Intelligible, too, is what may be called their dual reference.

Messages frequently convey information, which, so far as can be conjectured, could not possibly have been within the medium's own knowledge. The messages seem, moreover, at times to emanate from a particular source which, both in regard to the nature of its communications and the information which it appears to possess, certainly *suggests* the mind of a person known to have died. On the other hand, the messages are rarely detailed or definite; in fact they are so little detailed and so little definite that it is always possible to doubt their origin and the personality of their sender. 'If,' the sitter cannot help thinking, 'it is really my friend who has passed over who is communicating, why does he not speak more exactly and in detail of his condition and experiences, refer to those private matters that were known only to me and to him, and send words of comfort and consolation which are not vague generalities but have a special message for *me*? Moreover, many of the messages seem to bear upon them traces of the medium's

---

[1] See chapter ii, p. 42.

Relation between Natural and Supernatural

personality, and to convey the sort of knowledge and to indicate the kind of outlook which, granted her training, education and social class, the medium might be expected to possess.

This double characteristic of appearing loosely to relate, yet relating neither clearly nor satisfactorily, to the dead person, and of appearing to relate to, without in fact expressing, the personality of the medium, would be plausible on the assumption that the entity responsible for sending the messages is neither the surviving mind of the person who would normally be called dead, nor that of the medium, but is a mind or 'mindlet' consisting of a loose 'bundle' of ideas which were formerly regarded as the mind of the dead person in temporary association with the body of the medium which the 'mindlet' animates.

(f) Ghosts. Fanciful though it is, I cannot resist the attractiveness of an attempted explanation of the phenomena known as 'ghosts' which springs from the same hypothesis. This is the hypothesis that the true self is a spirit which lies behind and beyond—I do not see how to avoid these spatial metaphors—both the body with which it is associated and the bundle of ideas in which, as a result of that association, it expresses itself, which bundle achieves a temporary, though far from perfect, unity in what we know as a mind. This bundle of ideas, this 'mind', I am suggesting, is not dependent for its being upon association with the brain which it would normally be said to animate, but may cut loose, as it were, and temporarily associate itself with other brains, thus forming a kind of temporary mind or 'mindlet' which is responsible for 'spirit communications.' But why only with other brains? Why not on occasion with non-cerebral matter? That this is the most plausible explanation of telekinesis I have already suggested.[1] In telekinesis it is with the matter of dice rolling down an inclined plane that in the experiments reported 'foot-loose' ideas are combined.

But what of the stuff of which ghosts are made? It is customary, even among those who in general maintain open minds in regard to abnormal or para-normal phenomena, to write off

[1] See pp. 198, 199.

ghosts as purely subjective. The man who 'sees' a ghost does not, they believe, really *see* anything at all. He only *thinks* that he sees one, whereupon they proceed to give an elaborate account of the ways in which the hallucination may be generated, an account which is even extended to cover the case of multiple hallucination as when a number of people see the same ghost.[1] But unless they are on general grounds prepared to adopt an idealist theory of perception, I am unable to see why those whose attitude is in general hospitable to the reception of abnormal, psychical phenomena should 'draw the line', as it were, at ghosts, denying to them, and to them alone in the whole range of psychical phenomena, objective existence. If we were to accept at its face value only a tiny percentage of the formidable mass of records that have come down to us, records of all ages and from among all peoples, we could not avoid the conclusion that certain persons at certain times have really 'seen' something; and by using the word 'seen' I mean to imply that the retinas of their eyes and their optical nerves were stimulated by events which were independent of the seer, which stimulation was conveyed by neural channels to the seer's brain and was thereupon followed by the sensation of seeing—in a word, that what they saw was an objective occurrence and not a subjective projection. What strongly predisposes me in favour of accepting this, the common-sense—as it might be called—view of the ghost, is the testimony in regard to animals. Animals cower and howl and shiver and bristle and show signs of the most overwhelming terror, not only at the same time as, but often in advance of human beings. I find it difficult to believe that animals are the victims of subjectively projected hallucinations. What remains, then, but the hypothesis that the sense organs of the animals are stimulated by objective occurrences? They, too, *see* something. Even more, they feel it, sense it, as it were, in the air.

What, then, is the something? A shape, of white (? sheets), of shifting specks (? dust), a shape, which wears sometimes

[1] See, for example, Dr. Tyrrell's account in chapter vi of his fascinating Pelican, *The Personality of Man.*

clothes, sometimes even armour. I cannot enter further into detail without being betrayed into the temptation of telling tall stories. Let me, then, record my belief that the most plausible explanation of what it is that the observer sees is that certain ideational elements, foot-loose, as it were, from the bundle which once was a mind and temporarily surviving its disruption, combine with and proceed to animate the matter of the sheets, the dust, even the clothes, to constitute an apparition. Readers of Plato will remember the celebrated passage in the *Phaedo* where he introduces the conception of earth-bound souls which, unable to free themselves from the clogging influences of the flesh-generated cravings and emotions by which in life they were dominated, haunt the scenes in which their cravings were felt and found, but find no longer, their satisfaction. Such is Plato's explanation of the graveyard ghost. I hope it is not too fanciful to suggest that some element of truth may be embodied in this suggestion of Plato's, and that what are wrongly termed 'souls' may for a time 'hang about' the scenes in which strong desires or emotions were experienced, when their owners were in the flesh. I am suggesting further that the most plausible psychological explanation of the fact that they do so is that clusters of ideas, surviving the break-up of the bundle which was once a mind, achieve temporary embodiment in association with matter in precisely these places.

SUMMARY

These various suggestions all pre-suppose a particular view of the relation between the mind and the body or, as I would prefer to put it, between the soul and the body. The relation in question is a particular case of the general transcendence-immanence relation which, I am suggesting, constitutes the most fruitful explanatory hypothesis of the phenomena of the natural world that the mind of man has yet hit upon.

In brief, I am suggesting that the individual soul or spirit transcends the body in the sense of being other than it, of being independent of it and in all probability of surviving it. It is, nevertheless, immanent in the body in the sense that for a limited period and no doubt for a special purpose the soul is incarnated in matter. How this comes about, and what the resultant relation between soul and body may be, we do not know and, if I am right in thinking that the relation is devised by a divine mind, will probably never know. The incarnated soul expresses itself in ideas; these ideas cluster in bundles and are known to us under the name of mind or consciousness, whose interaction with the body constitutes our normal mode of conscious experience. The closeness of the clustering varies from one individual to another, and ideas may become detached from the bundle to which they normally belong and associate themselves temporarily with other bodies and brains and even with non-cerebral matter. It is in this tendency of ideas to wander, as it were, from the cluster to which they normally belong that the most plausible explanation of many super-normal phenomena is to be found. I venture to add that none of the explanations of these phenomena that rely upon and confine themselves to the concepts normally employed by the sciences seem even remotely satisfactory. Hence science has either to ignore these phenomena or to write them off as illusory.

II. FORMS AND PARTICULARS

It will have been quickly apparent to those familiar with philosophy that arguments used from time to time in the preceding pages have a Platonic flavour, nor is it difficult to see that the two-level structure of the universe which the last two chapters envisage, and in particular the transcendence-immanence relation between the two levels of reality, is conceived fairly closely on Platonic lines. Those, however, who accept the Platonic scheme must encounter one prominent difficulty which is often regarded as insuperable. This is the difficulty of envisaging the nature of the relation between the Forms and the particulars. Let us suppose that we hold the Platonic view that reality consists of an assembly of changeless and eternal Forms.

Relation between Natural and Supernatural

Suppose, further, that it contains also or consists also of an indeterminate featureless flux, a surd element, as it were, which appears and reappears in Platonic Dialogues under a number of different aliases, as the flux of Becoming and the Not-Being of *The Republic*, as the 'Unlimited' and the 'Indeterminate' of the *Philebus* and as the 'Indefinite Dyad' of the *Seventh Letter*. Suppose, further, that we follow Plato in holding that the features of the qualitatively differentiated world of becoming, that is, the familiar world, are due to the presence or manifestation of the first order in the second. How is this relation of manifestation to be envisaged?

Plato gives us broadly two answers. The first is that the flux of becoming 'partakes of' or 'participates in' the Forms, while the Forms 'manifest' in the particulars. The second is that the things of the familiar world 'imitate' or 'copy' the Forms. Both types of relation encounter formidable difficulties. According to the first, the world of Forms which Plato explicitly affirms to be 'apart' and 'self-sufficient' is supposed to enter into the flux of becoming. This 'entering' appears to infringe the notion of apartness. The world of Forms which is wholly and completely 'real', is also required to be the immanent cause of the being of that which is something less than real. A curious function, one would have thought, to prescribe for 'reality'.

According to the second, while apartness and self-sufficiency are preserved, it is hard to see how a particular region of the flux succeeds in imitating or copying just the Forms which it does copy—why the Forms of squareness and brownness, for example, in the case of a table and not those of ovalness and whiteness? Nor, unless the flux is itself credited with a dynamic urge and is imbued with teleological aspirations, can we see, on the copying theory, why the things of the familiar world should *try*, as Plato so often says that they do, to realise the Forms more completely? Most Platonists appear to take the view that some active principle is required to mediate between the Forms and the particulars and make the most of Plato's suggestion in the *Timaeus* that Mind performs this office. But if

211

Relation between Natural and Supernatural

Mind, presumably an omnipotent or near-omnipotent mind, is to be seriously introduced into the Platonic scheme, the whole situation, as I shall argue later, becomes transformed.

Meanwhile, I am content to make the point that the relation between the Forms and particulars has hitherto defeated every attempt to make a satisfactory formulation of it. I add that this is precisely what one might expect if the Forms belong, as Plato holds that they do, to a supernatural world, more particularly if, as I shall maintain in the next section, what we call the Values—and it is under this term that the Forms may, I think, be most appropriately referred to in respect of their most outstanding manifestations as Truth, Goodness and Beauty— are the modes of God's revelation of His nature to man. For if this is, indeed, the case, the relation must be regarded as the immanence of a transcendent Being in a medium which, though it manifests, is itself other than, the Being manifested. Now, we cannot, I suggest, expect to achieve a 'know-how' of the mode of manifestation of a Divine Being.

III. VALUE AND FACT

The current view of values is that they are subjective. To say 'this is good' or 'this is beautiful' means, on this view, that I, or most people, or most people who have ever lived, or most of those who have the knowledge and experience which entitles them to pass judgment, or most of the governing classes of the community to which I belong, approve of it or appreciate it or derive enjoyment from it. Thus good, bad, beautiful, ugly (and, presumably, true, false) are relational qualities, that is to say, they are related to human beings. They are also psychological in that they are defined with reference to mental states. It follows that if there were no human minds and no feelings, therefore, of appreciation, approval and the reverse, nothing would be good, bad, beautiful, ugly, true or false.

I have criticised this view at length elsewhere[1] and do

[1] See my *Decadence, A Philosophical Enquiry*, chapter vii.

Relation between Natural and Supernatural

not propose to restate the criticisms here. I confine myself to three points.

(i) It is the view which most scientists hold and for a good, indeed, a necessary reason. If you believe that the universe consists of matter or energy or force and that mind is somehow derivative from matter, then all the qualities of things will be physical qualities and all our experience of those qualities will be sensory, at least in origin. Now Beauty, Goodness and Truth are not physical qualities, nor is it with our senses that we comprehend them. (This, as I have already pointed out,[1] is clearly the case, even in regard to beauty. My eye tells me that a picture is large, square, highly coloured, of a landscape, but it is with my mind that I apprehend the aesthetic quality in terms of which I judge it to be beautiful. Beauty, then, is not a quality which stimulates the sense organs and initiates neural messages to the brain, as do qualities of shape and colour.) If the qualities are not physical and apprehended with our senses, it is difficult to see what account of them science could give, except a subjectivist account and this, in fact, in so far as it deals with them at all, is the account that science *does* give. Thus psychology treats of aesthetic values in terms of emotions of tranquillity or of the balance and harmonisation of impulses.

(ii) It is contrary to the common sense view which holds that some works of art are really better than others, Shakespeare, for example, better than the contemporary ephemeral farce, Beethoven than the latest swing tune from the U.S.A., and that they would be so, even if most people at any given moment happened to prefer the farce and the swing. Also in regard to morals; common sense holds emphatically that some things are right and others wrong, and that we approve and disapprove of them accordingly. It does *not* hold that to say that anything is right means merely that we approve of it.

(iii) The instinct of common sense in this matter is sound, since a world devoid of ethical and aesthetic value, a world, moreover, in which nothing was true and nothing false, would

[1] See chapter iv, pp. 145–7.

213

Relation between Natural and Supernatural

be a world robbed of most of what makes our experience valuable and significant. It would not only violate our most deep-seated preconceptions; it would be totally unable to account for the fact that our experience is as it is.

The popularity of the subjectivist view of values is at least in part due to the sterility of many forms of objectivism. Proclaiming the existence of the values of Truth, Goodness and Beauty, thinkers have, nevertheless, unduly emphasised their apartness from and transcendence of the familiar world. The invisible world of values has floated like an impotent mirage above the solid world of moving matter. Thus, the world of values was dismissed as being merely abstract, a figment of thought or a refuge from the vulgarities and deficiencies of the world of fact. The values, in short, were the philosopher's version of 'pie in the sky'. That they are transcendent is, indeed, the case, for they are, as I shall urge later, the forms under which God permits Himself to be revealed to man. 'In ultimates,' as Goethe said, 'we see God.' But they are also immanent.

Consider, for example, the value Goodness. Unless we are prepared to take a subjectivist view of ethics, according to which the characteristic of being good is one that we have invented and then imputed to things because we happen to like or approve of them, goodness must be a something given, something, that is to say, which is recognised as presented.

But the good man is never content with his goodness. That he should be so would savour of complacency since, if Christianity is true, we are imperfect beings who compass during our time here on earth such virtue as we may. The good man, then, in so far as he is good, is a man given to the pursuit of goodness. He aspires, in short, to be better. Indeed, as Socrates argued, all of us in our degree pursue the good, our frequent apparent preference for evil being due to our mistakes of judgment in regard to the nature of good and of that wherein it consists. For whatever at any given moment we may happen to be pursuing, it seems to be good to us while we are pursuing it. This much, at least, seems to be true, that *other things being equal*, we do tend to

214

desire and pursue the good. We lie and cheat in order to secure some end beyond the lying and the cheating; we forge a cheque in order to obtain money which is not ours. But other things being equal, we tell the truth and are honest; that is to say, we do not need any incentive for *not* forging cheques. Right conduct is, therefore, seen to be an end in itself, whereas wrong conduct is always a means to an end beyond itself.

But by means of what part of his nature does man aspire after goodness? Clearly that in him by means of which he aspires after the good must itself be good, for, as I have just remarked, it is a characteristic of the good man, or of man in so far as he is good, to aspire after and desire goodness, and that in his nature which leads him so to aspire and desire is a part of him. Therefore, goodness is immanent in man and is the source of that in him which we know as moral aspiration and endeavour. Hence goodness is not only transcendent but immanent, being the source of that in us which aspires after greater goodness—a point, this, which Plato was surely trying to bring out when he spoke of the individual soul as not only modelling itself upon the Form of goodness as its exemplar, but also partaking of it in the sense that the soul was the medium of the Form's manifestation.

As with Goodness, so with Beauty; it is the presence of beauty in works of art which causes them to have value. Consider a picture. The matter of which it is composed, the canvas and paints, are in themselves aesthetically worthless. The idea or concept of the painter, unless it finds expression in matter, is also aesthetically worthless. For unless there were paint and canvas, unless there were words, unless there were sounds, the inspiration of the painter, the poet and the musician, would remain unrealised and, because unrealised, impotent. They would constitute a mere potentiality of value, not value itself. It is not, unless and until it becomes immanent in matter, that the artist's 'idea' achieves value. Yet the idea transcends the matter in which it finds expression. *Hamlet* would still be a play even if there were no books to print it in or actors to speak its lines.

Relation between Natural and Supernatural

This consideration carries an important implication in relation to the nature of the process which we know as creation.

THE NATURE OF CREATION

Excepting motherhood, art is the most familiar form of creation which is known to us on earth, which is perhaps why Plato says in the *Phaedrus* that the Form of Beauty is the only one of the Forms which the soul, while incarnate in the body, is permitted to know as it really is. Hence the procedure of the artist is the best, perhaps the only model of the creative process which is available for our consideration. Now the procedure of the artist is to create *in* something which is other than the artist and other than the 'idea' which is expressed in it. If there were no such something, no raw material of paint or sound or stone or even words, there would be no art. Moreover, the material stuff, though it serves as a medium for bringing to birth the artist's conception, may also impede it. The artist thinks of it as something intractable which at best obscures, at worst distorts the full realisation of his design. Technical accomplishment in the practice of an art is the instrument by means of which the artist seeks to overcome this intractability, but the victory is never absolute. It is the best he can do with the material at his command, but 'the best he can do' is less than the best.

Beethoven is pre-eminently an artist who gives us this sense of struggling with his material. Yet there are moments, especially in the works of his last period, when he conveys the impression that he has at last managed to subdue it and, having cast aside the shackles of form and structure which normally limit a composer's creativity by constituting the framework, the necessary framework within which it normally functions, breaks through, as it were, into a world of pure sound.[1] The restraints imposed by the medium having been temporarily laid aside, we have a glimpse of pure creativity or, rather—for the medium of sound is still, as it were, there—a hint of what pure creativity might be.

[1] The end of the third movement, the Adagio, of the Archduke Trio, Opus 97, may be cited as an outstanding example.

Relation between Natural and Supernatural

In general, however, Beethoven, like other artists, struggles, struggles perhaps more than other artists, to embody his conception as best he can in a medium which seems, in spite of his mastery, to thwart his intentions.

IV. THE VALUES OF SCIENCE

The transcendence-immanence formula for the relation of value to fact can also be applied to the values of science. For science, too, has its values—coherence, for example, order, relation, even elegance and that canon of economy which, given two or more hypotheses, each of which covers the facts, prescribes the choice of the most economical. These are truly values in the sense that their discovery and establishment may be said to constitute the end at which the scientist aims. Having established them, he formulates them in laws which purport to determine the behaviour of phenomena not immediately under his observation and to predict the behaviour of phenomena which have not yet occurred.

What account, then, is to be given of these values and their relation to the phenomena in which they are embodied? Broadly, there are two possibilities, that they are contributed or imposed by the mind and that they are found by it present, as it were, in the subject matter which the mind studies. The first hypothesis is plausible enough and many scientists have embraced it. In its most tenable form the doctrine approximates to the Kantian, since the view that it is the scientist's *individual* mind which imposes *its* order and coherence on the phenomena it studies entails a hopelessly anarchical subjectivism. Thus Kant has often been claimed by modern physicists but not, interestingly enough, by the practitioners of any other science, as the thinker whose philosophy fits most appropriately the conclusions to which their own thought has led them.

But we cannot accept what suits us in Kant and ignore its implications. If one is prepared to go all the way with the idealists, excising from one's system the Kantian *noumena* as vestigial relics of an outmoded realism, well and good. One ends up, I suspect, in a universe not very different from Hegel's or, it may be, from Schopenhauer's. But what one must not do is to pick up and choose, selecting the Idealism that suits one and then assigning arbitrary limits to its application. Hence, if the scientist follows the Kantian line, he must be prepared to scrap the *noumena*, if only because independently existing things cannot be bound as regards their behaviour by laws which are at bottom only mental constructions.

The difficulty has, of course, been made familiar by Kantian criticism. According to Kant, it is the mind which orders the raw material of sensation, imposing upon it the attributes which exemplify the categories, imposing, in particular, spatio-temporal relations. These are entirely of the mind. Why, then, does it order the material as it does? If it is *we* who prescribe the temporal relations to a non-temporal given raw material, why do we impose that kind of temporal relation which is exemplified by a missed train; if it is we who prescribe spatial relations, why do we prescribe that kind of relation between hand and ball which is exemplified by a 'dropped' catch? More technically, the difficulty is this. When I experience the sensation of seeing and touching an object, something, Kant maintains, is given to me from outside. This something is the celebrated 'thing in itself' which *causes* my sensation. The raw material of that which I take myself to see and to touch is, then, other than and independent of me; it is really 'out there', as it were, in the universe. But the qualities and the relations which I perceive it to have are contributed by the mind. But why, it may be asked, *should* these relations bind between non-mental entities; why should mental relations hold between non-mental facts and why should mental laws govern their behaviour? But if we reject, as I think we must, the Kantian view of the matter, what is the alternative? If mental laws cannot bind objective facts, it would seem to follow that the order, the relatedness, the coherence, the regularity which science postulates in its dealings with the external world and which, in so far as it is successful, it succeeds in establishing, must be given and cannot be wholly supplied.

These, then, which are the 'values' of science, are not imposed by the scientist but are presented in the phenomena which the scientist studies. What is more, they are discovered as presented. In other words they are immanent; but since no particular configuration of matter on any particular occasion exhausts them, they are also transcendent. Thus, the world studied by science cannot be reduced without remainder to material particles in motion. It contains also non-material laws which the particles obey, and these non-material laws constitute the values of science.

V. GOD AND THE WORLD

I would suggest that the various examples I have considered are paralleled by the relation of God to the world, a relation of which they constitute special cases. I do not want to stress the analogy between God and the artist to the point of asserting a metaphysical dualism, yet there is much in the universe to encourage us to think of God's creation after the same fashion as that of the artist. Genesis, no doubt, tells us that 'In the beginning God created the heaven and the earth', created them, that is to say, not as the artist creates in a subject matter which precedes and is other than his creation, but created them out of nothing. Nevertheless, granted the prior existence of the subject matter, whatever its origin,[1] the mode of God's subsequent creativity would appear to illustrate the transcendence-immanence formula. The Incarnation of Christ, whereby the Word was made flesh would, on this view, be no more than a particular and extreme case of such creative immanence.

God's relation to the world, in so far as it is a relation of immanence, would also typify the other instances of the transcendence-immanence relation at which I have glanced in respect

[1] See chapter v, p. 131, where I suggest a logical and, perhaps, a chronological priority for the creation by God of the brute material stuff of the universe.

219

of the fact that the method of the 'entering in' is unknown to us and will presumably remain so. So, too, with the Incarnation of Christ. We do not understand how it could have happened. If we did, it would not be a miracle, nor would the so-called miracles of Christ be miraculous. Yet if the general line followed in this chapter is right, the miracles are a particular case of the immanence of the divine in matter and we have, therefore, no right to *expect* them to be intelligible. At the same time we have no more right to dismiss them because they are *not* intelligible, than we have to write off the mind as a by-product of the brain, merely because its mode of interaction with the brain passes our comprehension.

God's Motive

There are, moreover, two matters of great difficulty which the transcendence-immanence conception helps to illuminate without enabling us wholly to understand. The first is the question of God's motive in creation. This has seemed to many to constitute a difficulty of such magnitude that they have denied that God created the world. There is, for example, the celebrated argument in Plato's *Republic* to the effect that God, being perfect, could not desire change, for change is either for the better or for the worse. If the change were for the better, then there would be some element of good, that, namely, in which the betterment consisted, which God lacked before He caused the change to come about, and God would not have been perfect to begin with. But if God is good, he could not desire change for the worse. Indeed, it is difficult, as Aristotle pointed out, to credit God with desire of any kind, since desire implies lack, lack of that which is desired, and we cannot conceive what good thing God, who is assumed to be perfect, can lack.

The Problem of Evil

As for the problem of evil, that has seemed to many to be so insoluble that they have either denied that God could have created a world that has evil so palpably in it, or they have taken

Relation between Natural and Supernatural

Leibniz's heroic course of denying the evil and maintaining that in spite of appearances to the contrary this is the best of all possible worlds. The Christian view makes at least some attempt to grapple with the problem. Its explanation runs, I take it, briefly as follows. Virtue and love are goods. Therefore, the more of these goods that exist in the universe, the better. God, therefore, since He is good desires to increase the total amount of virtue and love. This desire would not, however, be satisfied by creating wholly virtuous beings who could do no wrong, for, since these would be automata and not the initiators of freely willed choices, their virtue, too, would be automatic. Now virtue that cannot help itself is not moral virtue as we know it, is not, that is to say, the kind of virtue that is morally desirable. As for love, it may be doubted whether the love of beings who have no alternative but to feel and to offer it is worth having. God, therefore, created man a moral agent having freewill. Freewill means the freedom to choose, to choose evil as well as to choose good, wrong as well as right. Evil must exist in the world, since otherwise it could not be chosen, or, perhaps, evil consists simply in the making of bad choices, where one might have made good ones. God, however, is willing to take the risk of men choosing wrongly and as a consequence introducing evil and becoming evil, even perhaps of men going wholly to the bad, in the interests of His desire to increase the amount of love and goodness that there is in the universe by the creation and development of freely choosing and freely loving beings who act morally and feel and give love when they need not have done so. Thus, not only does He increase the amount of love felt for Himself, He also increases the number of beings who are worthy objects of His love.

THE SURD ELEMENT

This explanation, though many think it far-fetched, does at least hang together; it makes sense, though difficult sense, but it presupposes that we have in principle solved the difficulty as to how potentially imperfect beings *could* have been created. It is

Relation between Natural and Supernatural

in connection with this difficulty that the analogy with the case of artistic creation cited above[1] offers its most fruitful application. We may suppose either that the universe contains as an aboriginal factor, in addition to God, a featureless stuff which in a previous chapter[2] I have called the 'brute-given', or, as Christianity would insist, that God Himself first created such stuff to be the medium of His own later creations. In this event, the universe, as I remarked in an earlier chapter,[3] though dualistic is not irreducibly so. In the beginning, as the Bible asserts, there was only God and to this extent the artist analogy breaks down.

It is in this stuff that God creates, as the artist creates in stone or paint or sound. Parenthetically, the Indian philosopher, Sankarachaya, finds in the practice of the artist the best analogy on which to conceive the practice and nature of God's own creation. The artist's creation is, he points out, an expression or overflow of himself.

We may, if we choose, think of it as a *necessary* overflow. As the artist, unable to contain his own inspiration, pours himself out, as it were, in works of art, so God, unable to contain the plenitude of His own goodness, pours Himself out into the world of His creation. God has no motive for His overflowing, any more than the artist has a motive in writing, painting or composing; the universe which He creates is the necessary expression or externalisation of Himself.

But just as his material proves intractable, thwarting the artist's intention and botching his execution so, it may be, the material stuff of the universe, which God uses as *His* medium and in which *His* Creation is embodied may thwart *His* intention or, rather, may prevent His creatures—who, since after all they *are* originally God's creatures, cannot in their *intention* be other than wholly good—from fully realising the Creator's intentions in regard to them. On this view, we are all of us designs that have been botched by the stuff in which the design had to be embodied

[1] See above, p. 130. [2] See chapter v, pp. 127-9.
[3] Ibid., p. 131.

in order that it might be realised. Or it may be—for it is scarcely necessary to draw attention to the purely speculative character of these suggestions—that having expressed Himself in the stuff of the universe, breathed life, as the Bible has it, into dust, God left the divine spark which is a human soul to fend for itself, endowed with the gift of freedom so that it may struggle as best it can against the obstacles and limitations which the 'stuff' imposes upon it. Thus the stuff, the material medium in which God creates, may be not so much the *necessary* condition of creation, as the condition which God has chosen to make use of for the making possible of human freedom, a condition which it fulfils by interposing, as it were, a barrier between us and the universal, creative Mind of which we are the expressions. Moreover, it may be just this barrier which, cutting us off, as it were, from the creative source of our being, confers upon us our individuality.

To put the point rather differently, matter which I have identified with the surd element in the universe, may be the instrument by means of which God secures the freedom of His creatures. If the universe consisted exclusively of God and of expressions of and emanations from God's nature, expressions and emanations which were not expressed in, embodied in or contained by anything other than themselves, it would be difficult to see how they could, as it were, cut loose from God. But if they did not cut loose, they would not be free, they would not be individual and they would, presumably, be perfect even as God is perfect.

If this world is to be regarded as a cosmic laboratory in which the experiment of character formation and development in morally free individuals is being conducted, conditions of the operation of the experiment may be that they should be less than perfect, that they should be genuinely individual and that they should have a brute, intractable environment, not amenable to their wills against which to struggle. These conditions are in general provided by the material environment in which their lives are set and in particular by their material bodies.

223

Relation between Natural and Supernatural

I am suggesting, then, that the facts of experience may be most satisfactorily covered by the hypothesis that God and God's creatures are not all, but that there is also matter, a brute intractable stuff derived we know not whence—save that it, too, must originally have proceeded from God—and that our souls are emanations of the divine temporarily incarnated in matter.

VI. HUMAN HISTORY

No set of facts have seemed to me more resistant to the Christian hypothesis, that man was specially created by God in pursuance of a purpose, than those provided by human history. For human history presents to all appearances nothing but a procession of societies emerging from time to time into civilisations which, after enduring for a certain period, decline and finally break up, to be succeeded by other civilisations which decay in their turn. So persistent in human history is the recurrence of this pattern, that one is sometimes tempted to wonder whether the growth and development of human societies may not bear witness to the operation of some law in terms of which man is enabled to raise the condition of human life to a certain level of prosperity, well-being, refinement and enlightenment, but is unable to hold it *at that level* for more than a certain period. When the period comes to an end, the level falls back and in due course the process begins all over again. Perhaps there is something incorrigible about us, some taint, it may be, which we have inherited from the primeval slime from which the biologists say we took our rise, which makes it impossible for us to push the progress of mankind beyond a certain point.

The evidence for this view of man's past is so impressive that many have seen in history nothing but a meaningless repetition. Thus, Aristotle thinks of history not as a drama unfolding itself in time but as an eternal recurrence in which the cosmos as a whole, and social and political phenomena, therefore, as part of the cosmos, repeat themselves indefinitely, while in our own

Relation between Natural and Supernatural

time Spengler's brilliant *Decline of the West* paints a picture of the past in which civilisations go through a fixed timetable of closely similar phases. Again and again, without rhyme or reason, meaning or purpose, they arise, develop, decline and founder. Such, it must be admitted, is the appearance which history, or at any rate that part of it with which we are, however imperfectly, acquainted, indubitably presents. And it is, of course, intolerably difficult to reconcile with the view that history in general and human history in particular are witnesses to the working out of a definite plan which is immanent in the process.

WHAT DIFFERENCE DID CHRIST MAKE?

And there is another difficulty. To the Christian the events which took place in the first half of the first century A.D. are crucial. They constitute for Christianity an historical watershed in the sense that nothing that has happened after them can have quite the same significance as anything that happened before them. Yet, apart from the fact that human history appears to go on very much in the same way as it did before—it certainly does not exhibit any outstanding change of type or pattern from the beginning of the Christian era onwards—it is difficult to see what kind of difference the coming of Christ made or, indeed, could have made to the lot or destiny of individual men.

Let us for the sake of hypothesis grant the truth of the Christian view that man is a soul created by God and sent into this world in order that, having learnt through trial and suffering, he may become in the long run less unlike God, more pleasing to God and closer to communion with God, until in the end he achieves salvation, conceived as a condition of timeless blessedness in communion with God. The world, then, is a school for the improving and strengthening of our moral characters. From the point of view of our moral education Christ is first and foremost an example, in that he provides a model of a life rightly lived. But, according to Christian doctrine, he was more

P
225

than an example, since through his suffering and sacrifice he redeemed mankind from sin. This does not mean, presumably, that all sinners will automatically achieve salvation because of Christ's suffering and sacrifice. What it does mean is that if they genuinely repent of their wrong-doing and sincerely try to be better, they will be forgiven their sins which have been expiated by Christ's suffering and death. Such, I take under correction, for I do not profess fully to understand this mystical doctrine, is the essence of the Atonement.

What account, then, are we to give of the innumerable individuals who preceded Christ and to whom the illumination of his life and teaching was not vouchsafed? Are we to suppose that, lacking the spiritual illumination and the moral strengthening which those who believe in Christ enjoy, with their sins unrepented of—for it may be that they did not know they were sinners—and presumably unexpiated—for the sacrifice and suffering of Christ had not yet occurred—they were born and died without the chance of achieving that moral salvation which, if Christianity is right, is the true end of man? Such a view is highly repugnant to our sense of justice and is inconsistent with the conception of God as having created man in order that he might achieve salvation and sending Christ into the world in order that he might be assisted to do so.

If, on the other hand, salvation were available to Christ's predecessors, what difference did his suffering and death make?

My difficulty in regard to human history has, then, been a double one. First, what sense, if Christianity is true, are we to make of the process by which human civilisations appear, develop and break up? Secondly, what difference have the example and sacrifice of Christ made to man's destiny or, rather, to his chance of achieving it?

PROFESSOR TOYNBEE'S INTERPRETATION OF HISTORY

An answer to these questions—the first that has seemed to me to be even remotely plausible—is suggested in the work of

Relation between Natural and Supernatural

Professor Toynbee. I cannot here enter at length into the nature of this answer or the reasons for it. I have not the qualifications, and even if I had, to do so would take me too far beyond the scope of this book. The upshot of Toynbee's interpretation of history is, however, very briefly as follows:

First, to say that the process of the rise and fall of successive human civilisations is no more than a meaningless succession is to generalise on grossly insufficient evidence. On the time scale established by cosmogony and geology the period during which human civilisation has existed is too short to justify any such generalisation. According to that time scale, the past of life upon the earth may be plausibly estimated at about a thousand million years, of human life, giving all doubtful human types the benefit of the doubt, at something under a million; of human civilisations, again giving doubtful examples the benefit, at four or, at most, at about five thousand. Scale down these figures to make them manageable. Let is put the past of life at about a hundred years. Then the past of human life works out at about five weeks and of human civilisation at between one and two hours. On this reduced time scale the period during which conditions suitable to life as we know it may be expected to continue on the earth is about one hundred thousand years, that is to say nearly a thousand times as long as the whole past history of life.

The period of time during which those species of human societies that we call civilisations have endured is thus too short, relatively to the history of life in general and of human life in particular, to permit of any easy generalisations to the effect that the succession of human civilisations is and must necessarily remain meaningless. Because a number of specimens of the species, which must be regarded in the light of very early experiments, a dozen or perhaps twenty, have failed, we are certainly not entitled to assume that civilisations *must* from their very nature pass like living organisms through a necessary succession of temporary phases, in which decay and disruption will necessarily succeed development.

Relation between Natural and Supernatural

Secondly, the fact that most civilisations that have hitherto existed have risen, fallen and been succeeded by others does not mean that the process of human history is meaningless. Civilisations may rise and fall in fulfilment of a divine plan according to which man learns through suffering, learning being defined as improvement of moral character. Thus, the suffering caused through the fall of civilisations may be a potent means of progress; as Toynbee says, 'after all, if a vehicle is to move forward on a course which its driver has set, it must be borne along on wheels that turn monotonously round and round'.[1] How, then, is the course to be conceived? The validity of any answer which is given to this question depends, it is obvious, upon the acceptance of some proposition in regard to the goal for man, since the goal for a civilisation which is composed of human beings can have no meaning except in terms of the goal, whatever it may be, for human beings. If the teaching of Christianity is true, the goal for man must be regarded as the achievement of moral salvation conceived in terms of man's increasing likeness to God, and culminating in his ultimate communion with God. It must be added, however, that this goal must not be selfishly sought by the individual for himself alone, but also by him for his neighbours.

THE FUNCTION OF CIVILISATIONS

Assuming, then, that the advance of civilisations must be measured by the criterion of improving moral character and the goal identified with salvation, the particular rôle which Toynbee assigns to civilisations is that of providing the conditions for the generation of religions in general and of the higher religions in particular. He shows in detail how the higher religions tend to be born as the result of the meeting and clash of two civilisations and the subsequent decline of one or both of them. It is through the rise of a religion that the tradition of civilised humanity, together with such degree of virtue and enlightenment as mankind has attained in the past, is preserved

[1] A. J. Toynbee, *Civilization on Trial*, p. 15.

Relation between Natural and Supernatural

and continued during the dark ages which tend to follow the decline and collapse of civilisations.

If it is the function of civilisations to provide the conditions for the birth and growth of religions, in what sense can the sequence of civilisations be said to progress? Toynbee emphasises the traditional Christian view that man is born in sin; he deduces that 'there is no reason to expect any change in unredeemed human natures while human life on Earth goes on'. But though the *raw material* of human nature may remain constant, the opportunities for moral and spiritual improvement during life upon earth may improve. If being born in the flesh upon the earth is to be interpreted as a kind of going to school, the school may become a more advanced one in the sense that higher forms, a fifth and a sixth, perhaps, even one day a seventh, may progressively be added to it.

It is in these terms that Toynbee invites us to view the *rôle* of religion and the function of civilisation as a pre-condition of the birth and growth of the higher religions. Each of the higher religions unfolds for man a pattern and prescribes a model, a pattern and model of how life should be lived. Christianity, the highest, provides in the person of Christ the perfect model. By trying to form his life on this model man solicits, comes to deserve and finally obtains grace to live a better life. Thus a virtuous circle is set up in which increase of moral virtue solicits increase of grace, and increase of grace impels the recipient to seek yet greater increase of virtue.

I have put this in terms of moral endeavour; but the concept is incomplete without the addition of the element of cognition. What the higher religions in general and Christianity in particular have done is to increase man's knowledge of the nature and purposes of God. Therefore, as civilisation succeeds civilisation, religion, religion, there is vouchsafed to man what Professor Toynbee calls 'a growing fund of illumination and of grace—meaning by "illumination" the discovery or revelation or revealed discovery of the true nature of God and the true end of man here and hereafter, and by "grace", the will or inspiration

229

Relation between Natural and Supernatural

or inspired will to aim at getting into closer communion with God and becoming less unlike Him. In the provision of increasing spiritual opportunity for souls in their passages through life on Earth, there is assuredly an inexhaustible possibility of progress in this world.'[1] Thus the function of the higher religions is to provide ever greater opportunities for men on earth to become less unlike God and, therefore, to qualify for salvation. The function of civilisations is to act as a vehicle for the birth and growth of the higher religions. Ultimately we may look— though one or more, perhaps many, dark ages may intervene— to a single world-wide civilisation to provide the conditions for a single world-wide religion. Church and State might then become one in 'the world-wide and enduring reign of the Christian Church Militant on Earth'.

THE SIGNIFICANCE OF CHRIST

This concept of the function of civilisation and the meaning which it gives to the notion of progress in civilisations incidentally provides an answer to the second of the two questions which I posed above, what difference did the coming of Christ make? The answer, Professor Toynbee suggests, is that under the Christian dispensation, a dispensation which through the continuing tradition of the Christian Church has bequeathed to man a great and growing fund of illumination, if he wills to avail himself of it, and of grace, if he can be at the moral pains to win it, man, while still on earth, enjoys greater opportunities for qualifying for salvation than he enjoyed before. He can, in other words, make greater progress here on earth in the direction of becoming less unlike God. This suggestion has the advantage of not excluding from the advantages of spiritual grace and enlightenment and, therefore, from the chance of salvation, the men whose lives preceded the coming of the higher religions in general and of Christianity in particular. It merely draws attention to the fact that to us is vouchsafed the opportunity of travelling further along the road than was

[1] Toynbee, op. cit., p. 249.

possible to them. To revert to the school metaphor, we have the chance of rising to a higher form, if only because we have better instruction.

Thus Toynbee sees in the rise and fall of civilisations and in the birth and growth of the higher religions whose relation to civilisations he explores, not a meaningless succession but the gradual working out of a divine plan, whereby man—who is properly to be regarded as a moral experiment in that, though he is a creature born *for* salvation, it nevertheless depends upon his own efforts whether or not he attains it—enjoys, as civilisation succeeds civilisation, a greater opportunity of achieving his destiny while yet on earth by reason of his fuller and more enlightened conception of what his destiny is, and receives greater assistance towards its achievement by reason of the fact that the suffering and sacrifice of Christ have rendered grace more readily available to him than to his predecessors.

History, then, in Toynbee's words, is 'the masterful and progressive execution on the narrow stage of the world of a definite plan which is revealed to us in this fragmentary glimpse but which transcends our human power of vision and understanding in every dimension'.[1]

CONCLUSION. GOD AND THE WORLD

It is time to draw these scattered observations to a point. I have sought to exemplify what I have called the transcendence-immanence relation in the relation of mind to body, of forms to particulars, of value to fact, of the artist to his work and of divine plan to human history, because these familiar problems seem to me to be less inexplicable—I would put it no higher—in terms of this relation than in that of any other. The relation of God to the world, I have suggested, also illustrates this relation. God is, in the first place, immanent. If He were not, we should have to reject the whole testimony of man's spiritual experience according to which it is possible for us to make contact with a source of spiritual influence which, if we solicit its assistance

[1] Toynbee, op. cit., pp. 14, 15.

231

by prayer, will help and strengthen us in the continual moral conflicts of which our lives here on earth are composed. The help and strengthening take the form of what we know as divine grace.

Moreover, unless God is immanent, we are left with the alternatives (a) of a straightforward materialism which, if it admits spirit at all, treats it as epiphenomenal upon matter, or (b) if we are prepared to admit the causal efficacy and partial independence of spirit, of envisaging the cosmos as a field in which a number of detached and isolated spirits originating we know not whence arbitrarily interfere with the movements of pieces of matter, either to no end at all—save perhaps that of their own self-satisfaction—or in pursuit of values which are themselves arbitrarily given, pieces of spiritual furniture which just happen to be lying about in the cosmos, their number being as arbitrary as their characteristics and the pattern of arrangement, if any, which they constitute.

On the other hand, God cannot, I think, be *wholly* immanent for the reasons given in chapter vi. Briefly, they are that if God is wholly immanent, (i) there is no even remotely tolerable explanation of the problem of evil. (ii) It is impossible to set limits to God's pervasion of the universe; yet to assert that my toenail is also God, or part of God, seems to me to make nonsense of religion and to reduce the concept of God to meaninglessness. Further, a wholly immanent God is fatally entangled in the death, whether from heat or cold, of the physical universe. But a God who is doomed to die with the world that He pervades is not the God of religious experience, nor is He a God whom man could worship.

If the transcendence-immanence relation be accepted, we cannot expect to comprehend its nature. One conclusion of great importance follows. If God created the world and is or may be immanent in it, it might be expected that He would from time to time intervene in its affairs. In fact, He intervenes continuously, if only through the instrument of grace by means of which he works upon us. But it is also on this assumption

Relation between Natural and Supernatural

quite reasonable to expect certain special interferences such as Christianity, with its record of the series of God's mighty acts, affirms. The culmination of these interferences, which is also the supreme expression of God's immanence, is the Incarnation of Jesus Christ. The transcendence-immanence conception also covers Christ's miracles, which may be interpreted as interferences by the spirit with the behaviour of matter in unforseeable and inexplicable ways. It may even, though their acceptance is by no means necessary to the truth of Christianity, be extended to explain the stories of God's interventions in the Old Testament.

All these—the Incarnation, the miracles, even the Old Testament stories—would only be special and dramatically picturesque examples of the functioning of a relation which, if the conception developed in this chapter can be accepted, is normal and continuous, but which transcends our powers of comprehension.

CHAPTER IX

The Church of England

I add a chapter on the Church, not because a discussion of the position of the Church in Britain today is an essential part of the theme of this book—there are already many books devoted to such discussion, and even if there were not, I have no competence to undertake it—but because of the large part the Church has played in my own conversion to the Christian faith. I am properly grateful for what it has done for me, and would like to pay my tribute to its work.

The Church of England, it is common knowledge, is passing through a difficult time. The number of those who in Great Britain have any continuing connection with it is small, amounting to not more than one tenth of the population, and shows no signs of growing larger. The number of its clergymen is small (it is now about 15,000 in a population of 50,000,000 as compared with 21,000 in a population of 39,000,000 in 1914) and they are for the most part miserably poor. (Their average stipend, after making allowances for necessary expenses,[1] is about £450 a year; some six thousand curates receive on an average £300 a year.) Their lot is not one that any man would envy or that any man who lacked an intense religious conviction would choose. Day in and day out, the parson must swim against the tide of opinion, striving to make headway against apathy and neglect, a persistent seller of goods that the public doesn't want. Many men, especially in country parishes, are made desperate by loneliness. An educated man does not want

[1] Maintenance of house and glebe, telephone, postage, etc.

to spend *all* his time discussing farm prices and the prospects of the harvest; he needs occasionally to exchange ideas with men of common interests and equivalent education. Yet in many parishes the parson finds nobody of his kind or, if he does, is debarred by his poverty from intercourse on the normal footing of entertaining and being entertained. Lonely and discouraged himself, the parson must yet maintain a cheerful readiness to shoulder the troubles of others. Burdened by the grossest poverty, he must continue to keep up an appearance of decent sufficiency. Whatever else it may be, his is not an easy life. These are men who do fine work in circumstances of the greatest difficulty and deserve more credit than they normally obtain. I, for one, am glad to pay tribute to them.

CONTEMPORARY CRITICISMS OF THE CHURCH

Much has been written on the causes of the Church's decline. Admittedly, the times are hostile to the Church and to its ritual of worship. The bonds of the family, that tight little church-going Victorian block, have relaxed and the invention of the internal combustion engine gives its members the chance to disperse on a Sunday on motor cycle, motor car and motor-bus. Young people in particular take advantage of the chance and no longer spend their Sundays at home. There are rival attractions which the Victorians never knew, and in many large towns there is in the evening the competition of the cinema. These are reasons of circumstance.

More important, perhaps, is the shift of belief. As I have shown in previous pages, the temper of the times formed, as it has been, by science, is sceptical in regard to the things of the spirit and contemptuous of any so-called reality that is not accessible to sensory perception. I have sought to examine the grounds for this attitude and tried to show that, in so far as they are afforded, or thought to be afforded, by science, they are baseless. The attitude, nevertheless, is widely prevalent and is likely to remain so for as far ahead as one can foresee.

More, however, than the reason of circumstance, more than the

The Church of England

shift of belief, is required to account for the definite hostility with which many today regard the Church and all that it stands for. The reader of *English Life and Leisure* by Rowntree and Lavers, published in 1951, is struck by the extent of this hostility. A number of representative opinions is quoted, of which the following are not untypical:

'A working-class family that is religious is working against its own interest.... Everyone knows religion isn't true, but the nobs try to make working folk believe it so that they won't kick up a fuss. . . .' 'Nobody believes all the nonsense they read out in church. The parsons just do it to earn their living. . . .' 'Don't talk to me about parsons! They've got a pretty soft job, if you ask me. Telling decent folk how to behave! Never done an honest day's work in their life, most of them.'

Whence does this active hostility, compounded in equal measures of hatred and contempt, derive? The opinion that religion is the opium of the people carries little weight today. It dates from an age when working people were miserably poor, knew their place and went to church to learn their duty to their betters. None of these conditions obtains in contemporary Britain.

For my part, I would assign the active hostility with which in many quarters the Church is today regarded to two main causes. The first is the Church's attitude to war. Thirty-seven years ago, on the outbreak of the 1914 war, Shaw wrote in *Common Sense about the War*: 'We turn our Temples of Peace promptly into Temples of War, and exhibit our parsons as the most pugnacious characters in the community. I venture to affirm that the sense of scandal given by this is far deeper and more general than the Church thinks, especially among the working classes, who are apt either to take religion seriously or else to repudiate it and criticise it closely. When a bishop at the first shot abandons the worship of Christ and rallies his flock round the altar of Mars, he may be acting patriotically, necessarily, manfully, rightly; but that does not justify him in pretending that there has been no change, and that Christ is, in effect, Mars. The straightforward course, and the one that would serve the Church best in the long run, would be to close our professedly Christian Churches the moment war is declared by us, and reopen them only on the signing of the treaty of peace.'

Since these words were written, war has become the over-riding problem of our age and another war bids fair to destroy us. From time to time the churches issue denunciations of war, yet, when war comes, they cease to preach the gospel of Christ and become the voice of an embattled nation. Clergymen bless the guns, pray for victory over the enemy and bestow their approval upon young men who are perfecting themselves in the art of efficiently slaughtering their fellows as a preliminary to giving an exhibition of their skill.

The absurdity of the attitude that the churches of all nations adopt when war comes has been pilloried for all time in Sir John Squire's quatrain written at the beginning of the 1914–18 war:

> *To God the embattled nations sing and shout,*
> *'Gott strafe England' and 'God Save the King.'*
> *God this, God that and God the other thing.*
> *'Good God', said God, 'I've got my work cut out.'*

Now all this is so flagrantly at variance with the teaching and spirit of Christ that even those who have little interest in the Church and its doings sense the discrepancy and conclude that a body which, professing a particular faith, approves on occasion so different a practice, cannot be taken seriously.

The other main reason is on the score of belief. It is not clear what the Church of England today believes. In particular, there is a feeling that she has for years been fighting a losing battle against science, surrendering decade by decade under the growing pressure from science a few more positions, positions insisted upon in the past with passionate intensity as strongholds of the faith. That the elasticity and vagueness of the Church's creed have played no small part in the decline of its influence, the comparative popularity of the Roman Catholic Church which

The Church of England

has made few, if any, concessions, to 'the spirit of the times' and has withstood the challenge from science, convincingly demonstrates. The Church of England, on the other hand, loses both on the swings of belief and the roundabouts of doubt. While to the would-be believer its continued concessions to science and to common sense seem to rob its doctrines of the supernatural backing which alone gave them sanction, so that it runs the risk of dwindling into a mere purveyor of vague ethico-religious uplift, to the scientist and to those whom he influences, the doctrines which the Church still upholds appear as a mixture of superstition, of make-believe and convention. There are many good men today who regard the Anglican Church as dishonest. It trims its sails, they feel, to every shift of the winds of modern thought without explicitly acknowledging that the shift has taken place. Has the Church abandoned the history and geography of the Bible or has it not? If it has, why does it not explicitly say so? Does it believe in the physical ascension of Christ's body or does it not? If it does not, why does it not explicitly say so? Thus, the Church, getting no credit for the concessions that it has in fact made, is condemned either as an obscurantist institution which insists on teaching 'truths' which science has shown to be false, or as a time-serving organisation making desperate bids for popular favour by concessions which cut at the very foundations of the faith it is supposed to profess.

On these criticisms, and on the attitude of mind which underlies them, I venture to make four comments.

In Defence of the Church

A word, first, on the propriety of doing so; for 'the Church' it might well be said, 'is perfectly well able to look after itself and needs no defence from such as you.' I agree. But my life is normally set in circles hostile to the Church. I know what the young men say about it when they deign to think of it at all, and I should like to indicate very briefly how I should try, how I do try, to answer them—briefly, for this whole book is in its true sense and intention an attempted answer.

The Church of England

First, then, on the point of belief. A creed, that is, a set of propositions which are believed, is the backbone of a religious faith, though the backbone needs to be clothed with the flesh and blood of emotion, of spiritual fervour and faith. The Church, then, must believe something, and since its subject matter is the supernatural order of reality and man's relation to it, what it believes cannot be established or verified by the tests recognised by science. Most of its teaching has come down from a comparatively remote past and, so far as the statements which it includes about the natural order are concerned, some at least, will be at variance with what science has found out about the natural order. In a word, they are related to the science of the times. Some, then, are in need of revision.

That the Church has done its best to be accommodating in this matter nobody could deny. In 1922 a Commission on Christian Doctrine was set up by the two Archbishops. After fifteen years' deliberation, it published its report in 1938. Those who do not realise how much water has flowed under the clerical bridges during the last fifty years would be surprised to find what opinions may be held and taught without censure by ordained clergymen.

To mention one or two outstanding examples, the tradition of the verbal inerrancy of the Bible is abandoned. It is no longer necessary to hold that Creation consisted of a series of sudden, successive acts; many believe it to be a continuous process. To believe in the existence of Satan and evil spirits is no longer obligatory; on such matters the language of the Liturgy may be interpreted in 'a purely symbolic sense'. So, too, with the belief in Hell. The belief in Christ's miracles is optional. Many hold that 'it is more congruous with the wisdom and majesty of God that he should never vary the regularities of nature'. The Virgin Birth disappears, leaving the manner of Christ's Incarnation indefinite. So, too, with the *physical* resurrection of Christ and his *physical* ascension into Heaven, of which the Commission report that its physical features are to be interpreted symbolically, 'since they are closely related to the conception of Heaven as a place locally fixed beyond the sky'.

The Church of England

There are enough abandonments here, in all conscience, to satisfy the most confirmed 'mover with the times'. A doubt might, indeed, be hazarded whether too much has not been abandoned. Indeed, it is difficult to see how the Church could give up more without surrendering its claim to be a vehicle for the revelation of supernatural truth. The body of the Church's teaching must, therefore, stand. The science of the future will, it is obvious, discover much about the natural world which is unknown today. But the Church cannot, it is equally obvious, alter its teaching every time science rectifies its earlier picture of the natural world to accommodate some newly discovered fact. The central core of the Christian faith is either absolute truth or it is nonsense. Being absolute, the truths which it proclaims also claim to be eternal. If they were not absolute, if they were not eternal, they would not be worth believing. Scientific knowledge, on the other hand, is relative, relative to what at any given moment happens to have been found out about the natural world. A religion which is in constant process of revision to square with science's ever-changing picture of the world might well be easier of belief, but it is hard to believe that it would be worth believing.

Secondly, to revert to a point made earlier in another connection,[1] a belief which has been established and persisted over many generations becomes charged with emotion; it comes, in fact, to acquire a sacramental value. Change it (if you can) and substitute another in closer accordance with contemporary science and the emotion disappears, the sense of holiness evaporates. It must not be forgotten that one of the purposes of religion is to affect our lives and actions. A religion which trimmed its sails to every fresh wind that blew from the laboratory would no more affect men's lives than a belief in evolution or in the creation of matter from inter-stellar gas.

Thirdly, it seems to me that those who expect—if ever they did, and in the nineteenth century I think that they clearly did —Christianity to become a universal religion, are in error. I,

[1] See chapter v, pp. 110, 111.

240

at least, can find no warrant for this expectation in Christ's own teaching. So far from Christianity becoming a world-wide religion, Christ taught that it would be a religion only of the few. So far from it being a creed to convert the world, His followers would, He intimated, be persecuted and rejected by the world.

Moreover, as I pointed out in a previous chapter,[1] it is not in this world that man's regeneration will occur. Hence, to judge the Church by the counting of heads, to point out that in Britain its numbers decline and that its influence wanes, is to apply to it a criterion whose relevance is, to say the least, doubtful. The Church has declined before and recovered. Some fourteen hundred years ago, a Dark Age descended upon Europe in which whatever remained of culture, knowledge and human charity was preserved and guarded by the Church. It is not inconceivable that history should be repeated.

I have been speaking hitherto—for a reason which I shall mention in a moment—of the Anglican Church. This, it should be unnecessary to point out, is only a small part of the whole Christian community. There is, I imagine, little evidence that the Roman Catholic Church is declining either in influence or in numbers. On the contrary, it is growing in respect of both.

Fourthly, and this, for me, is the pith of the matter, religion is, for most of us, a corporate activity. Few of us have the strength of will to practise it alone. Alone we cannot collect ourselves for meditation or constrain ourselves to utter prayers that are more than perfunctory. I speak, of course, for myself; yet also, I suspect, for many like myself. It is only when we come together that we come near to God and we come together in corporate worship. The worship is prescribed by the ritual of a Church which is, in my own case, the Church of England. Indeed, for me, it must be so. Religion is not like a language, something that you acquire; it is bound up with the ancestral elements of your being. (It is for this reason, I suspect, that in so many of my generation it 'comes out' late in life, when the things that are

---

[1] See chapter iii, pp. 80, 81.

Q   241

The Church of England

ancestral take increasing possession of the stage of one's personality, and the things that are acquired fall away.) The countryside of England and the life of its villages are also, for me, bound up with the ancestral elements of my being. My people have for generations been 'on the land'.

Prominent in the life of the English village has been the church. In the past—though scarcely at all today—those who earned their living on the land had an affection, an affection which deepened on occasion into reverence, for the village church. Hence, when I came, as I recounted at the outset, to consider again the whole question of religion, it was natural that the process of reconsideration and reflection should take place within the framework of the Anglican Church, and that my worship, when at last I began to worship, should find its appropriate setting in the parish church. Indeed, I formed the habit of intermittently attending the services of village churches long before I came to believe in the truth of what they taught. I would, I used to tell myself, go out of curiosity because I wanted to learn what still went on in them. Or—and this, perhaps, was a little nearer the truth—I was attracted by the beauty of the setting and by the beauty of the Liturgy. And both of these did, indeed, have their way with me, calming my spirit and preparing me, albeit unconsciously, for a change of heart, until at last they prevailed and, after the doubts and hesitations described in an earlier chapter, I became the diffident and halting Christian that I now am.

I am grateful, more grateful than I can say, to the Church of England and more particularly to its country churches, and to the men who, in spite of every discouragement, persist in teaching there the Christian religion as the Church understands it. Without them; I should not, I think, have come to Christianity.

Postscript on Christianity

Having finished this book, I am conscious of a sense of insufficiency. For some years past I have done my best to practise the Christian religion according to the ritual of the Anglican Church. I have gone regularly to church on a Sunday and partaken of Holy Communion. I should have liked, then, to have made this book an apologia for, a defence of, Christianity. Judged from this standpoint the book fails. It puts forward, as I hope and believe, a strong plea for the theistic view of the universe, but for the particular version of it which is maintained by the Christian Churches, though it holds a brief, it makes no case.

Wishing that this were not so, I have been led to consider why it is so. The reason is, I think, that the main doctrines of Christianity, the Incarnation, the Resurrection and the Ascension are strictly unbelievable on grounds of reason alone, unbelievable at any rate by a modern. They must be accepted, if accepted at all, on faith—*credenda*, in fact, *quia impossibilia.* Now, faith, as I suggested in the first chapter, must for a modern justify itself at the bar of reason. From this point of view there are three reasons which, as I think, make faith not unreasonable; at least, there are three which have had weight with me, and I should like to conclude this book by saying what they are.

First, it seems to me impossible to explain the history of Christianity, *unless* it is of supernatural origin and has had divine backing. The two main relevant considerations here are, first, the ignorance and pusillanimity of the disciples and, secondly, the record of the Church. How, in the first place, it

might be asked, could such a handful of unlettered and discouraged men have made the impact they did upon the Roman
world, *unless* they were convinced of the truth of what they
proclaimed, more particularly of the truth of the Resurrection,
and *unless* they received continuous assistance from God as
mediated by the Holy Ghost?

Consider, secondly, the record of the Church which seems
at times to have seized upon the Christian creed as a new,
divine-sent medium for the display of human nature in its
least agreeable aspects. As has often been pointed out, man's
inhumanity to man has never risen to greater heights than
among Christians, and no sin in the whole calendar has been
committed more flagrantly and more continuously than by the
professed servants and ministers of the Church. Moreover,
theirs have been precisely the sins specifically condemned by
Christ himself. Nevertheless, the Church has survived the
excesses of its ministers and members. How, one is tempted to
wonder, could it have done so unless God Himself kept it alive?
There is a story of a Jew who, becoming discontented with
Judaism, went in search of a new religion. Having tried and
rejected many, he came at last to Rome, then in the heyday of
its Renaissance wickedness: indulgences were shamelessly
sold, murder stalked the streets, there were venality and
corruption in high places, sexual perversion was rampant, the
poisoner lurked behind the arras, while on every side the luxury
and ostentation of the few outraged the misery and poverty of
the many. Having witnessed these things for some months, the
Jew joined the Catholic Church. When asked why he did so,
'Only a religion which is true,' he said, 'could survive such
behaviour on the part of its exponents.'

The same argument may be applied in a different form today.
The Church, we know, is in a poor way, and its influence,
compared with what it has been, is small. Nevertheless, people
do attend it, it *does* have influence. Regarded objectively, the
circumstance cannot fail to arouse surprise. Look at a congre-
gation of village people attending a country church. The

Postscript on Christianity

doctrines they are taught, the creed they profess, the truths they enunciate, are to them either meaningless—for example, the doctrine of the Trinity or of the Atonement—or, like the injunction to turn the other cheek or to take no thought for the morrow, run completely counter to all their natural human propensities and desires. Yet they attend; yet the Church survives. Its doctrines, it may be said—and I believe with truth —have so little relation to men's working lives that during the rest of the week they do not give them a thought; yet they attend; yet the Church survives.

In the second place, it seems to me that any creed must from its nature as a creed be arbitrary, arbitrary not only in what it affirms but in what it denies; for in affirming anything about the universe, you implicitly deny the opposite of what you affirm. In this sense, as Spinoza pointed out, any statement about the universe limits it and, if the universe is, indeed, infinite, may be said to falsify it. Considered from this point of view a creed is a kind of box, a strait-jacket in which men have sought to confine the infinite variety of what is.

Now, Christianity is a box of a very peculiar and, you would have thought, of a highly restricting kind. It makes no concessions to infinity or universality and so far from being timeless, is the dramatic record of a development in time, a development which begins, presumably, with the calling of Abraham to be the father of the chosen people, and will end with the Second Coming. This drama is punctuated from time to time by the arbitrary interventions of God which take place at specific times in the shape of a series of mighty acts. Of these, one was the sending of His Son into the world. Now it is precisely these elements in Christianity, its arbitrariness, the impression which it conveys of 'boxing' or 'strait-jacketing' the universe, its assertion that history is to be regarded as a drama, the progressive working out of God's will in the world, which makes it for the modern mind so hard of belief.

Dissatisfied with materialism, seeking some assurance that a world consisting exclusively of pieces of matter moving about

245

Postscript on Christianity

in space is not all, insisting, therefore, that the spiritual and akin must somehow underlie and even determine the alien and the brutal, the modern mind is prone to embrace some form of Hindu mysticism.

Aldous Huxley's statement of belief in *Ends and Means*—'that which' the mystic 'discovers beyond the frontiers of the average, sensual man's universe is a spiritual reality underlying and uniting all apparently separate existence—a reality with which he can merge himself', since it is 'possible for individuals to transcend the limitations of personality and to merge their private consciousness into a greater impersonal consciousness underlying the personal mind'—has touched a chord in the minds of many disillusioned westerners, especially among those who are called intellectuals. They have found it easy to believe with Huxley that the world is a unity of spiritual consciousness and that it is possible for us to realise our oneness with, indeed to merge ourselves into, this cosmic one here and 'now' in this life. (I put the word 'now' in inverted commas since, on this view, reality, the universal spiritual consciousness, is not in time at all. Time, then, belongs only to the world of appearance.)

What attracts in this view is precisely what it denies. By denying the reality of time, it refuses to limit the world as Christianity does, to the unfolding of a drama in the time series. By identifying the reality which underlies the world of appearance with a universal consciousness, it denies that God is a Person. 'Ultimate reality,' Huxley writes, 'is impersonal. Belief in a personal moral God has led all too frequently to a theoretical dogmatism and practical intolerance.' In his monograph, *Variations on a Philosopher* (Maine de Biran), Huxley describes the process of enlightenment from 'immediate knowledge of an "I" in relation to a passive "not-I", to belief in a substantial soul, and from this belief to belief in an unconditioned Being underlying and giving support to the substantial soul'. Now a God who sends His Son into the world at a specific moment of time is not an 'unconditioned Being'.

Postscript on Christianity

The attraction which this kind of view has for the modern mind springs precisely from its denial of limitation, from its escape from arbitrariness. Here are no miracles, no arbitrary interferences of God with nature, no appearances at points of time of supernatural Personages. Such a view is, I dare say, quite easy to believe, but apart from the intellectual difficulties pointed out in chapter VI of this book, it is, for me, put out of court by one overwhelming deficiency—I do not see how it can possibly affect one's life. Here is a man, myself, faced with a specific temptation. I would like to resist it, but it seems likely to prove too strong for me. Is there, I wonder, any source of strength upon which I can draw outside myself? I think, we will suppose, of religion. I remember, perhaps, having recently read in the *Philosophia Perennis*, that the reality of the universe is a universal impersonal consciousness, that this is somehow present in myself and that by adopting a suitable discipline and following a certain way of life, I can merge into it. Does the remembrance of these truths, if truths they are, help me here and now? Not in the least. What is a universal impersonal consciousness that it should help *me*, even if it is aware of my existence, or why, after all, should I desire to lose my individuality by merging into it, or even believe that the resistance of the temptation would assist my merging?

And then I turn to Christianity. 'Oh God,' I read, 'Who knowest that we have no power of ourselves to help ourselves.' Again, it is because 'through the wickedness of our mortal nature we can do no good thing without' God, that we are bidden to pray to Him, 'Grant us the help of Thy grace'. For is not God 'the protector of all that trust' in Him? In these and in innumerable, similar phrases I am assured that God is a Person, that He has an interest in me, that He wants me to be a better man and that if I pray to Him and trust Him, He will help me to be one. Here is a creed which can affect a man's life; a creed to live by; a creed to afford comfort in trouble and help in danger. Now any account of the universe which makes provision for a God of this kind, a God who concerns Himself with that which is

247

Postscript on Christianity

finite and is in time, who is constantly intervening in the affairs of the finite in time is *ex-hypothesi* limiting and arbitrary. It cannot help but be a box. Yet it is only such a creed that can fulfil the *practical* function which Christianity postulates and upon the performance of which it lays stress.

All of which brings me to the third reason which I state with the greatest diffidence. The proof of the pudding is in the eating. Does the thing, then, work in practice? On the whole and subject to considerable doubts and reservations, I should say that it does. It is, I have found, in fact the case that if you try, however unsuccessfully, to do what is right and pray regularly for assistance, you are assisted—not perhaps directly in the way you expected and which you at the time would have thought most helpful but, it may be, in some other way by a strengthening of character or by a tranquillising of the spirit which, on looking back afterwards, you realise to have been the best thing that could have happened to you.

I speak of 'doubts and reservations' simply because there have been, there still are, times when I have wondered and do wonder whether the thing has ever happened at all. I am told that many Christians go through such times. On the whole, however, I think I can subscribe to the testimony of the innumerable people who have tried to practise Christianity— the thing does, at least sometimes, work.

Index of Names

249

Index